SUSTAINABILITY IN AGRICULTURAL AND RURAL DEVELOPMENT

Dedicated to our parents, who represent the previous generation and generations long gone ...

... and to our children who represent the next generation and generations yet to come...

Sustainability in Agricultural and Rural Development

Edited by
GERARD E. D'SOUZA
TESFA G. GEBREMEDHIN
West Virginia University, USA

Ashgate

Aldershot • Brookfield USA • Singapore • Sydney

© Gerard E. D'Souza and Tesfa G. Gebremedhin 1998

Published by
Ashgate Publishing Ltd
Gower House
Croft Road
Aldershot
Hants GU11 3HR
England

Ashgate Publishing Company
Old Post Road
Brookfield
Vermont 05036
USA

British Library Cataloguing in Publication Data
Sustainability in agricultural and rural development
   1. Rural development 2.Sustainable development 3.Sustainable
   agriculture
   I. D'Souza, Gerard E. II.Gebremedhin, Tesfa G.
   338.1

Library of Congress Cataloging-in-Publication Data
Sustainability in agricultural and rural development / edited by
   Gerard E. D'Souza and Tesfa G. Gebremedhin.
      p.   cm.
   ISBN 1-85521-977-8 (hb)
   1. Sustainable agriculture. 2. Sustainable development. 3. Rural
   development.   I. D'Souza, Gerard Eugene. II. Gebremedhin. Tesfa G.
   S494.5.S86S85   1998
   307.1'412--dc21   97-51331
                                                     CIP

ISBN 1 85521 977 8

Printed in Great Britain by The Ipswich Book Company, Suffolk.

Contents

Tables

Figures

Foreword

A precise, consensus definition of sustainable development is illusive, however most advocates recognize three interrelationships as crucial to the goals of sustainable development. These are the relationships embedded in economic systems, ecological systems, and socio-cultural systems. The concept of sustainable development, at least as labeled as such, appears to have begun in the United Nations in the mid-1960s, and it has since gained prominence as a central feature of the United Nation's development environmental philosophy.

Most view the key criterion of sustainable development as that provided by the so-called Brundtland Report—the 1987 World Commission on Environment and Development. That is, sustainable development meets the needs of the current generation without compromising the ability of future generations to meet their needs. Sustainable development includes the sustainability of agricultural systems and agro-ecological integrity. However, much of the agricultural systems analysis has been directed at the difficulties of protecting ecosystems in the face of expanding agriculture in the developing world.

While the concept of sustainable development was gaining supporters, a parallel but apparently independent evolution was occurring with respect to the concept of sustainable agriculture. In the developed nations, starting around the 1970s, there began a reaction to chemically dependent, large-scale, commercial agriculture. This reaction was propelled further by cost-price squeezes in North American and European commercial agriculture that periodically created "farm crisis" situations and threatened the incomes and futures of smaller scale family farms.

The search for alternatives to commercial agriculture harbored many names; including alternative agriculture, low-input agriculture, biological agriculture, and organic agriculture, as well as sustainable agriculture. While some adherents considered sustainable agriculture to only be a set of substitute technologies to commercial agriculture practices, others offered sustainable agriculture as an alternative belief system to that underlying commercial agriculture. As an alternative belief system, sustainable agriculture tended to emphasize reduced chemical use, family and group self-reliance, a global village view of the world, a respect for nature and ecosystems, a high value on the family farm, and voluntary simplicity. Similar to sustainable development concepts, sustainable agriculture concepts provided a more holistic philosophy that emphasized systems and connections, and tended to eschew reductionist thinking and analysis. With this holistic philosophy, multi-disciplinary systems-based science was considered essential to creating a new understanding and a new set of appropriate technologies for agriculture.

Oddly, many are just beginning to recognize that the two emerging philosophies of sustainable development and sustainable agriculture have much in common. The nuances of that recognition are just beginning to be explored. That this volume is dedicated to that exploration is refreshing and overdue. The book explores, from many disciplinary perspectives, the definitional difficulties—what is sustainable agriculture and rural development? It then goes on to explore the most challenging question of "how do we get there from here?". Much of this latter exploration is appropriately offered as an exploration in the related question of "What makes people make the choices that they do?". Since the answer to that question includes gender differences, cultural differences, domestic and trade policy incentives, land markets and tenure arrangements, personal characteristics, available technologies, the costs of information, the nature of adaptive learning and the like....the volume is of necessity, suggestive rather than conclusive. Yet, its multidisciplinary nature and its breadth are most welcome.

Since World War II, our concerns with natural resource use have broadened from that of quantitative adequacy to the sustainability of systems' functioning. There is increasing recognition that economic growth, as conventionally defined, will not necessarily assure ecosystem integrity, broad improvements in the well being of all peoples, or obtainment of justice. The choice of our future development path requires informed judgments, wise policy, and wise investments. Multidisciplinary contributions such as this one are fundamental to this choice.

Sandra S. Batie
Elton R. Smith Professor in Food and Agricultural Policy
Michigan State University

Preface

In a world where growth and development often come at the expense of resource degradation, it is imperative to understand the nature of this degradation and explore possible solutions. The preferred approach to development is one that is sustainable. However, the path to sustainable development is neither obvious nor simple; for one thing, sustainability has many, interrelated, components. This book examines the links between sustainability and various other topics, in the process exploring and integrating many of the components. Thus, our purpose is to provide a broad but in-depth discussion of the issues, concepts, methods of analysis, and empirical results related to the sustainable development of agriculture and rural communities.

Ideal for a seminar course, the book is intended for undergraduate and graduate students studying production agriculture, rural sociology, economics and public policy, environmental sciences, geography and land use planning, and other social sciences. It can serve as a source of information for policy makers. It can also be used as a reference by professional economists and other researchers interested in issues relating to sustainable agricultural and rural development. While the coverage of some topics is, by necessity, more technical, the book is compiled with a general audience in mind. Thus, it should be of interest to anyone concerned with agriculture and rural issues, particularly as they relate to the future of agriculture and of rural communities.

The book is comprised of 12 chapters contributed by authors from a variety of disciplines, with sustainability as the common link. The perspective is either national (U.S.) or international, but global implications can be drawn. Each chapter addresses one or more of the following components of sustainability: economic, social or demographic, community, environmental, and human health. Specific chapters explore the links between sustainability and related topics such as industrialization, farm size, role of markets versus government regulation, production technology, community, gender, population growth, economics, public policy, land use, and information. The final chapter is devoted to synthesizing some of the issues in the context of identifying areas for, and challenges of, future research in the area. The topics have not previously been explored together in one publication. The approach of the book is to present the evidence (using a combination of case studies or case examples, sample and literature surveys, and observation) and then interpret it in light of individual understanding and experience. Since the authors approach the issues from different backgrounds and perspectives, the conclusions are not necessarily consistent across chapters. The fact that different viewpoints are espoused perhaps reinforces the notion that there are several pathways to sustainable development.

Editing of chapters was minimized to preserve the unique flavor and sentence rhythm of the individual authors. The chapters have been integrated to some degree through annotation; however, they can be read independently of each other, and in any order. We should also note that the conclusions of the individual chapters are the authors' own, and are not necessarily shared by the editors or other authors. As editors we have strived for, but not necessarily achieved, infallibility, and apologize in advance for any errors or omissions.

While we have attempted to integrate as many issues relating to the sustainability of agriculture and rural communities, our coverage is by no means comprehensive. Indeed, sustainable development is a broad topic and means different things to different people, as the definitions of sustainability sprinkled throughout this volume suggests. However, we can perhaps best capture the essence of sustainability by invoking the Seneca saying: *before acting, we must consider the consequences of our actions for the next seven generations*. If we add to this "and the next seven watersheds", then we can explicitly capture both the temporal and the spatial dimensions inherent in sustainable development.

This book is by no means a panacea; however, like all work, it has a larger purpose. The larger purpose of this work is to lead us to reflect on the opulence of our natural inheritance, and on our apparent reluctance to value it for its true worth to this generation and to those who are only a gleam in our eyes.

G.E.D. and T.G.G.

West Virginia University
October 1997

Acknowledgements

We owe a debt of gratitude for this work to many individuals and organizations. First, the individual authors and co-authors of this volume who gave generously of their time and effort to bring this work to fruition. Our employer, West Virginia University and, in particular, the Division of Resource Management and its Director, Peter Schaeffer, for the moral and financial support of our academic pursuits. Lisa Lewis, who did the type setting efficiently and courteously, with her trademark good humor. Gloria Nestor, for assisting with graphics. Our colleague, Jerry Fletcher, for computer support. The Blue Mountain Center in New York for the one-month residency awarded to Gerard D'Souza during which much of the editing for this book was accomplished. Finally, our spouses (Susan and Meheret) and children (Ryan, Kellie, and Alexi, and Abnet, Luwam, and Adam) for sustaining us through the development of this volume and, no doubt, beyond. THANK YOU!

Abbreviations and Conversions

AGNPS	Agricultural Non-Point Source Pollution model
ANSWERS	Areal Non-Point Source Watershed Environmental Response Simulation
BEA	Bureau of Economic Analysis
CAST	Council for Agricultural Sciences and Technology
CEEP	Cropland Environmental Easement Program
CGIAR	Consultative Group for International Agricultural Research
CIMIS	California Irrigation Management Information System
CREAMS	Chemicals, Runoff and Erosion from Agricultural Management Systems
CRP	Conservation Reserve Program
CRSP	Collaborative Research Support Program
CSA	Community-Supported Agriculture
ECP	Environmental Compliance Program
EPIC	Erosion-Productivity Impact Calculator
ERS	Economic Research Service
FAIR	Federal Agricultural Improvement and Reform
FAO	Food and Agriculture Organization
FBFM	Farm Business Farm Management
GATT	General Agreement on Tariffs and Trade
GDP	Gross Domestic Product
GIS	Geographic Information System
GPS	Global Positioning System
GREAN	Global Research on the Environmental and Agricultural Nexus
IPM	Integrated Pest Management
ISAN	Illinois Sustainable Agricultural Network
LISA	Low Input Sustainable Agriculture
MCL	Maximum Contaminant Level
mmt	million metric tons
NARS	National Agricultural Research System
NGO	Non-Government Organization
NNP	Net National Product

NRC	National Research Council
NRCS	Natural Resources Conservation Service
NRM	Natural Resource Management
PCSD	President's Council on Sustainable Development
PDRs	Purchase of Development Rights
PRB	Population Reference Bureau
ROTO	Continuous Water and Sediment Routing model
SANREM	Sustainable Agriculture and Natural Resource Management
SAREP	Sustainable Agricultural Research and Education Program
SWAT	Soil and Water Assessment Tool
SWRRB	Simulator for Water Resources in Rural Basins
UN	United Nations
US	United States
USAID	United States Agency for International Development
USDA	United States Department of Agriculture
USEPA	United States Environmental Protection Agency
WCED	World Commission on Environment and Development
WEPP	Water Erosion Prediction Model
WHO	World Health Organization
WWF	World Wildlife Fund

Sucre (Ecuador): 4528 sucres=1 U.S. dollar (February 2, 1998 exchange rate)
1 Kilogram = 2.2046 pounds
1 Hectare = 2.47 acres
1 Meter = 1.094 yards
1 Metric ton = 2,204.622 pounds
1 (U.S.) ton = 2,000 pounds

1 Sustainability and Agricultural Industrialization: Issues and Implications

Tesfa G. Ģebremedhin and Ralph D. Christy

Introduction

There is increasing evidence that agriculture and other natural resource industries have been preoccupied with increasing productivity much to the detriment of environmental degradation. Agriculturists have been eager to claim high-yield farming benefits, but they have been strangely silent on the need for environmental constraints. It has been believed that investing heavily in yield-increasing technologies for agriculture would meet the rapidly increasing demand for a resource-costly modern lifestyle. Consequently, scientific advancements and innovations have motivated and accelerated structural changes in production agriculture and caused major industry restructuring and relocation of production and processing activities. Such restructuring can be devastating to rural communities and areas dependent upon production agriculture because technical and management factors combine in ways that can adversely affect the environment. The issue of increasing productivity in agriculture so as not to undermine the environment is a complex one. Thus, rather than attempting to provide answers to all questions pertaining to sustainability in production agriculture, the purpose of this chapter is mainly to explore issues relating to the survival and sustainability of farms, given the structural changes currently taking place in production agriculture. In particular, the focus is on the characteristics and problems of small farms in an industrialized agriculture.

Structural Changes in Production Agriculture

The U.S. economy has gone from one based heavily on production from many small family farms, to an industrial and service based economy with agricultural production taking place on fewer but larger farms. The trend

1

toward greater economic concentration in agricultural production has been of considerable interest to agricultural researchers and public policymakers. Much of this interest is centered around: (a) the alarming rate at which the number of small to medium-sized farms has been declining and the increasing rate of average farm size over the years; (b) the disproportionate percentage of total agricultural production now being generated by a relatively small percentage of farms, in the larger size categories, followed by a steady downfall of social and economic conditions of the small farm sector; (c) the constant rising percentage of farm family income which is derived from nonfarm sources; (d) the migration of farm population from rural to urban centers for better economic opportunities and social services; and (e) the adverse impacts of large-scale farming on the environment (Brown, Christy, and Gebremedhin, 1994).

The movement toward greater concentration has been a persistent feature of production agriculture (Heady and Sonka, 1974). At the national level, average farm size has more than doubled in the past 50 years, from 216 acres of land in 1950 to 491 acres in 1992 (Table 1). The average farm size for farms with sales of less than $100,000 (considered "small farms") was 271 acres compared with 1,542 acres for farms with sales of $100,000 or more (considered "large farms"), in 1992. On the other hand, land in farms has been declining slowly since it reached a peak of 1,161 million acres in 1950. In each succeeding year, the total land in farms has fallen somewhat so that in 1992 (946 million acres) land in farms returned to about the same total (956 million acres) as in 1920. It is projected that this trend of slow decline will continue into the next century.

The number of U.S. farms has been declining since 1935, when it reached an all-time high of nearly 6.8 million. By 1992, this number declined to 1.93 million (Table 1); the number of U.S. farms is projected by the U.S. Department of Agriculture (USDA) to decline to 1.8 million in the year 2000. Another forecast, in a 1986 study published by the U.S. Congress/Office of Technology Assessment projected that the number of farms will shrink to about 1.25 million by the year 2000. This projection means that more than half a million farms now in production will disappear by the turn of the century. The number of large farms grew six fold in the past 25 years, increasing from 51,995 in 1969 to 333,865 in 1992. At the same time, the number of small farms declined by almost half from about 2.68 million in 1969 to 1.59 million in 1992. Large farms are more likely than small farms to be operated by full-time farmers, receive government payments, be organized as corporations, and generate large returns (U.S. Department of Commerce, 1994).

Table 1. U.S. farm numbers, land in farms, and average farm size, 1920-92

Year	Number of Farms (million)	Land in Farms (million acres)	Average Farm Size (acres)
1920	6.40	956	148
1930	6.30	987	157
1940	6.10	1,061	174
1950	5.40	1,161	216
1954	4.80	1,158	242
1959	3.71	1,124	303
1964	3.16	1,110	352
1969	2.73	1,063	389
1974	2.31	1,017	440
1978	2.26	1,015	449
1982	2.24	987	440
1987	2.09	964	462
1992	1.93	946	491

Source: U.S. Department of Commerce, Census of Agriculture, (1950-92).

Statistics show that the number of farms and the value of production are highly concentrated at opposite ends of the size scale (USDA, 1994). Smaller operations accounted for most farms, whereas larger operations accounted for most farm sales. Small farms comprised nearly 83% of all farms. The latter account for about 46% of the total land in farm use but only 17% of total farm products sold. However, in 1992, large farms comprised less than 20 percent of all the nation's farms. These farms operated 54% of the total land in farm use and accounted for approximately 83% of all farm products sold. It was also reported that large farms earned average net cash returns of $83,812 compared to $1,836 per farm for small farms in 1992 (USDA, 1994).

Agriculture in the U.S. is continually changing. Like most other sectors, agriculture has become industrialized. It is characterized by increased concentration. The current structure of agriculture, in correspondence with the decline in the number of farms, is a reflection of the interaction of multiple institutional and economic forces: acccess to new technology for production, economies of size and capital requirements, the land distribution and forms of ownership, operators' managerial ability, the availability of markets both within and outside the country, price instability, credit financing, opportunities for employment outside agriculture, transportation networks connecting urban to rural areas, government regulations, and commodity programs. Since all of these factors have immediate and dramatic effects on the farm sector, the trend has given rise to widespread concern for the future of small family farms and the general rural economy.

The structure issue has more than a direct relationship to the agricultural sector and rural communities; it is also linked to broader problems beyond the farm gate and rural limits. Historically, farming has been the principal occupation and the primary source of family income in rural America. With the decline in the number of farmers, the agricultural link to the general economy has dramatically changed over the years. Currently, many rural economies are not as dependent on agriculture as was the case several decades ago; indeed, agriculture in many areas has become dependent on the general economy for nonfarm jobs. Off-farm employment has become an integral part of the emerging structure of production agriculture and its effects are of vital concern to rural communities because of the labor, farm input and product market linkages of agriculture to the rest of the rural economy. Consequently, the shifting structure of production agriculture, which is characterized by technological and economic changes, has forced many small farmers either to grow, leave, or find off-farm work (Gladwin and Zabawa, 1985). For instance, in 1950, off-farm income contributed 31% of total farm household income compared to 87% in 1993 (Table 2). Families operating small farms usually depend more on off-farm employment than those operating large farms (USDA/ERS, 1993; Tweeten, 1995).

In addition, the structural transformation in production agriculture has resulted in massive migration of farm families from rural areas to urban centers due to better economic opportunities and social services. U.S. farm population has decreased drastically in the past 50 years, from 30.5 million in 1940 to 4.6 million in 1992 (Table 3). Today, farmers represent less than 3% of the total population. Historically, higher wages and salaries, more attractive jobs, and better educational opportunities and other public services in cities—compared with limited employment opportunities, lower relative farm wages, and low returns to agriculture in some rural areas—have produced a large exodus of the farm population from rural agricultural communities to urban centers. African American farmers have participated more than any other population group in the dramatic exodus from agriculture. For the most part, many of these individuals received low levels of formal training and

Table 2. Off-farm income as a percentage of total household income, 1950-93

Year	Percent
1950	31
1960	43
1970	55
1980	61
1982	62
1992	72
1993	87

Sources: U.S. Congress/Office of Technology Assessment (1986) and Tweeten (1995).

Table 3. U.S. farm population, 1940-42

Year	No. (Million)
1940	30.5
1950	23.1
1960	15.6
1970	9.7
1980	7.2
1990	4.7
1991	4.6
1992	4.6

Source: USDA/ERS, No. 446, 1989.

education, thus creating adjustment problems in urban areas (Brown, Christy and Gebremedhin, 1994). In general, this situation has both facilitated farm growth over the years, as well as created many problems for the low skilled and undereducated workers who have been displaced from their rural settings and forced to adjust to the labor and lifestyle of urban settings. However, recent studies have noted a substantial population growth in rural and small towns, as a result of the search for a better quality of life and the prospects for economic opportunities, even though employment growth in the nation's rural and small town communities is expected to continue to lag behind growth in metro areas (Tweeten, 1995).

Impacts of Industrialized Agriculture

While much attention has been given to the overall question of structural change in agriculture, relatively little emphasis has been placed on the implications of this change for small farms. It has become increasingly difficult for small farms to compete with large farms as viable economic units in the shifting structure of production agriculture. It is reported that full-time small farm operators have abandoned production agriculture at an alarming rate. Also, since entry costs are relatively high, new farmers find it difficult to begin farming. Structural changes in production agriculture have had the greatest negative impact on small farms. Furthermore, small farms are plagued with limited accessibility to capital markets, inadequate educational opportunities, and insufficient technical assistance from public and private institutions (Brown, Christy, and Gebremedhin, 1994).

The historical increase in farm size, mechanization and accompanying reliance on off-farm inputs, specialization, and globalization is often referred to as "industrialization" of agriculture. Industrialization not only affects the number and size of farms, the ownership and control of farm resources, and the marketing of inputs and outputs, but also has a direct impact on the broader issues of families and rural communities (discussed elsewhere in this volume). These changes in the structure of production agriculture and the general economy have had profound impacts on aggregate and individual welfare. The structural transformation of production agriculture will cause a great deal of uncertainty about the survival of small farms as viable economic units and as a "way of life" for many rural farm families (Brown, Christy, and Gebremedhin, 1994). Thus, it appears that the direction and rate of change in production agriculture have important policy implications on a variety of issues: resource use, enterprise combination, environmental sustainability, population distribution and labor mobility, the future survival and well-being of farm families, the economic viability and social vitality of agricultural and rural communities, and the effectiveness and nature of public policy.

Role of Small Farms in an Industrialized Agriculture

The term "small farm" is neither precisely defined for the agricultural research community nor for the general public. The definition of what constitutes a small farm and the concomitant categorization by size have gone through several metamorphoses in the United States (Crecink, 1986). The definitions of small farms are by necessity arbitrary, numerous, and vary by type of farm, geographic location, and even by the individual researcher. Farm size has been defined by various criteria, including acres of land operated, units of livestock in operation, value of farm output produced, total assets controlled, level of farm income to level of total family income, and days worked off-farm and on the farm (Lewis, 1978). However, most investigations of small farm characteristics combine two or more of these classifications to arrive at a more limited and conclusive definition. Over the last several decades, small farms have been generally described as family farms with limited resources, farms with a small volume of farm product sales, part-time farms, and retirement farms. Also, these farms have been—rightly or wrongly—closely identified with poverty situations. A common thread running through each of these characterizations is that somehow small farms fall outside the mainstream of commercial agriculture.

A farm is considered small in the U.S. if its size does not allow for efficient utilization of existing agricultural technologies. U.S. farms have become more and more capital intensive, and yesterday's large farms have become today's small farms. The 160-acre farm of the 1862 Homestead Act appears to have been considered a small operation at the time, even though it was large enough to use the most sophisticated technology of the time. Later, with the advent of new technology, came improvements in farm tools and techniques which increased the skills and capital investment to operate a much larger farm. However, farm size after 1950 was most commonly measured in terms of farm product sales, not acres of land operated or total assets controlled. In the 1960s, small farms were said to be production units selling less than $10,000 in annual gross farm products. The dividing line crept up to $20,000 in annual gross farm product sales by the mid-1970s and to $40,000 in the 1980s (Brewster, 1982). In the 1990s, the most frequently used definition of a small farm is one selling over $1,000 but less than $100,000 in annual gross farm products.

The gross farm product sales persists as the most commonly used method to distinguish between large and small farm groups. However, this criterion can easily be misleading because of variations in input requirements among small farms and the extent to which inputs are purchased or produced on the farm (West, 1979). In addition, inflation shifts some farms with constant real sales volume from one pecuniary sales class to another. A farm can be considered small one year and large the next year due to volatile farm product prices. Indeed, farmers are particularly vulnerable to inflation because their costs are likely to rise faster than their revenues. Much of the increase in number of larger farms took place due to the rise in the index of prices received by farmers rather than a rise in the real output per farm (Tweeten, Cilley, and Popoola, 1980).

In assessing the structure of production agriculture, it appears that large farmers as a group are probably more alike than small farmers, since the large farmers usually rely on the farm to provide family income and are expected to devote most of their time and energy to farm work and management (Hinson, 1983). Conversely, farms with a low level of farm product sales, or limited resources, make up a more diverse group. Some farms may have sufficient resources and growth potential to generate an acceptable level of family income. Some farmers who are full time and have few resource limitations may lack the basic economic incentives and motivation for farming or may be preparing for retirement. Still others are part time farmers because their income is derived mostly from labor or resources devoted to the nonfarm sector.

On most small farms, one or more resources is limited. Some farmers are able-bodied and young, but have low farm product sales because they have just started farming with small operations, and may expand as they gain experience. Some farms may be growth and goal limited, but low-skilled farmers have few opportunities for additional farm and nonfarm earnings. Others may be aged and retired, have some physical disability, or may even depend heavily on social welfare, social security, or veteran payments. Many of these persons live under deplorable poverty conditions in the rural communities. In many cases, these are the people who the federal and state cooperative extension workers and agricultural researchers find the most difficult to reach and serve (Marshall and Thompson, 1976). Many additional situations may also exist that make the characteristics of small farms more complicated and ambiguous.

In general, small farms are a part of the pluralism of rural America and their structural characteristics vary by type of operation, goal or purpose of farming, and geographical location. Small farms differentiate in terms of total family income from both farm and off-farm sources and the family's reliance on farm generated income. Accordingly, small farms may be classified into four categories: (1) **limited resource farms** which have a low total income and a high reliance on farm-generated income; (2) **successful small farms** which have a high family income and a high reliance on farm-generated income; (3) **part-time farms** which have a high family income but a low reliance on farm-generated income; and (4) the **farm or rural poor** which have a low family income and a low reliance on farm-generated income. Most small farm operators are in the upper age brackets and occupationally or geographically immobile due to age, health, and/or training constraints. They are often educationally disadvantaged, economically poor, and many face institutional barriers, such as access to financial credit, and input supply and product markets. Thus, small farms tend to be a heterogenous group (Gebremedhin, 1990; Carlin and Crecink, 1979).

Implications for Sustainability of Production Agriculture

The trend toward fewer but larger farms and the grim reality of continuing financial crises in agriculture are the result of the interaction and changes of numerous economic and non-economic factors. Affecting all size farms, especially those with a low equity, are the macro-level economic forces which cause economic concentration (Gladwin and Zabawa, 1985); past increases in the value of farm land and equipment which make it difficult for the beginning farmer to get started (Eginton and Tweeten, 1982); inflationary increases in the cost of production inputs and credit, which decrease farmers' profit margins and raise their level of permanent indebtedness (Van Blokland, 1981); technological changes which lead adopters to expand, create a market surplus of commodities, thus depressing crop prices (Carter et al., 1981); monetary policies that contribute to a strong dollar and a downturn in exports (Schuh, 1984); and changes in international markets which may result in a minor squeeze or major collapse of the local market (de Janvry, 1982). Some of the principal forces that shape the structure of production agriculture particularly as they impact small farms are discussed in the following sections; the relationship between farm size and agricultural sustainability is a subject that is explored in more depth in the following chapter.

Agricultural Technology and Resource Endowments

The technological revolution in agriculture has led to increasingly larger farms over the years. Enterprise specialization and increased uniformity of farming, resulting from the adoption of the techniques of regional monocultural production, have increased the vulnerability and reduced the adaptability of such changes especially in small farm operations. Utilizing economic principles to guide production, the larger farmer has adopted new technology and better cultural practices generated from agricultural research and development. Technological developments in agriculture have increased the nation's agricultural output and accrued benefits to large and rich farmers, but not without great cost. As a result of these technological developments, displaced farm workers and small farmers have incurred massive social and economic costs (Hightower, 1972; Singh and Williamson, 1985).

Small farmers are often alienated from the mainstream of modern agricultural activities. They are confronted with many difficulties because they produce in an industry geared toward serving large-scale production units. Tradition plays a large role in the day-to-day management of the small farm. New technology is very slow in replacing old techniques which have been handed down for generations. Factors inhibiting adoption of technology on small farms include lack of knowledge, limited quantities of resources (land, capital, and skilled labor), fear of risk, limited managerial ability, as well as inability to justify economically the adoption of certain types of technology for use on small-scale farm operations (West, 1979). All these factors weaken small farmers' survival and their competitive position, causing many to leave agriculture in search of off-farm jobs.

The ownership and control of land and technology plus the distribution mechanisms are becoming increasingly concentrated in the hands of a few individuals and/or corporations. This is a trend which, if carried to an extreme, could have severe implications for the survival of small farms (Madden and Tischbein, 1979). The social, ecological, and economic vitality of rural and urban communities is directly related to patterns of ownership, control, use, and distribution of agricultural resources. Prices and technology, along with initial resource endowments, managerial ability, and environmental factors, determine the ability of individual farmers to generate income. The process of adjustment to price changes and technology explains changes in the size and productivity of farms and the farming industry over the years. In a competitive market economy, low productivity and low income earnings often lead small farms to a long-run situation of disinvestment and eventual relocation into other off-farm economic sectors.

Farm Credit Financing

Small farmers are continuously plagued by credit problems. Without an adequate source of credit, they cannot invest in land or modern technology to increase production and expand the farm base. The capital investment possibility has become a question of survival for many small farms. Traditionally, most small farms have financed the major share of capital requirements for farming operations from internal savings. Other farms, because of their small size and nonfarm income earnings, can be equity financed. Still others minimize credit requirements by reducing input use and selecting low cash cost enterprises. Some farms have cut back production by selling land when faced with a huge debt load and with no other alternatives.

Despite the fact that there is a low borrowing rate observed among small farmers, the need for credit remains one of the overwhelming characteristics in the small farm business. Interest among many small farmers to borrow for such purposes is found to be lacking, as they wish to remain debt-free and tend to have a complacent attitude toward the present pattern of farm capital investment for production purposes. Family subsistence and risk avoidance are necessarily first priority considerations for survival of small farm families.

Even though no shortage of loan funds in the farm sector is evident, marginal farm operators who perceive credit financing as an essential factor in farming continue to have problems getting farm credit from conventional lending institutions. Small farm operators are usually disqualified from farm credit loans because of their disadvantaged economic condition and the general conservative lending practices of financial institutions. The farmers have low equity positions and can offer little security, which implies high cost for lenders. To obtain a loan, small producers may have to pay a higher rate of interest. Since most small farmers possess limited information about available sources of credit, they usually do not compare interest charges or other measures of credit's true cost.

Only a few lending agencies currently have the ability and the mandate to serve low-equity or beginning farmers. In general, many lending institutions seek only large borrowers in order to minimize their service costs per dollar loaned. These lending institutions often limit access of small farm operators to the capital market by imposing rigid rules on credit lending in order to fully protect the loan capital, thereby restricting the risk of loss. Nevertheless, small farm operators continue to survive with traditional financing practices and sources for reasons of convenience and choice (Singh and Williamson, 1985).

Farm Input Prices

In recent years, the price of agricultural inputs has risen more rapidly than that of agricultural output, causing a cost-price squeeze. Small and large farmers alike are affected by the cost-price squeeze, but the impact of this problem is felt most severely by small farmers. Small farms produce at higher private cost per dollar of output than larger farms. Unlike large farmers, small farmers do not receive quantity discounts and other preferential treatment by input supply and marketing firms. To solve this problem, many small farms have turned to production activities that are labor-intensive rather than capital-intensive.

The price paid for inputs varies among individual farms and changes over time. Recent changes in the prices of energy inputs are an example. As input prices vary among firms or change over time, the relative competitive positions of a farm business are affected. The optimum input mix changes and farms may be better or worse off depending on their relative use of the input involved (West, 1979).

Farm Product Marketing and Structure

The market structure for most farm products has changed in response to the development of highly efficient communication and pricing systems. These developments and changes have a significant impact upon the survival of small farms. Small farms are seldom in a position to benefit directly from the developments of these technological practices. General developments in marketing services—such as developments in transportation, storage, the advent of mass retailing patterns, accompanying volume and standardization requirements, integration of segments in the production and marketing systems, and public regulation of marketing activities—have also created serious problems for small farm operators.

Successful marketing is essential for the survival of farm operations. Lack of markets where small farmers can sell their products is a growing concern. As marketing activities have shifted from a decentralized to a centralized system, production has shifted to areas capable of amassing large quantities for shipment. Mass retailing, product standardization, and volume specialization are methods which small farms cannot compete with and are unable to exploit. Marketing firms have increasingly turned to large farms or have developed an integrated system which bypasses the small farms (West, 1979). The new methods of marketing, which have replaced organized open markets, set volume requirements so high that small-scale producers are often excluded from the marketing process. However, direct marketing outlets, such as roadside markets, farmers' markets, and pick-your-own operations, have increased market access for some small farms (West, 1979).

Another market problem faced by small farmers is lack of bargaining power and market information. They need to know the advantages and disadvantages of each market outlet, the ease and difficulty of access to each outlet, and information on the relationships of price levels among and within outlets. Price variation in each market outlet translates directly into income variation. Since most small farmers have limited reserves to carry them through a bad year, price variation is quite important to their survival.

Non Farm Employment and Income

The most critical problem confronting small farmers today is maintaining a sufficient level of income. As a growing proportion of the total farm family's income comes from non farm sources, off-farm employment has become a critical and an important alternative income source to small farmers (Brown, Christy, and Gebremedhin, 1994; Sharples and Prindle, 1973). Off-farm work is prevalent among operators of all farm sizes, but most prominent on smaller farms. The average farm family in the U.S. depended on off-farm income for 87% of its household income in 1993 (USDA, 1993). However, families operating small farms usually depend more on off-farm employment than families operating large farms. In many cases, the availability of off-farm employment is essential to the continuation of small farm operations. The lower the total household income, the more dependent farmers are on off-farm income to maintain family well-being.

Currently, most small farm operators seek a job away from their farms for at least a short time in order to earn supplementary family income. Some small farm operators hold full-time jobs in the cities and do their farming in the evenings and on weekends. But, many of the off-farm jobs they hold in rural small towns are in the secondary labor market, paying low wages commensurate with their basic educational backgrounds and practical experience. In some cases, off-farm earnings have provided small farm families with an adequate standard of living, in addition to providing an opportunity to continue operating their farms and living in the community of their choice. Furthermore, for these few farmers, the farm business is used as a means of reducing tax liability in addition to providing residential, community, or other satisfactions (Lin, Coffman, and Penn, 1986). Many small farmers have chosen farming as an occupation because of the values they attach to farm work, including the opportunity to be one's own boss.

Government Support Programs

Federal programs are often supported by farmers because of the inherent benefits they supply, such as additional farm income through acreage allotments, farm commodity programs, and tax policies. Although these commodity price and support programs have the stated objectives of benefitting all farmers, the distribution of benefits is skewed toward the larger producer. Furthermore, such programs frequently have adverse long-run economic effects on the farm sector, encouraging excessive output and substitution of capital for farm labor—which in turn increases the size and decreases the number of farms. However, a number of provisions tend to lower the tax burden on farm income by allowing the use of cash rather than accrual accounting, the offsetting of non farm income with farm losses, investment credits, lower taxes on capital gains, low corporate taxes, and accelerated depreciation. The major beneficiaries of the special farm tax preferences appear to be those farms with high incomes or those farms in the strongest position from the standpoint of assets and technical efficiency (Singh and Williamson, 1985).

It has also been reported that the decline in the number of farms can be linked to the unequally large share of government payments that went to the largest farms (Schertz, 1979). Large-size commercial farms received 39%, mid-size family farms received about 33%, and the remainder, 28%, went to smaller farms, who are not totally dependent on agriculture for all their income. Despite the increasing amount of federal government spending, commodity programs have done little to halt the decline in the number of small farms or to improve the incomes of these farms. While technical problems make it impossible to measure the precise impact of government policies, there can be little doubt that past and present policies have had a net effect of displacing small farmers. Thus, national agricultural policies are not necessarily applicable to all small farms. Government programs have often benefited those farms that were already in the strongest position from the standpoint of assets or volume of production. Most small farmers benefit very little from farm commodity programs because income from the farm is only a small fraction of their total family income. Small farms represent enterprises that often have been adversely affected by public policy, and operate in an environment geared toward serving large-scale producing units. Small farms are a segment of the impoverished rural population that is often ignored by public policy (Gebremedhin, 1990).

Agricultural Research and Extension Services

Most agricultural research, conducted by land-grant institutions, has been directed toward the development of crops, livestock, and agricultural machinery and equipment—but this research has not necessarily addressed the needs of small farmers (Marshall and Thompson, 1976). The research was conducted under the belief that benefits would filter down, and the small farmer would also be able to use the results of the research conducted. This trickle-down has not occurred; instead, the research has strengthened the concentration process even more than before (Hightower, 1972; Singh and Williamson, 1985).

Agricultural research and cooperative extension services have provided the basis for highly innovative agriculture which is geared to capital-intensive, large-scale farming. While the U.S. Department of Agriculture and the land-grant institutions have made a limited effort to solve problems impeding the economic improvement of small farm operations, they have not evaluated the economic and social impacts of production efficiency, nor have they determined the assistance that small farm operators need to adjust to the change brought about by such research.

In general, established means of communication, both in research and extension, have failed to work for low-income farmers. The Agricultural Research Service and the Cooperative Extension Service are supposed to be responsible for disseminating research results to all categories of farms. However, small farmers do not seek information from these agencies as readily and frequently as do large farmers. Although agency personnel have claimed to work with the most receptive farmers on the premise that knowledge would "trickle down" to others, this strategy has proven unsuccessful over the years (Singh and Williamson, 1985; Marshall and Thompson, 1976).

Conclusions

The changing structure in production agriculture, as a response to ongoing economic adjustments, is not a temporary phenomenon. It is an arena in which the economic and natural resource base of farming and rural communities will be changing constantly. Emerging modern agricultural technology will move and change the structure of production agriculture in the same profound ways and directions as before. Production agriculture will change toward more sophisticated management and marketing, larger and fewer commercial farms, greater capital intensity, greater separation of management from farm ownership, and further concentration of land and capital into a new agriculture. Like most other sectors, agriculture will continue to become more "industrialized" and the rural community will rapidly become an industrial and service economy.

To this effect, the direction and speed of these changes in the structure of production agriculture raise public policy questions in light of the survival of small farms and agriculture in general. The survival of small farms is important because of their social and economic role in the rural community. Despite the relatively meager earnings derived from the farm, small farms are positive and substantial contributors to both the agribusiness and consumer industries of rural communities. Small farms constitute the majority of farm enterprises in the country. Their survival implies more viable rural communities which have been overlooked over the years. Rural communitiees comprised of small and part-time farms are expected to have a greater potential demand for public and private goods and services than would be the case with a greater proportion of large farms (Heady and Sonka, 1974). Small farms fill an economic need by providing local market niches and establishing a competitive yardstick against which prices and quality of products of the commercial farm sector can be judged by consumers. Small farms with skilled labor are linked to the rural economy through the labor market and serve as a stable source of labor for attracting new business ventures in the rural community. Also, the continuous decline in the number and economic vitality of small farms adversely affects the quality of life in small towns and rural communities. A study by Goldschmidt (1978) showed that a town surrounded by family-operated small farms was superior in all measures reflecting the quality of life more than a town surrounded by large-scale farm enterprises. Coughenour and Christenson (1983) observed that small or part-time farmers and non-farmers are more supportive of community growth and economic development than are large-scale, full-time farmers. Likewise, Coughenour and Tweeten (1986) found that the shift toward large-scale agriculture accelerates environmental degradation and reduces the rural quality of life for both farm and non-farm families, themes that are echoed in the following chapter. They add that small farms promote community vitality to a much greater extent than do large farms. Part-time farms are linked to the rural economy through the labor market and serve as a stable source of labor for attracting new businesses in rural communities.

Emphasis on low-income families is appropriate for public policy purposes because public policy also concerns itself with people who are not likely to benefit from market or nongovernmental forces. Small farms are diverse and vary in their characteristics and geographic locations. For many small farm families who are poor or aged or disabled, social welfare programs are more important than income from farming or commodity programs. Thus, in order to understand the characteristics and needs of small farms and to make the necessary public policy choices, it is essential to decide whether the concern is solely about the production of food and fiber or whether it encompasses the well-being of families living on farms and the communities in which they reside. It is important to understand that farms are not just places where farmers eke out a living; they are composed of families. Both farms and families are deeply rooted in the values of rural America. Therefore, small farms are more than a social institution that ought to be maintained for humanistic, or perhaps sentimental, reasons.

Acknowledgements

An earlier version of this paper was published in the July 1996 issue of the *Journal of Agricultural and Applied Economics*. The authors gratefully acknowledge the review comments of Dale Colyer and Denny Smith on an earlier draft of the manuscript.

References

Brewster, David E. 1982. "What Is a Small Farm?" *Research for Small Farms.* USDA/Agricultural Research Service, Miscellaneous Publication No. 1422, Washington DC, July.

Brown, Adell, Ralph D. Christy and Tesfa G. Gebremedhin. 1994. "Structural Changes in U.S. Agriculture: Implications for Survival of African American Farmers". *Review of Black Political Economy* 22:4:51-71.

Carlin, Thomas A. and John Crecink. 1979. "Small Farm Definition and Public Policy". *American Journal of Agricultural Economics* 61:5(December):933-939.

Carlin, Thomas A. and David Houston. 1981. "Small Farm Policy: What Role for the Government", in *Increasing Understanding of Public Problems and Policies-1981*. Farm Foundation, Oak Brook, Illinois.

Carter, Hall, Willard Cochrane, Lee Day, Ronald Powers, and Luther Tweeten. 1981. "Research and the Family Farm". A paper prepared for the

Agricultural Experiment Station Committee on Organization and Policy, Cornell University, Ithaca.

Coughenour, Milton C. and James A. Christenson. 1983. "Farm Structure, Social Class, and Farmers' Policy Perspectives". In David E. Brewter, Wayne D. Rasmussen and Garth Youngberg, eds. *Farms in Tradition*. Ames: Iowa State University Press.

Coughenour, Milton C. and Luther G. Tweeten. 1986. "Quality of Life Perspective and Farm Structure". In Joseph Molnar, ed. *Agricultural Changes: Consequences for Southern Farms and Rural Communities*. Boulder, Co.: Westview Press.

Crecink, John C. 1986. "Small Farms: Their Distribution, Characteristics and Households". Agricultural Economics Research Report 161, Agricultural and Forestry Experiment Station, Mississippi State University, April.

de Janvry, Alain. 1982. "Historical Forces That Have Shaped World Agriculture". In *Agriculture, Change, and Human Values*, R. Haines and R. Lanier, eds., pp. 14-28. Gainesville Humanities and Agricultural Program, University of Florida.

Eginton, Charles and Luther Tweeten. 1982. "Impacts of National Inflation on Entrance and Equity Growth - Opportunities on Typical Commercial Farms". Paper presented at the annual meetings of the Southern Agricultural Economics Association, Atlanta, Georgia.

Gebremedhin, Tesfa G. 1990. *A Profile of Small-Scale Farm Operations in West Virginia*. R.D. Publication No. 772, College of Agriculture and Forestry and Cooperative Extension Service, West Virginia University, June.

Gladwin, Christina H. and Robert Zabawa. 1985. "Survival Strategies of Small Part-Time Farmers: A Response to Structural Change". In *Strategy for Survival of Small Farmers -- International Implications*. Tuskegee Institute, Human Resources Development Center.

Goldschmidt, Walter. 1978. "Large-Scale Farming and the Rural Social Structure". *Rural Sociology*, 43:3:362-366.

Heady, Earl O. and Steven T. Sonka. 1974 "Farm Size, Rural Community Income and Consumers Welfare". *American Journal of Agricultural Economics* 56:3(August):534-42.

Hightower, Jim. 1972. *Hard Tomatoes, Hard Times: The Failure of The Land Grant College Complex*. Agribusiness Account Ability Project Washington, D.C..

Hinson, Roger A. 1983. "Characteristics of Small Commercial Farms in Three Louisiana Farming Areas". DAE Research Report No. 622. Louisiana State University, Baton Rouge, Louisiana, November.

Lewis, James A. 1978. "Implications of Alternative Definitions of Small Farm". In *Toward A Federal Small Farms Policy*. Washington, D.C., National Rural Center NRC, Report No. 9, November.

Lin, Williams, George Coffman, and J.B. Penn. 1986. *U.S. Farm Numbers, Sizes, and Related Structural Dimensions, Projections to Year 2000*.

USDA/ASCS, Technical Bulletin, No. 1625, Washington, D.C., July.

Madden, J. Patrick and Heather Tischbein. 1979. "Toward an Agenda for Small Farm Research". *American Journal of Agricultural Economics* 61:5(December):940-946.

Marshall, Ray and Allen Thompson. 1976. *Status and Prospects of Small Farmers in the South*. Atlanta Southern Regional Council, Inc..

Schertz, Lyle P. 1979. "Another Revolution in U.S. Farming". U.S. Department of Agriculture, Economic Research Service, Washington DC.

Schuh, G. Edward. 1984. "Policy Options for Improving the Trade Performance of U.S. Agriculture". Washington, D.C., National Agricultural Forum.

Sharples, Jerry and Allen Prindle. 1973 "Income Characteristics of Farm Families in the Corn Belt". *Agricultural Finance Review* 34:13-18.

Singh, Surenda P. and Handy Williamson, Jr. 1985. "Perspectives on the Small Farm (Small, Low-Income Farms in Tennessee)", School of Agriculture and Home Economics Cooperative Research Program, Tennessee State University, Nashville, Tennessee.

Tweeten, Luther G. 1995. "The Twelve Best Reasons for Commodity Programs: Why None Stands Scrutiny". *Choices* (Second Quarter): 4-7, 43-44.

Tweeten, Luther G., G. Bradley Cilley and Isaa Popoola. 1980. "Topology and Policy for Small Farms". *Southern Journal of Agricultural Economics* 12:2:77-85.

U.S. Congress, Office of Technology Assessment. 1986. *Technology, Public Policy, and the Changing Structure of American Agriculture*. OTA-F-285. Washington, DC: Government Printing Office, March.

U.S. Department of Agriculture, Economic Research Service. 1993. *Economic Indicators of the Farm Sector: National Financial Summary, 1992*. USDA/ERS, Washington DC: Government Printing Office.

U.S. Department of Agriculture, Statistical Reporting Service. 1994. *1993 Agricultural Statistics*. Washington DC: Government Printing Office.

U.S. Department of Commerce. 1950-52. *U.S. Census of Agriculture*. USDA/Economic and Statistics Administration, Washington DC: Government Printing Office, Various years.

Van Blokland, P.J. 1981. "Trends in Agricultural Finance with Reference to Florida". Florida Food and Resource Economics No. 38, Institute of Food and Agricultural Sciences, University of Florida, Gainesville, Florida.

West, Gerry G. 1979. "Agricultural Economics Research and Extension Needs of Small Scale Limited-Resource Farmers". *American Journal of Agricultural Economics* 61:1(July):49-56.

2 Sustainability and Size: Are Small Farms More Sustainable?

Gerard E. D'Souza, John Ikerd and Lynndee Kemmet

Introduction

All farms have some impact on the environment and the local community of which they are a part. The type of impact (positive or negative) and the intensity (high, medium, or low) are likely to be different for different sizes of farms. The role that farm size plays in sustainable agricultural and rural development is something we address in this chapter.

A sustainable system is one where current production and consumption activities do not come at the cost of future activities, and activities undertaken at one location do not come at the cost of activities at other locations. Thus, our definition recognizes that sustainability has both a temporal and a spatial dimension. Given this definition, which category of farms, small or large, is likely to be most sustainable? Our study focuses on the U.S., with implications for sustainable agricultural and rural development elsewhere.

Obviously, factors other than size, such as type of farm (e.g., grain, livestock, fruit, combination), operator characteristics, and geographic location are important determinants of sustainability. Why, then, look at size in isolation? For one thing, the relationship between farm size and sustainability has not been examined in detail before. Second, as discussed in the previous chapter, there has been a trend toward fewer, larger, and more "industrialized" farms, particularly in the U.S., in the past few years, a trend that some would argue has been accompanied by an unsustainable agriculture. Third, by examining size in isolation, it may be possible to shed light on whether characteristics associated with sustainable farms are observed more frequently on farms at one end of the size spectrum compared to the other and, therefore, whether or not the trend toward fewer and larger farms should be reversed.

Just as there are many definitions of sustainability (some articulated elsewhere in the chapter and in other chapters in this volume), there are many definitions of small and large farms. Consistent with the definition in the previous chapter, we define a small farm as one having less than $100,000 in annual gross farm sales (the average land holding for this sales class is 271 acres), and operated by a household where one or more family members likely works off the farm perhaps full-time.[1] Conversely, large farms are those where annual gross sales consistently exceed $100,000 (the average land holding for this sales class is 1,542 acres), and are generally synonymous with "industrial farms". We make a distinction between management and stewardship. Good management does not necessarily encompass good stewardship; however, good stewardship implies good management.

We rely on the literature and the data available to us, substantiating our arguments with our own observations as well. While there is a large literature on sustainable development and on farm structure, little attempt has been made to tie the two together.

Is There a Problem?

One is tempted to look around at the bountiful food supply in countries such as the U.S. and conclude that all is well with the food supply chain. Does this "chain" have any weak "links"? If we think of the food chain as being comprised of economic, social, and environmental links, there is enough evidence to suggest that the economic links are strong. Unfortunately, the same cannot be said about the social and environmental links. Witness the declining rural infrastructure and environmental quality in many parts of the country—and world—today. Certainly, not all of this is attributable solely to agriculture. However, of that portion that can be attributed to agriculture, what proportion is attributable to small farms versus large farms?

Some might argue that the increase in farm size, and accompanying reliance on off-farm inputs, mechanization, specialization, and globalization in the recent past are contributing to the strength of the "economic link" in the food chain. Others might argue that this trend toward fewer and larger farms coincides with the trend toward the declining sustainability of agriculture, in the process undermining the "social links" and the "environmental links". That agriculture in the U.S.—and perhaps globally as well—is on an industrialization trajectory is generally acknowledged (e.g., Barry, 1995; Drabenstott, 1995; Davis and Langham, 1995).

Ikerd (1993) attributes environmental concerns from agriculture mainly to the industrial paradigm of agricultural production, manifested in large-scale, commercial units. Industrial methods have accounted for most of the productivity increases in agriculture (as conventionally measured) but, on the other hand, are an important source of environmental and, some would argue, rural development, problems. Environmental problems include non-point source pollution, loss of biodiversity and habitat, and risks to human health and wildlife. Rural development problems as a result of industrialization include reduced employment and income generation, and less diversified local economies, increasing vulnerability of rural communities to economic hardships. However, whether or not industrialization of agriculture, on balance, is good or bad for rural areas is complex to determine (Barry, 1995; Drabenstott, 1995). In the meantime, as long as the natural resource base is viewed as costless in the market place, the short term benefits from using industrial methods are likely to continue to exceed the short run costs, thereby encouraging their continuing adoption. Coase (1937), in defining firm size in terms of the number of transactions, observed that a firm will tend to expand "until the costs of organizing an extra transaction within the firm become equal to the costs of carrying out the same transaction by means of an exchange on the open market or the costs of organizing in another firm". To the extent that the intra-firm and perhaps inter-firm "costs of organizing transactions" are underestimated, in addition to weakening the social and environmental links, they would result in larger firm sizes than optimal, with the ensuing misallocation of resources ultimately weakening the economic link as well. Over time, as economic valuation of non-market resources gains in precision and acceptance, the relative economics of industrial methods will also change.

The *hypothetical* tradeoffs among size, economic efficiency, rural quality of life (as proxied by, say, rural development), and environmental quality can be illustrated with the aid of a diagram (Figure 1). Some explanation and caveats are necessary. In Figure 1A the relationship perhaps should show a local maximum to reflect the potential for diseconomies of size. Figure 1B reflects the fact that as farm size increases, so does the trend toward specialization and industrialization and the associated reduction in environmental quality; smaller farms, on the other hand, tend to be more mixed, many including a combination of livestock, crop, pasture and woodland activities (literature to support this contention is presented later; a later chapter, by Capalbo and Antle, provides some evidence regarding the existence of economic and environmental tradeoffs, more or less substantiating the relations hypothesized in panels (A) and (B), and extending these tradeoffs into the human health arena as well). Perhaps the best evidence to support Figure

1C comes from the work of Goldschmidt (1978). In a comparison of two California towns, one surrounded by large-scale enterprises and the other surrounded by family-operated units, the author found the latter town to be "superior in all measures reflecting the quality of life" (p. 363). Goldschmidt subsequently found evidence that this relationship could be extrapolated to the U.S. as a whole as well as evidence showing a significant and positive correlation between the prevalence of large-scale farming and economically poorer families. Figure 1D merely sums up the relationships in the other three figures. The relationships embodied in the graphs are intended mainly to provide a framework for the analysis; they also are intended to reinforce the need for more empirical analysis to either affirm or negate the hypothesized relationships.

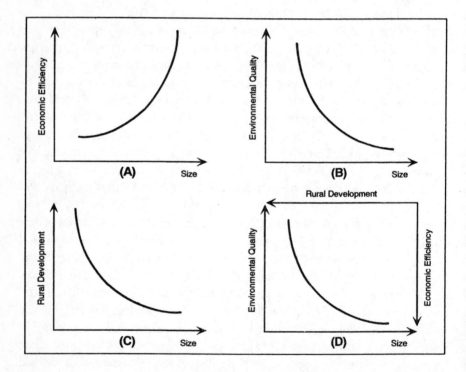

Figure 1. Hypothetical tradeoffs between (A) economic efficiency and size; (B) environmental quality and size; (C) rural development and size; and (D) economic efficiency, environmental quality and rural development, and farm size

Is There a Solution?

Sustainability is increasingly viewed as the post-industrial paradigm guiding agriculture. The sustainability paradigm emerged as a possible solution for such problems created by the industrial model as declining quality of rural life and the environment, and resource base degradation. In the remainder of this chapter, we will examine how and why farm size plays a role in this process.

Conway (1987) defines sustainability in agriculture as "the ability of an agroecosystem to maintain productivity when subject to a major disturbing force", which we shall refer to as "Conway sustainability".[2] Examples of "major disturbing forces" include frequent pesticide applications, a new pest, and a price shock such as the oil price increases of the 1970s (Conway). The discussion so far leads us to the following proposition:

> *Proposition 1:* To the extent that, the larger the farm, the greater the natural ecosystem it displaces or landscape it dominates, large farms individually and collectively create greater ecological "disturbance".

It is not difficult to visualize, for example, the disruption that could result from a (new or old) pest outbreak on a large, specialized, farm. Further, one of the reasons why agriculture has become increasingly viewed as unsustainable is because farms have tended to become closed, self-contained units, something fostered by the "industrialized" concept of agriculture.

Before examining whether or not small farms can be part of the solution to putting agriculture on a more sustainable track, it may be useful—without merely duplicating a similar effort in the previous chapter—to profile small farms, domestically and globally.

Nature of Small Farms

While there is perhaps no "typical" small farm (Thompson, 1986), it may be illuminating to compare small and large farms in terms of some aggregate measures. Slightly over 80 percent of U.S. farms are small (Table 1). However, small farms together account for 26 percent of gross sales (which translated into an annual monetary value of $48 billion in 1992), even though they control over half the value of all farm assets. Both the total number of U.S. farms and the number of small farms have shown a declining trend, while the number of large farms has shown an increasing trend (Figure 2).

Table 1. Profile of U.S. small farms[a]

Item	Value in 1992	Percentage	Change in Value, 1982 - 92 (%)	Change in Value, 1987 - 92 (%)
Number (1,000)	1,724	82	-17	-10
Gross Cash Income (billion $)	48	26	9	9
Net Cash Income (billion $)	8	14	14	-20
Govt. Payments (billion $)	3	33	50	-100
Assets (billion $)	454	53	-20	5
Debt (billion $)	60	43	-30	-12
Debt/Asset Ratio (average %)	13	80	-13	-19
Part Owners and Tenants	566	33[b]	-9	-11

[a] Small farms are defined as farms with annual sales not exceeding $100,000. All monetary values are in nominal terms.

[b] Percentage of all small farms that are operated by part owners or tenants (the comparative number for large farms is 74 percent).

Sources: U.S. Dept. of Agriculture and U.S. Dept. of Commerce (1994*a*, *b*).

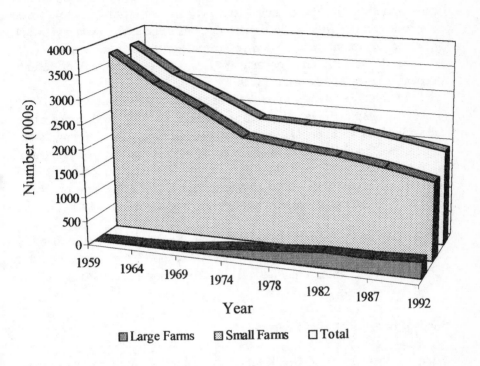

Figure 2. Trends in number of U.S. farms by size group

Source: U.S. Department of Commerce (1994).

Although the farm-generated cash income of small farms as a group is positive and sizable, an examination of the size distribution of income in the U.S. will inevitably reveal relatively large disparities, with negative net cash incomes not uncommon both for specific sub-groups and for individual farmers across the group. However, to the extent that many small farms rely heavily on off-farm income, history would indicate that the lack of positive net farm income by some farmers in this group, in and of itself, does not appear to threaten their survival as a group. Glover and Kusterer (1990) identify a major goal of small farm operators to be to increase the "security and income of their families while retaining their independence as owners and operators of a farm enterprise" (p. 1). This goal provides a motivation that might ensure their long-term economic sustainability, even if cash returns fail to always cover cash costs. Furthermore, the desire to be independent should somewhat counteract the recent trend toward vertical integration in some sectors (such as in the U.S. poultry and hog industries) and the *de facto* loss of farmer independence usually associated with it.

Globally, statistics on small farms are less readily available. Wharton (1969) (as cited in Valdes, Scobie, and Dillon, 1979, p. 168), reports that "about half the world population is dependent on subsistence farming, about 40 percent of total cultivated land is worked by small farmers, 60 percent of all farmers are small, and they account for less than 40 percent of all agricultural output". Peasants are said to account for a "major proportion" of basic food crop production in most developing countries (Valdes, Scobie, and Dillon).

One way to examine the contribution of small farms to sustainability objectives is to explore the scope of societal "benefits" and "costs" of small farms as a group, at least qualitatively, which we now proceed to do.

Societal Benefits of Small Farms

Whatever they are called (small farmers, peasants, or subsistence farmers), they have several characteristics other than size that commonly distinguish them from their larger counterparts. Among these are: (a) the intensity of the man-nature relationship, (b) the diversity of plant and animal life, and (c) the diversity of income sources on small farms relative to large farms. Carlin and Saupe (1993) have found that many small farms contribute more to local economic activity in rural areas than a few large farms. This leads to our next proposition:

> *Proposition 2*: If an emphasis on environmental and rural quality, biodiversity, and income diversity, in turn, are among the necessary conditions for sustainable development, then small farms could, individually and collectively, enhance the likelihood of sustainable agricultural and rural development.

One way to explore the contribution of small farms to sustainability objectives is to match the characteristics of a sustainable system with those of small farms and large farms, respectively. Tisdell (1994) associates the following characteristics with sustainable systems: (a) maintenance of intergenerational economic welfare, (b) existence of human beings indefinitely, (c) resilience of production and economic systems, (d) sustainability of community, and (e) maintenance of biodiversity. The characteristics of small farms have previously been articulated. Following Tisdell, characteristics of "modern" or "industrialized" agricultural systems include: (a) high energy-using, (b) high chemical-using, (c) intensive management, (d) premium on uniformity rather than diversity of both products and environments, and (e) dependence on research for productivity maintenance. Based on these listings of characteristics, it would seem that small farms match the characteristics of sustainable systems more so than large ones (assuming the synonymity between large farms and industrialized ones). Table 2 summarizes this matching of characteristics.

Table 2. Properties of sustainable systems and consistency with the goals of small-scale farming, and "industrialized" farming

Properties of Sustainable Systems[a]	Consistent with Goals of Small-Scale Farming?	Consistent with Goals of Industrialized Farming?
Maintenance of inter-generational welfare	yes	no
Existence of human species indefinitely	?	no
Resilience of production and economic systems	yes	no
Sustainability of community	yes	no
Maintenance of biodiversity	yes	no

[a] Properties as defined by Tisdell (1994).

The following are some specific benefits of small farms within a sustainability context (Thompson, 1986):

● *Buffering effect*. Thompson (1986) points out that small farms can act as buffers against urban encroachment and that the economic vitality of a community is directly proportional to the number of small farms in that community. This is attributed to the fact that small farms, particularly in urban states, do not depend substantially on income from farming and, therefore, do not face the same economic pressure to sell land for development as their larger counterparts. As it turns out, small farmers own a relatively high proportion of farm land in the Eastern states where urban pressures are also greatest.

Some U.S. state tax systems designed to protect small farms and open space also seem to have encouraged property owners to protect farmland. For example, New Jersey's Farmland Assessment Act has made it possible for large landowners, including corporations, to greatly reduce their property tax bills by keeping their land in agriculture. While some have criticized the law because it allows wealthy property owners to reduce their property tax burden, others have argued that it is the reason why New Jersey, as urbanized as it is, still has open space and farmland.

● *Scenic attributes*. Although difficult to quantify, the aesthetic appeal of small family farms to tourists as they drive around clearly exists. Thompson cites the case of Lancaster County in Pennsylvania, where the "attraction" is the large concentration of Amish and Mennonite farms. He adds that this is the most productive farm county east of the Mississippi river, with gross sales of $700 million annually from farming, and an estimated $250 million annually from tourists. Thompson also finds small farms fulfilling a role as "goodwill ambassador" from the farm sector to the public by virtue of the roadside markets many of them operate. Woods (1997), in turn, finds a link between public farm markets and tourism. In parts of Europe, particularly the U.K., agriculture is going through a transition where subsidies are no longer based on production, but rather are paid out to maintain the scenic and environmental characteristics of the farm (Odle, 1997). Such programs are designed to benefit wildlife, the landscape, and public recreation, in addition to maintaining a healthy farming economy.

While scenic attributes are not necessarily precluded for large farms, their net amenity values are often perceived to be negative. Take the case of the trend toward "mega" hog and broiler farms in the U.S. Critics cite the odor and water pollution problems often experienced not just by people who live around them, but even across large distances. Instances of accidents such as ruptured waste pipes in large hog facilities and the associated spills of hog waste and fish kills in surrounding bodies of water are not uncommon.

● *Lower land use intensity.* Thompson notes that small farms tend to use their land less intensively than large ones, which potentially is less environmentally damaging (other authors, including some in this volume, point out that *higher* intensity of land use is perhaps more desirable to combat such things as deforestation, for example). Larger proportions of land are devoted to woodland on small farms (17 percent versus 5 percent); less cultivable land is actually cultivated and harvested on small farms (50 percent versus 80 percent); a greater percentage of cropland is used for pasturing livestock (31 percent versus 8 percent); and small farms maintain almost twice as much cropland (although accounting for only a small fraction) in cover crops, legumes, and other "soil improving uses" (Thompson, 1986). Small farms tend to involve more "site specificity" and are more in tune with peculiarities of the landscape of which they are a part.

● *Greater reliance on conservation practices.* Thompson points out an interesting dichotomy. On the one hand, an implication of the lower intensity of land use by small farmers is that they may be contributing less to soil erosion than larger operations. For example, in a comparison of soil degradation under small holder farming and large scale irrigated land in Nigeria (Eussiet, 1990) over a 13-year period, it was confirmed that soil degradation, qualitatively and quantitatively, was more severe on the large farms. On the other hand, there is the possibility, in the aggregate, that small farm cropland is more inherently erodible, necessitating its maintenance in pasture or cover crops to minimize erosion. On balance, Thompson argues that small farmers "*must* be better land stewards than their larger counterparts" because small farmers tend to be less dependent on row crops that are inherently more erosive, they farm fewer acres and can devote more time to caring for them.[3] The last characteristic is consistent with the "management-intensive" nature of sustainable systems.

● *Intergenerational transfer of practices.* Associated more with small farms, indigenous peoples and less-developed countries. By relying more on natural phenomena, these practices are more sustainable from an ecological standpoint.

Societal Costs

Some would argue that small farms are less efficient and slower to adopt new technologies in comparison to larger farms. It may be useful to re-examine these perceptions, particularly from a societal perspective.

• *Inefficiency*. It is generally recognized that economies of size accrue in farming. However, to the extent that environmental and other social costs are excluded from conventional efficiency measures, the economies of size are overstated. Kislev and Peterson (1982; 1996), and later Peterson (1997), find evidence to support their hypothesis that scale economies do not fully or consistently explain farm growth; in fact, when measurement problems affecting scale economy estimates are factored in, Peterson finds that estimated scale economies in agriculture disappear and, in fact, diseconomies occur as farm size increases.   Peterson categorizes measurement problems stemming from: (1) combining the farm dwelling with capital inputs, (2) correlation of environmental and management characteristics with size, and (3) the effect of off-farm employment on small farm output and production costs.

Then there is an argument that large, commercial, farms are more "efficient" than their smaller counterparts because the commercial farms make decisions based primarily on economic considerations.   Therefore, for example, they would not use more than the "necessary" level of purchased inputs such as fertilizers and pesticides.   Even if this were true, it does not ensure that commercial farms are sustainable in the long run.   In fact, to the extent that the short-run and cumulative environmental consequences of farm management decisions are ignored, it would likely ensure the long-term unsustainability of such operations.   This would be true, albeit on a different scale, of small operations that ignored social production costs as well.   To the extent that small farms tend to depend more on off-farm income, the buffering effect associated with such income is generally recognized as an advantage that makes small farms more competitive while keeping food costs lower than they otherwise would be.

• *Slower adoption of technologies*. Large farmers are generally the first to adopt new production technologies (Bieri, de Janvry, and Schmitz, 1972) because of their easier access to credit particularly for large-scale innovations (Price, 1983).   However, while technological use can be economically beneficial—especially in the short run to early adopters—technical change can reduce societal welfare if distortions, including externalities, are present (see

Alston and Martin, 1995, for example). From a sustainability perspective, there are two types of technologies, desirable and undesirable, depending upon the nature of the social benefit/cost valuation. (The relationship between sustainability and production technology is explored elsewhere in this volume.) The correlation between farm size and type/rate of technology adoption has not been explored to any significant extent. There is some evidence to show that large farms are actually less likely to adopt "environmentally-friendly technologies" (Owens, Swinton, and van Ravenswaay, 1997), although this does not necessarily imply that small farms are quick to adopt such technologies. Thus, whether or not the perceived slower rate of adoption of new technologies by small farmers as a group is good or bad from a societal standpoint depends importantly on the type of technology.

For some interesting counter-arguments to the above discussion on benefits and costs of small farms, the reader is referred to a discussion by Henry (1996).

Benefits and costs notwithstanding, is it possible for a community to meet its food needs from small-scale production units? Examples can serve to illustrate that it is possible.

An Example

The "ultimate" small farm, of course, is a kitchen garden. It must be stressed that it is impractical for an "advanced" society to revert to kitchen gardens for the population as a whole, and this is certainly not being advocated here. However, it serves as a useful vehicle to illustrate the relatively benign effect small-scale production has on the environment. Thus, in a kitchen-garden setting, equipment needs are greatly reduced, and so is transportation. Use of manure and composting, and recycling in general, is quite common in such settings.[4] At the other extreme, "industrialized" farms rely heavily on a transportation and retailing infrastructure that is energy- and capital-intensive, that potentially contributes heavily to environmental degradation, and that requires constant investment in infrastructure, including new technologies. While perhaps consistent with the Solow or Hartwick view of sustainability, the industrial model of farming is inconsistent with the Holling (and Conway) view of sustainability.[5]

While reverting to individual kitchen gardens to meet our food needs is not a practical solution, a system that is both small-scale and community-oriented is more so. An example of such a system is the "Community-Supported Agriculture" (CSA) concept which is becoming increasingly popular under a variety of names in many areas of the country.[6] The basic idea is for small farms in the community to market their products, often although not necessarily "organically" produced, to other CSA members, which consist of farmers and others in the community. By marketing directly, farms are able to cut costs and increase profit margins. In a typical CSA, members buy "shares" at predetermined prices, entitling them to a "subscription" of a market basket comprised of an assortment of commodities ranging from fresh fruit and vegetables, to flowers and even meat at regular intervals throughout the growing season. This is an example of a system that can meet the needs of the local community in a manner that potentially is economically, socially, and environmentally sustainable (such programs can even be successful in large cities such as New York City, where six CSAs supply a 3,000, and ever-growing, customer base). The Pennsylvania-based Biodynamic Farming and Gardening Association estimates that the number of CSAs in the U.S. has grown from only a handful around 10 years ago, to over 500 now.

Looking to the Future

In the 21st century, the dovetailing of several problems and new opportunities is going to mean a transformation of the way agricultural production takes place. Blum (1994), for example, cites (a) increasing competition for space for food production brought about by "exponential growth" of urban spillover and socioeconomic problems into adjacent rural areas, (b) competition between food production and groundwater production, and (c) reduction of biodiversity through "large scale monocultural approaches" that are likely to severely constrain large farms. Blum also cites factors such as decreasing land surfaces in many developing countries due to increasing soil erosion as well as "sealing of fertile land for infrastructural development" that, in the future, are likely to translate into more small-scale farms, perhaps reversing the declining trend of the last few decades.

It is obvious that farmers in general, and across the entire size spectrum, for a myriad of reasons, are paying closer attention to the environmental impacts of their farming practices, earlier with an emphasis on soil quantity and water quality, and more recently on water quantity and soil quality. D'Souza, Cyphers, and Phipps (1993), for example, found that water quality surrounding the farm is significant in a producer's choice of agricultural practices. Van Keulen (1997) finds that the source of water quality problems often is a water *quantity* problem. Much uncertainty remains about the effectiveness of many practices in controlling pollution as well as the fate and transport mechanisms of agriculturally-caused pollution sources themselves. What is less uncertain is the existence of (a) an upper bound to the waste-absorption capacity of the environment, (b) a lower bound on the natural capital stock needed to sustain life, and (c) a low degree of substitution between natural capital and manufactured capital.

Can Small Farms Compete?

Effects of Globalization

When analyzing the effects of farm size on sustainability it is important to consider not only farm size but also the organization of and links within the agriculture industry. As with other industries, agriculture is feeling the effects of increased globalization. One of these effects is that links between multinational agribusinesses and small, independent growers are increasing. By linking themselves with a major agribusiness, which serves as their marketer and distributor, small farmers are able to sell their produce in a world market, rather than just a local one. For the agribusiness, direct links with farmers provides a secure supply of produce.

Such links are most common in the fruit and vegetable industry. The fresh produce market has grown tremendously in the United States as more Americans change their diets to include more fresh fruits and vegetables. As a result, marketers and distributors of fresh produce have sought to expand their production links into a variety of climatic zones. They do this through essentially two methods. One is to establish production facilities in countries around the world. The other is to contract with independent growers worldwide. Growers agree to sell their produce to agribusinesses, which assures growers of a market. Such links provide multinational agribusinesses with a steady supply of fresh produce for the American market throughout the year. Dole Foods proudly advertises its global links as the reason why it can provide the American consumer with summer produce in the winter months.[7]

These strong links between agribusiness and independent producer are not always visible in the data on farm size and organization. Yet, in some cases the links are so strong that the agribusiness refers to the contract growers as "our growers".[8] It is through these contracted relationships that a large agribusiness can gain some control over the independent producer. In its 1996

Annual Report regarding global operations, Dole Foods notes that in countries where it does not control production "it assists independent growers to successfully improve productivity and the quality of crops, enabling Dole to maintain the highest standard of the industry in the countries in which it operates".[9]   While such assistance might be extremely beneficial to the independent grower, it could also threaten that grower's freedom to make decisions regarding production methods.

This linking of multinational agribusinesses with small, local growers is not new. In the early 1900s in Mexico's Mexicali Valley, located in the Colorado River region, American agribusinesses developed direct links with Mexican growers. The American agribusinesses provided the growers with the credit to produce cotton. The growers provided the land and labor and agreed to sell their cotton to the agribusinesses, which processed the cotton and handled   marketing and distribution.[10]   In more recent years, American agribusiness distributors have developed similar links with Mexican vegetable producers, allowing them to provide fresh produce to the American market throughout the year (Mares, 1987).

While the close links between independent producer and large agribusiness provide benefits to both, they can also present a threat to the sustainability of smaller, independent farmers. The security of a contract with an agribusiness is an attractive proposition for growers, but it could lead smaller growers to switch from sustainable agricultural practices to more industrial methods. As noted above, a contract might reduce a grower's control over production methods on his farm. Once under contract, the freedom to shift to other crops, or diversify, might be gone.

But a shift away from sustainability might not always be the result of pressure from the agribusiness that holds a grower's contract. The prospect of guaranteed sales and expanded markets could entice many small growers to specialize, seek greater yields from their land, and expand. This is exactly what seems to be occurring in the cranberry industry. The demand for cranberry products in the American market has soared, making it difficult for current producers to keep up with the demand. As a result, distributors of cranberry products are seeking contracts with growers and they are willing to pay a hefty price, which is pitting distributors against one another in the competition for grower contracts. This is financially quite good for the growers, but many are reacting by shifting more land into cranberry production, increasing yields on current land, and buying more land for production—a fact that is causing alarm among some environmentalists concerned about attempts to convert wetlands to cranberry bogs (Carton,

1997).

An important point here is that when analyzing the link between farm size and sustainability one must consider the organization within the agriculture industry. It is possible to find cases where farms categorized as small are as industrialized as larger farms, which could lead one to conclude that smaller farms are no more sustainable than large farms. But if it is found that such farms are linked with larger agribusinesses then one can question whether they fit the definition of a small, independent farmer. Perhaps what is needed is a different definition of farm size.

It is also important to note that small farmers do not necessarily threaten their sustainability by linking themselves to the global market. Perhaps what matters most is how they link themselves. A number of small-scale coffee growers in Latin America have successfully tied into the global market through companies and cooperatives that promote sustainable agricultural practices and market organic coffees to European and American consumers.[11] If it is true that consumer demand drives production, then, as this coffee case—together with the earlier discussed CSA movement—implies, consumers can encourage sustainable agricultural production by supporting those who practice it.

General Trends

Small farms have some clear ecological advantages over large farms, but will small farms of the future be able to compete economically? After all, the trend toward more specialized, larger farms has been driven by competitive forces of the market place. If the industrial era of human development were just beginning, or was even in its prime, there might be little hope for smaller *farms*, or smaller *firms* in general, into the foreseeable future. However, there is growing evidence that past trends toward larger, more specialized, industrialized enterprises are slowing, stopping, and even reversing.

Toffler (1990), for example, observes that many forecasters simply present unrelated trends, as if they would continue indefinitely, while ignoring how the trends are interconnected or the forces likely to reverse them. He contends that the forces of industrialization have run their course and are now reversing. The industrial models of economic progress are becoming increasingly obsolete. Old notions of efficiency and productivity are no longer valid. The new "modern" model is not mass production, but to produce customized goods and services aimed at niche markets, to constantly innovate, to focus on value-added products and specialized production.

Toffler adds that "the most important economic development of our lifetime has been the rise of a new system of creating wealth, based no longer on muscle but on the mind" (p. 9). He contends that "the conventional factors of production—land, labor, raw materials, and capital—become less important as knowledge is substituted for them" (p. 238). Toffler also provides some insights into the nature of knowledge-based production. He states that separate and sequential systems of production are being replaced with synthesis and simultaneous systems of production. Synergism is replacing specialization as a source of production efficiency.

The view that society has shifted to a knowledge-based order is shared by Drucker (1989), who subsequently dramatically describes the "sharp transformation" that has resulted in society (1994). Reich (1992), like both Drucker and Toffler believes that power and wealth of the future will be created by mind work, rather than by routine production.

Drucker points out an important fundamental difference between knowledge work and industrial work. Industrial work is fundamentally a mechanical process, whereas the basic principle of knowledge work is biological. He relates this difference to determining the "right size" of organization required to perform a given task. "Greater performance in a mechanical system is obtained by scaling up. Greater power means greater output: bigger is better. But this does not hold for biological systems. There, size follows function" (p. 259). It would surely be counterproductive, for instance, for a cockroach to be big, and equally counterproductive for an elephant to be small. Drucker concludes that differences in organizing principles may be critically important in determining the future size and ownership structure of economic enterprises. Other things equal, the smallest effective size is best for enterprises based on information and knowledge work. "'Bigger' will be 'better' only if the task cannot be done otherwise" (p. 260). The smallest effective size for farms will likely be different across space and time, and is that size that will best contribute to economic/market, environmental, and social objectives.

So what does all this say about the future of small farms? It says that farms of the future may need to be smaller, rather than larger, if they are to remain productive and competitive in the post-industrial, knowledge-based era of economic and social development. But if this is true, why are we currently seeing the rapid industrialization of some sectors of the agricultural economy?

Barker (1993) points out that new paradigms (including developmental models) tend to emerge while, in the minds of most people, the old paradigm is doing quite well. Typically, "a new paradigm appears sooner than it is needed and sooner than it is wanted" (p. 47). Consequently, the logical and rational response to a new paradigm is rejection. New paradigms emerge when it becomes apparent to some that the old paradigm is ineffective. Aging paradigms may also be applied in situations where they are ill suited, creating major new problems while contributing little in terms of new solutions. Industrial pollution of the natural environment is a prime example.

The industrialization paradigm appears to have outlived its usefulness, at least with respect to agriculture. This paradigm requires one to separate, sequence, analyze, and organize as a matter of standard operating procedure. Integration, simultaneity, synthesis, and spontaneity are missing from its problem-solving tool box. Thus, it automatically leads to specialization, never to synergism, as a logical solution, regardless of the nature of the problem. Consistent with this paradigm, problems caused by industrialization must be addressed by more sophisticated industrial methods, because there are no logical alternatives.

American agriculture provides a prime example of over application of the industrial paradigm. The early gains of appropriate specialization in agriculture lifted people out of subsistence living and made the American industrial revolution possible. But, the potential societal benefits from agricultural industrialization were probably largely realized by the late 1960s. More recent "advances" in agricultural technologies may well have done more damage to the ecologic and social resource base of rural areas than any societal benefit created by more "efficient" food production.

A new post-industrial paradigm for American agriculture is emerging under the conceptual umbrella of sustainable agriculture. The sustainable paradigm has emerged to solve problems created by the industrial model, primarily pollution of our environment and degradation of our rural and natural resource base. This new paradigm seems capable of creating benefits the industrial model is inherently incapable of providing, such as greater individual creativity, dignity of work, and attention to social equity.

Conclusions

The potential "benefits" of small farms appear to outweigh the potential "costs" when viewed in a sustainable development context. Further, the characteristics of small farms seem to most closely resemble those of sustainable systems. This leads us to the preliminary conclusion that small is more sustainable than large when it comes to agricultural and rural development issues. The conclusion that smaller is better is certainly not new, at least in a general context as evidenced by now classic works such as *Small is Beautiful*.

Although not dominant in production terms, small farms are numerically significant and an integral part of the rural community. Furthermore, small farms are consistent with both the Conway view of sustainability and the Holling view of sustainability. In general, they are not large enough to threaten the stability either of the system as a whole or of key components of the system. In contrast, the larger a farm, in general, the greater the geographic impact on the natural ecosystem, and therefore the more likely it is to interfere with ecosystem stability. It would be premature to conclude that *all* small farms are sustainable and *all* large farms are not; however, there clearly are tradeoffs among size, economic efficiency (as currently measured), environmental quality, and rural development.

In the past, public policy has been the "villain" of sustainable development. In the future, policy needs to be virtuous instead. Changing from a commodity- or acre-based system to an ecological- or landscape-based system may be necessary to accurately capture the essence of the relationship between a farm and the ecosystem of which it is a part. After all, a major reason why the current version of large-scale, commercial, agriculture is unsustainable is because of the artificial separation between the farm and surrounding landscape, a legacy of the many years of pursuing an "industrialized" concept of agriculture.

The sustainable agriculture paradigm is also consistent with the visions of Toffler, Drucker, Reich, and others of a post-industrial era of human progress. Sustainable agriculture is management intensive and, inherently, information and knowledge intensive.

Complexity, interdependence, and simultaneity are fundamental elements of the sustainable model, which is clearly biological rather than mechanical in nature. For such systems, size must follow function. In biological systems, individual elements must conform to their ecological niche. Big farms will be sustainable only if their "niche" is equally large. It is readily apparent that many of today's large farms are degrading both the natural and human resource base as they have expanded beyond their ecological and societal niches. It will take "mind work", not physical or economic muscle, for farmers of the future to find a niche where they carry out their function by means that are ecologically sound, economically viable, and socially responsible. The vast majority of those niches will likely be smaller than today's "commercial-sized" farm.

Can small farms compete? Other things equal, the smallest effective size will be the most competitive size, for farms as for other information—and knowledge—based enterprises of the future. The logical future trends in U.S. agriculture will be toward smaller, rather than larger, farms as we move through the great transformation toward the post-industrial era.

We began this analysis by questioning what role farm structure plays in sustainable agricultural development. In the process of addressing this question, we raised—and attempted to answer—other questions. These include: What characteristics must a farm possess for it to be sustainable? Are characteristics associated with sustainable farms more likely to be associated with small farms rather than large? Questions that remain include: What is the optimal size farm (or the "smallest effective" farm size)—and, more fundamentally, how should size be measured—in the sustainability era? Can a farm that adopts sustainable practices be sustainable regardless of its size? More generally, will small "continue to be beautiful?" And rather than a "silent spring" will we have "silent springs", as clean water, among other resources, become more scarce? While such questions have no easy answers, they do, however, reveal the shortcomings of this analysis and can guide further work in this area.

Finally, it is important to underscore, as we did at the outset, that sustainability has both temporal and spatial dimensions. The temporal dimension is perhaps best represented in the Seneca phrase, "Before acting, we must consider the consequences of our actions for the next seven generations..". If we add to this "... and for the next seven watersheds" then we can capture the spirit of the spatial dimension as well.

Notes

1. This definition of a small farm is generally consistent with one proposed by the American Small Farm magazine [http://www.smallfarm.com/], which defines a small farm (or ranch) as one with 5-300 acres that is owner-operated, earns income from agriculture, and has at least one full-time off-farm income. From a historical perspective, it is perhaps noteworthy that this size operation is considerably larger than even the 160-acre limitation embodied in the agrarian provisions of the 19th century U.S. Homestead Act.

2. The idea underlying this term originated with what Common and Perrings (1992) refer to as "Holling sustainability". A system is said to be "Holling-sustainable" if it is resilient enough to retain its basic structure

even when subjected to external shocks or strains.   Thus, "Conway sustainability" and "Holling sustainability" are operationally similar concepts.

3.   Thompson makes an interesting, and apparently important, distinction between *part-time* small farmers and *full-time* small farmers. The author expects the latter to use their land similarly to their large-scale counterparts.

4.   This point was made by Dave Finnie in an electronic mailing to multiple recipients of the Internet on-line discussion group, "AGROECOLOGY" (on LISTSERV@WVNVM) dated 23 August, 1995.

5.   Solow or Hartwick sustainability refers to constant consumption over infinite time as long as the Hartwick rule (rents deriving from exploitation of exhaustible resources must be reinvested in renewable resources) applies. Holling sustainability is defined in footnote 2.

6.   The idea underlying CSAs, "subscription" farms, "green markets", and other small-scale community-oriented farming approaches, at least in the U.S., was apparently originated by Booker T. Whatley, an Alabama horticulturist, in the 1970s. Worldwide, the "movement" is believed to have originated by a group of Japanese women some 30 years ago.

7.   Dole Food Company, Inc., *Annual Report 1996*, available at [http://www.dole.com].

8.   Co-author Lynndee Kemmet spent six years covering agriculture as a journalist in Southern California. During interviews, executives with several agribusinesses operating in the region frequently referred to independent growers as company growers because of the strong links those growers had with agribusiness.

9.   Dole Food Company, Inc., *Annual Report 1996*.

10.   For a discussion of the involvement of U.S. agribusiness interests with Mexican growers, see Whiteford (1986) and Sanderson (1986).

11.   "Green, As in Greenbacks", *The Economist*, 1 February 1997, p. 42.

Acknowledgements

This chapter is based in part on an article by D'Souza and Ikerd published in the July 1996 issue of the *Journal of Agricultural and Applied Economics*.

The authors thank Tim Phipps for helpful comments on an earlier version.

References

Alston, J.M. and W.J. Martin. 1995. "Reversal of Fortune: Immiserizing Technical Change in Agriculture". *American Journal of Agricultural Economics* 77: 251-259.

Barker, Joel. 1993. *Paradigms: The Business of Discovering the Future.* New York: Harper Business, a Division of Harper Collins Publishing.

Barry, P.J. 1995. "Industrialization of U.S. Agriculture: Policy, Research, and Education Needs". *Agricultural and Resource Economics Review* 24: 128-135.

Bieri, J., A. de Janvry, and A. Schmitz. 1972. "Agricultural Technology and the Distribution of Welfare Gains". *American Journal of Agricultural Economics* 54: 801-808.

Blum, W.E.H. 1994. "Sustainable Land Use and Environment". Symposium on Management of Land and Water Resources for Sustainable Agriculture and Environment, Indian Society of Soil Science, New Delhi, India.

Carlin, T.A. and W.E. Saupe. 1993. "Structural Change in Farming and Its Relationship to Rural Communities". In *Size, Structure, and the Changing Face of American Agriculture*, A. Hallam, ed., pp. 538-560. Boulder, CO: Westview Press.

Carton, B. 1997. "Forget Cattle and Corn: Let's Bet the Farm on Cranberry Crops". *Wall Street Journal* 23, July, p. A1.

Coase, R. 1986. "The Nature of the Firm". *Economica* 4(1937): 386-405. Reprinted in *The Economic Nature of the Firm: A Reader*, L. Putterman, ed. Cambridge, Mass.: Cambridge University Press.

Common, M. and C. Perrings. 1992. "Towards an Ecological Economics of Sustainability". *Ecological Economics* 6: 7-34.

Conway, G.R. 1987. "The Properties of Agroecosystems". *Agricultural Systems* 24: 95-117.

Davis, C.G. and M.R. Langham. 1995. "Agricultural Industrialization and Sustainable Development: A Global Perspective". *Journal of Agricultural and Applied Economics* 27: 21-34.

Drabenstott, M. 1995. "Agricultural Industrialization: Implications for Economic Development and Public Policy". *Journal of Agricultural and Applied Economics* 27: 13-20.

Drucker, Peter. 1989. *The New Realities.* New York: Harper and Row, Publishers, Inc..

Drucker, Peter. 1994. *Post-Capitalist Society.* New York: Harper Business, a Division of Harper Collins Publishing.

D'Souza, G., D. Cyphers, and T. Phipps. 1993. "Factors Affecting the Adoption of Sustainable Agricultural Practices". *Agricultural and Resource Economics Review* 22: 159-165.

D'Souza, G. and J. Ikerd. 1996. "Small Farms and Sustainable Development: Is Small *More* Sustainable?" *Journal of Agricultural and Applied Economics* 28: 73-83.

Eussiet, E.U. 1990. "A Comparison of Soil Degradation Under Smallholder Farming and Large-Scale Irrigation Land Use in Kano State, Northern Nigeria". *Land Degradation & Rehab.* 2: 209-214.

Glover, D. and K. Kusterer. 1990. *Small Farmers, Big Business.* New York: St. Martin's Press. Goldschmidt, W. 1978. "Large-Scale Farming and the Rural Social Structure". *Rural Sociology* 43: 362-366.

Henry, M.S. 1996. "Small Farms and Sustainable Development: Is Small *More* Sustainable? Discussion". *Journal of Agricultural and Applied Economics* 28: 84-87.

Ikerd, John. 1993. "Policy and Sustainable Agriculture". *Agricultural Outlook.* Jan-Feb. pp. 14-16.

Kislev, Y. and W. Peterson. 1982. "Prices, Technology, and Farm Size". *Journal of Political Economy* 90: 578-595.

Kislev, Y. and W. Peterson. 1996. "Economies of Scale in Agriculture: A Reexamination of the Evidence". In Papers in Honor of D. Gale Johnson, J.M. Antle and D.A. Sumner, eds., pp 156-170. Chicago: University of Chicago Press.

Mares, D.R. 1987. "The U.S.-Mexico Winter Vegetable Trade: Climate, Economics, and Politics," in B.F. Johnson, C. Luiselli, C.C. Contreras, and R.D. Norton, eds. *U.S.-Mexico Relations: Agriculture and Rural Development.* Stanford, CA: Stanford University Press. pp. 181-197.

Odle, J. 1997. "Life Outside the United States". *Progressive Farmer*, August. p. 2.

Owens, N.N., S.M. Swinton, and E.O. van Ravenswaay. 1997. "Will Farmers Use Safer Pesticides?" Selected paper presented at the annual meeting of the Southern Agricultural Economics Association, Birmingham, Alabama, February 2-5.

Peterson, W.L. 1997. "Are Large Farms More Efficient?" Staff Paper P97-2, Department of Applied Economics, University of Minnesota. January. [On-line version available at http://agecon.lib.umn.edu/mn.html]

Reich, Robert B. 1992. *The Work of Nations.* New York, N.Y.: Vintage Books, Random House Publishing.

Sanderson, S.E. 1986. *The Transformation of Mexican Agriculture: International Structure and the Politics of Rural Change.* Princeton, N.J.: Princeton University Press.

Thompson, Edward, Jr. 1986. *Small is Bountiful: The Importance of Small Farms in America.* Washington, D.C.: American Farmland Trust.

Tisdell, C.A. 1994. *Economics of Environmental Conservation.* New York, N.Y.: Elsevier Science B.V.

Toffler, Alvin. 1990. *Power Shifts.* New York, N.Y.: Bantam Books.

U.S. Department of Agriculture, Economic Research Service. 1992. "Economic Indicators of the Farm Sector: National Financial Summary 1991". Washington, D.C.

U.S. Department of Commerce, Bureau of the Census. 1994. *Statistical Abstract of the U.S.* Washington, D.C.: U.S. Govt. Printing Office. (1994*a*).

U.S. Department of Commerce, Bureau of the Census. 1994. *1992 Census of Agriculture: U.S. Summary and State Data.* Washington, D.C.: U.S. Govt. Printing Office. (1994*b*).

Valdes, A. G.M. Scobie, and J.L. Dillon, eds. 1979. *Economics and the Design of Small-Farmer Technology.* Ames, Iowa: Iowa State University Press.

Van Keulen, S. 1997. "Perceptions on Natural Resource Management in the North Fork Watershed, West Virginia, USA" M.S. thesis, Wageningen Agricultural University.

Wharton, C.R. 1969. "Subsistence Agriculture: Concepts and Scope". In *Subsistence Agriculture and Economic Development,* C.R. Wharton, ed. Chicago: Aldine.

Whiteford, S. 1986. "Troubled Waters: The Regional Impact of Foreign Investment in State Capital in the Mexicali Valley" in *Regional Impacts of U.S.-Mexican Relations*, Ina Rosenthal-Urey, ed., University of California, San Diego: Center for U.S.-Mexican Studies.

Woods, T.A. 1997. "Public Farm Markets and Tourism: Vendor and Consumer Perspectives on Developing Linkages Toward Improved Performance". Selected paper, annual meeting of the Southern Agricultural Economics Association, Birmingham, Alabama, February 2-5.

3 Sustainability: The Role of Markets Versus the Government

Luther Tweeten and William Amponsah

Introduction

Sustainable agriculture has many definitions. For example, Conway (1987) defines sustainability in agriculture as "the ability of an agroecosystem to maintain productivity when subjected to a major disturbing force" over time (p. 101). Some examples of "major disturbing forces" listed by Conway include frequent pesticide applications, a new pest, the cumulative effects of salinity or soil erosion, and the sudden rise of an input price such as the oil price increases of the 1970s. According to Markandya (1992), sufficient conditions to achieving sustainable development include correct economic valuations, appropriate legal and social framework, and environmental accounting or monitoring. Sustainability has economic dimensions (are farmers predestined to chronic low returns and financial failure?) and social dimensions (survival of family farms, rural communities, rural values, etc.), but here we focus solely on environmental and natural resource dimensions.

Recent decades provide compelling evidence that markets operate to allocate resources and products more efficiently than the public sector where goods are rival and exclusionary. Because all goods are not rival and exclusionary and for other reasons, a government role in a sustainable agriculture is essential. While an environmentally sound agriculture will rely mainly on the market for decisions regarding what, when, how, and where to produce, the public sector role is often pivotal in encouraging private firms to act in the public interest.

Market failures and appropriate policies to address them differ among problems that must be confronted for an environmentally sound agriculture. Consequently, the following issues are addressed: (1) renewable resource degradation, (2) wildlife habitat and biodiversity, and (3) nonrenewable resource depletion. Each of these issues is discussed under the following sub-headings: (a) conceptual issues, (b) current situation, and (c) policy options.

47

Renewable Resource Degradation

Conceptual Issues

Environmental issues of soil conservation and air, water, and food quality are closely tied to externalities driving a wedge between private and social costs (benefits) so that market allocations equating marginal private costs and returns do not serve the public interest. As indicated earlier, markets tend to work well where goods are *rival* and *exclusionary*. The latter terms cannot be separated from externalities: where goods are nonexclusionary, marginal private returns fall short of marginal social returns so that the private sector produces too little to maximize net social benefits. Where goods are nonrival so that consumption by one consumer does not reduce consumption available to another, marginal cost of good A is zero because no goods and services are foregone to expand output of A. Hence a private firm which charges a positive price to cover overhead costs will charge private marginal costs in excess of social marginal costs. The result is too little output to maximize net benefits for society.

In reality, other factors including lack of knowledge and economic equity (income/wealth) also constrain market choices and the role of public policy. For example, many farmers do not know and probably underestimate their soil erosion rate. Hence they are likely to underestimate payoffs from conservation and under-invest in "best management practices" for sustainable agriculture.

Low income/wealth farmers tend to have high discount rates favoring farming practices with low capital requirements and with quick payoffs. Unfortunately, some of the most socially beneficial sustainable agriculture practices require considerable capital outlays with positive net payoffs only in the long term — if profitable at all to the private firm. Thus it is not surprising that small farmers frequently lag behind larger farmers in sustainable practices including conservation tillage (see Tweeten, 1995).

However, an environmentally sound agriculture will not be forthcoming even if capital constraints are overcome and even if all farmers act rationally and the public is successful in providing every farmer with complete information on erosion rates, water quality, and best environmental practices. The reason is that much (over half by some estimates) of environmental costs are borne "downstream" rather than on the farm making decisions regarding soil erosion and water quality (Ribaudo *et al.*, 1989). These downstream externalities do not enter the private cost and return accounts of the offending farm, hence rational farmers acting to maximize profit, with complete information, and without capital constraints will not make socially optimal decisions. In short, the market acting alone will not properly care for the soil, water, and air quality and for wildlife and biodiversity.

The Situation

Land and Water Soil erosion compromises the sustainability of American agriculture. However, much progress has been made in cutting erosion in the U.S.: the average sheet and rill water erosion rate has fallen from nine tons per acre in 1938 (Magleby et al., 1995; U.S. Department of Agriculture, 1938, p. 595) to nearly 3 tons per acre in the mid-1990s (Pierce and Nowak, 1994, p. 2). Soil erosion per acre of cultivated cropland as estimated by the National Resources Inventory is shown in Table 1.

Table 1. Soil erosion per acre of cultivated cropland, selected years, U.S.

	1982	1987	1992
	(Tons per acre)		
Water erosion	4.5	4.1	3.5
Wind erosion	3.7	3.7	2.8

Source: Pierce and Nowak, 1994, p. 2.

Thus, soil erosion from water and wind fell nearly one-fourth in the 1982–1992 decade alone.

Most soil erosion does not reach lakes or oceans, but still entails costs. Studies in Alabama, Virginia, and Wisconsin indicate that over 90 percent of eroded soil remained in the region or watershed (see Committee on Long-Range Soil and Water Conservation, 1993, p. 96); if true, this imposes on-farm costs of lost nutrients and of diminished moisture holding and root-zone capacity. Sanders, Southgate, and Lee (1990, p. 14) cite four studies indicating that annual aggregate on-farm cost of soil erosion ranges from $500 million to $1.2 billion. Off-site damage from cropland erosion averages $2.2 billion per year according to estimates of Clark *et al.* (1985) and averages $7 billion according to Ribaudo *et al.* (1989). Thus off-site erosion costs to reservoirs, navigation, recreation, and plant and animal life appear to be at least double the on-farm cost of erosion (Colacicco *et al.*, 1989). Of course, not all erosion is from farmland, and costs vary widely among sites and regions.

Crosson (1992, p. 196) estimates that continuation of erosion at current rates would reduce agricultural productivity by 3 to 10 percent in a century. Annual farm output could drop 5 percent from erosion and 10 percent (as discussed later) from urban encroachment in a century, or on average by 0.15 percent per year. This could be offset at least 10 times over by future productivity advances that have averaged over 1.5 percent per year since 1950 (Council of Economic Advisors, 1996, p.388). This comparison highlights the importance of productivity gains through science and technology but by no means abrogates the need to control losses of farmland.

Turning now to water problems, reports of waterlogging and salt buildup under irrigation are common. Some irrigation reserves such as parts of the southern Ogallala aquifer have been depleted to the point where continued use is no longer economic. Many rivers have reached the limits of their capacity for irrigation. On the other hand, much water could be but is not exploited for agriculture. An example is millions of acres in the U.S. cornbelt that could receive supplemental irrigation from renewable water sources if crop and livestock prices were sufficiently favorable. Modern technology such as drip irrigation could conserve water and improve irrigation efficiency.

Chemical Contamination of Food and Water Much has been made of chemical contamination of food and water supplies by agricultural fertilizers and pesticides. In the U.S., approximately 2 percent of water wells have nitrogen and 0.6 percent of wells have synthetic pesticides above levels judged safe by the Environmental Protection Agency (EPA, 1990). The U.S. has been so successful in controlling synthetic chemical contamination of food supplies that American consumers get over 10,000 times as much carcinogens from natural as from synthetic sources! And even the natural carcinogens in food are not considered to be a problem (Ames and Gold, 1989).[1] Improved pesticides applied in ounces rather than pounds per acre, modern conservation tillage techniques, best management chemical application practices, and government regulations seem adequate to reduce currently low U.S. levels of synthetic chemical contamination of food and water to even lower levels.

Policies

Commodity programs that covered only one-third of all farms and one-half of the nation's land in farms (Padgitt, 1990, p. 49) in the mid-1980s were an inadequate delivery system for environmental programs. Much higher participation rates in the 1996 Federal Agricultural Improvement and Reform (FAIR) Act have extended environmental provisions to more farmland, but program participation and, hence, conservation compliance are expected to drop sharply if transition payments are terminated after the year 2002. What public policy is needed to follow up the sodbuster, swampbuster, conservation compliance, and water quality features of existing commodity programs?

Two options have been suggested by Tweeten and Zulauf (1997) to replace environmental features of commodity programs, the Conservation Reserve Program, and the Wetland Reserve Program. The suggested two options—(1) an Environmental Compliance Program (ECP), and (2) a Cropland Environmental Easement Program (CEEP)—ideally correct externalities while avoiding "taking" of property.[2] The two options would be designed to end supply management by the Conservation Reserve Program and to enroll the 18 million acres of cropland that cannot be cropped at tolerable erosion rates even using no-till (the CRP only enrolled 6 million of those acres [see Dicks and Coombs, 1994, p. 55]). These options would supplement and not replace current Environmental Protection Agency (EPA) programs and Natural Resources Conservation Service (NRCS) programs of technical assistance and cost sharing.

The ECP would be similar to but broader than conservation compliance. It would entail an environmental plan for all land on all U.S. farms by a prescribed date and implementation by a later prescribed date. To be manageable, it would initially address mostly soil erosion. In time, ECP might be extended to address water quality issues including synthetic chemicals, livestock manure disposal practices, filter strips, protection of stream banks, and the like.

ECP could be voluntary, financed by "green payments" from the government, or it could be mandatory. The attraction of green payments is that they would use the carrot rather than the stick to effect compliance. Green payments would maintain the long tradition of compensating producers for environmental measures deemed to serve the public interest.

An important constraint on identifying and implementing appropriate environmental programs is the inability of economists to calculate social benefits and costs of environmental measures with acceptable accuracy.

Improved models built for watersheds with detail for individual farms would be needed to allow more careful selection of environmental policies and to accurately compensate losers with green payments. But insurmountable problems in operationalizing a policy that varied taxes and subsidies with respect to both on-farm pollution levels and off-farm social costs of pollution have prompted a search for alternatives to green payments.

An option would be to require ECP of all operators in keeping with Napier's (1994) contention that "... [compulsory approaches] will be required to motivate a significant number of land operators to adopt and continue using farming systems that minimize degradation of environmental quality". The Committee on Long-Term Soil and Water Conservation (1993, p. 16) noted that "Nonvoluntary [conservation] approaches may be needed in problem areas where soil and water quality degradation is severe and where there are problem farms unacceptably slow in implementing improved farming systems". Only operators with problems above a specified threshold would have to implement a preventive plan. Several reasons for requiring compliance are listed below.

(1) Modern conservation tillage practices (including no-till) have greatly reduced the cost of protecting the soil while maintaining farm output, productivity, and profits (Hopkins *et al.*, 1996). In many cases the operator is only being asked to do what increases his income and saves his soil — actions in his self interest but currently not done because of lethargy, lack of knowledge, or other reasons. Millions of acres once classified as "highly erodible" can now be cropped with conservation tillage at tolerable erosion rates (see Dicks and Coombs, 1994).

(2) Requiring environmental compliance can reduce "taking". An operator has reason to control soil erosion on his farm that is reducing his net income and net worth. But as noted earlier, over half of the costs of soil erosion are borne by "downstream" parties subject to sedimentation or chemical contamination of their farmland, streams, urban reservoirs, and the like. Thus the farmer allowing erosion is "taking" from downstream parties. If he does not have to pay for such taking, downstream damage is an externality unlikely to change his behavior. The ECP only requires the operator to stop doing what he should not be doing — "taking" someone else's property.

(3) A mandatory ECP could avoid the high cost and administrative difficulty of monitoring non-point source effluents. The procedure could be for the NRCS to appraise environmental hazards and approve an environmental plan for a farm. Rather than monitoring effluent levels, the operator would be monitored for proper environmental practices. This would

reduce high transactions costs of administering a voluntary program paying farmers according to their reduction in effluents.

(4) Requiring compliance would bring agriculture in line with standard procedures applied to other industries. Of course, how to enforce ECP would be a delicate issue. As a start, the only penalty on violators might be denial of federal program benefits including catastrophic insurance and commodity loan rate support. If that does not bring sufficient compliance, enforcement using approaches employed for other industries could be instituted. It is important to note that at least two-thirds of all cropland (Padgitt, 1990, p.49) has already met requirements of the conservation compliance program, easing problems of compliance with the ECP.

(5) ECP would be the "stick" that could impose penalties required in some cases to move land to the Cropland Environmental Easement Program. An example is the 12 million acres or so of cropland outside of CRP that could not be cropped even with no-till at tolerable rates of soil loss in 1994. Using ECP to force such land into a program compensating them (as described below) would cut losses currently burdening off-site parties.

The companion Cropland Environmental Easement Program would compensate those who would experience a significant loss of earnings (taking) from implementing the ECP. CEEP would have similarities to the Conservation Reserve Program (CRP) but would interfere less with farm production. As with the CRP in 1997, an index of environmental hazards (or benefits from correction) might be constructed, and acres with the highest index per dollar of easement payment might be selected for participation. CEEP would focus solely on environmental hazards (benefits) and not on production control. To reduce economic and taxpayer costs, easements would allow haying, grazing, recreation, wildlife habitat, trees, or other uses consistent with soil, water, and wildlife protection. A carefully targeted CEEP of no more than 30 million acres encompassing 18 million of highly erodible cropland that cannot be farmed at tolerable erosion rates even with no-till plus 12 million acres removed to serve mainly water quality (including filter strips and other water quality control) would go far to address serious environmental problems while only minimally curtailing production. Perpetual and 30-year easements would be offered.

Other efforts ordinarily not viewed as environmental programs would continue. An example is agricultural research and development which has played an important role in allowing the nation to supply its food and fiber crop needs on only one-fifth of the nation's land area, leaving most of the remainder in grass or forest more supportive of wildlife. Continued improvements in technology will hold down requirements for cropland, thereby freeing land to be used for species preservation, forests, recreation, and other purposes favored by society.

Environmental problems of nonrenewable agricultural resources extend beyond soil loss and water and food quality. Problems include agricultural nuisances such as flies, odor, and waste disposal. The Environmental Protection Agency would continue to address problems of point-source pollution and associated air and water quality problems on large livestock farms.

Biodiversity and Farmland Preservation

Conceptual Issues

A second set of issues arises from loss of farmland, wildlife habitat, and associated biodiversity. Markets best reflect *use value* for market participants. The price system imperfectly accounts for the *option value* or *existence value* of biodiversity, farmland, and rural landscapes preserved for future generations when needs for food and open spaces might be greater. Although people will pay for option value because they might use amenities later or will pay for existence value even if they never plan to make use of the amenities, no market exists at acceptable transaction cost where they can vote with dollars for preservation. Free rider problems add to the market failure. Public involvement of some type is necessary to preserve option and existence value in the face of irreversible conversion of farmland to development.

The Situation

Globally, most fertile, environmentally safe land currently is being cropped. Bringing in new land would require higher real food prices. With good land already in short supply, further loss of cropland is of concern. U.S. cropland dropped to 460 million acres in 1992 after peaking at 478 million acres in 1949. The net loss of 425,000 acres annually averaged a 0.1 percent drop per year (U.S. Department of Agriculture, 1997). Thus, every year one in each thousand acres of cropland is converted to urban and other non-crop uses (Tweeten and Forster, 1993, p. 30). If that rate persists, in 1,000 years all prime farmland would be gone. Of course, higher returns on farming resources that would attend food and farmland shortages would slow the rate of farmland loss.

Up to 90 percent of the world's biodiversity is located in the tropics (World Resources Institute, 1994, p. 148). Interventions in nature to produce crops and livestock in the United States have lost or threatened few species compared to potential losses in the tropics. In many developing countries in the tropics the pressures of rapid population growth coupled with poverty (an issue that is discussed elsewhere in this volume) have forced subsistence farmers to follow loggers felling trees for lumber. The result has been substantial soil erosion, loss of biodiversity, permanent deforestation, and contribution to greenhouse gases and global warming.

American crop yields have tripled since 1925 (Council of Economic Advisors, 1973, p. 289 and later issues). Technological improvements making it possible to expand farm production at the intensive margin of more output per acre rather than at the extensive margin of more acres undoubtedly saved considerable forests, grasslands, and soil. Forests and grasslands are more supportive of wildlife than is cropland. These uses have replaced much fragile cropland especially in the eastern and southern regions of the United States.

Food demands of the future are unknowable and the public may want to avoid some irreversible conversion of prime farmland to residential development. Figure 1 shows that per capita local government spending rises sharply as annual population growth accelerates. The figure does not directly indicate rising marginal costs of services but undoubtedly captures some of the costs of providing new schools, access roads, utilities, and other services with community expansion. The figure probably does not catch full marginal costs because expanding communities frequently spread the high costs of community service expansion among established and new residents.

Based on data from several studies, Blaine (1997) concluded that residential area service demands were $1.30 to $1.40 per dollar of taxes paid whereas agricultural service demands were only $.30 to $.40 per dollar of taxes paid. Thus, farmland owners may experience higher taxes as city people establish residences in rural areas, but are not taxed enough to cover additional costs for schools and other services. Some communities place *impact fees* on new developments to more fully cover marginal service costs.

Policies

Several public policies to preserve farmland deserve attention. One is to charge rural residents the full marginal costs for public services. The distinguishing feature of "rural" areas is low population density that in turn

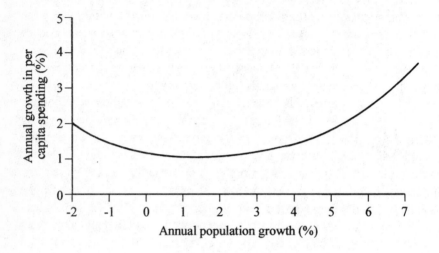

Figure 1. The relationship between per capita local government spending and population growth rate

Source: Ladd (1992).

implies high costs of services such as roads, school bus, mail, telephone, and electricity. Subsidizing these services might have made sense in an earlier era when rural areas had a high preponderance of low income farmers who could markedly raise their quality of life and reduce their isolation through access to services. Such conditions no longer characterize rural areas. Nonfarmers predominate and poverty rates are only modestly above national averages (Brown and Deavers, 1987, Table 5). Marginal cost pricing so that *new residents* pay their way would help to preserve prime farmland and rural amenities.

Failure to practice full marginal cost pricing has caused considerable resentment among long-term rural and farm residents and generated local NIMBY (not-in-my-backyard) policies to keep new residents out who would introduce LULUs (locally undesirable land uses), compromise rural amenities, and not pay their own way. Such local policies often merely send prospective new residents to other rural communities, with no net impact on overall farmland preservation.

Some examples of current policies encouraging urban sprawl and that governments can scrutinize and adjust are listed below:

Community services, including government subsidies for electrical, mail, school bus, water, solid waste disposal, and other services to rural residents: These could be phased out so the market would work better, enabling people to live where they wish subject to paying full costs and benefits. If required to pay their way, some current and potential rural residents and businesses would chose to reside in towns and cities where community services cost less and where prime farmland is not sacrificed.

Capital gain tax preferences and mortgage interest tax deductions: Preferential tax rates on capital gains and the mortgage interest deduction encourage investment in residences. Ability to escape capital gain taxes by applying proceeds to a new house of at least equal value is a further inducement to real estate expansion. The result is larger homes on larger acreages, often on land once cropped. Home ownership is a social good the public may wish to encourage, but tax advantages could be limited to families with *modest* real estate holdings.

Rural development programs: Government operated programs to promote jobs and place prosperity in rural areas typically use tax abatements, low interest loans, technical assistance, infrastructure and industrial park concessions, as well as other subsidies to attract and hold firms providing jobs in rural areas. New factories, shopping centers, and residences for workers frequently locate on prime farmland—often because such land has topography suited to low cost construction of streets and utilities. Once built up, such land is unlikely ever to return to cropland.

Measures such as *agricultural use valuation* (taxing at agricultural rather than development property value) and *agricultural districts* (current agricultural uses protected from legal challenges) may make life less stressful for farmers but are unlikely to preserve agricultural land in the long run. *Circuit breakers* (granting farmers property tax relief if property taxes are high relative to net income) as well as tax deferral schemes are likely to especially benefit wealthy landowners.

Some promising policy options: A notable policy to preserve prime farmland is public purchase of development rights (PDRs). Pennsylvania and Maryland have been at the forefront of use of PDRs to preserve farmland in the face of intensive urban pressure for development. On the whole, current farmers in aggregate would have higher incomes by allowing cropland to be sacrificed to urban development so as to raise food prices and farm earnings. Because the public at large rather than farmers gain by preserving land in agriculture as an option to deal with unforeseen future need for food, it is appropriate for the public to pay the cost through PDRs.

Local, state, and national interests in land use preservation do not necessarily coincide, however. Local residents may wish to discourage development to preserve rural amenities such as open space, uncongested roads, and scenic views while protecting against higher service costs. States may wish to preserve farmland to maintain a basic industry, agriculture. The national (and, perhaps, international) interest is in preserving prime agricultural land for food security of future generations. Local, state, and national interests in land use need to be coordinated. National funding can supplement local and state funding to purchase development rights making appropriate use of space and services while steering development away from prime farmland.

Some coordination of efforts among private agencies and public agencies is evident. Several states allow local jurisdictions to tax for the purchase of development rights. The Nature Conservancy and the American Farmland Trust are examples of private agencies buying development rights to farmland. The 1996 farm bill interjects the federal government into purchase of development rights with the modest Farmland Protection Program authorizing up to $35 million for purchase of up to 340,000 acres of farmland. The Farmland Protection Program will be most effective when coordinated with other public efforts and with private efforts at farmland preservation. Because development potential, such as road frontage, has been bid into land prices for years, current owners paid full market value, and the taking is less hypothetical. Should they be compensated for this?

Measures such as zoning can supplement efforts listed above but often entail "taking" of development rights from owners. A host of other programs such as *urban growth boundaries* (restrict city utilities to serve only those within the boundaries) and *agricultural zoning* can preserve cropland but can cause losses to farmland owners. Zoning is widely used to avoid loss of property value from incompatible uses such as mixing business (e.g. a hog farm) with residential property. In such cases each use compromises the value of the other, as for example, the business loses profit because local residents sue it for odors, and the odors reduce the value of residential property. An option is "setbacks" prohibiting residences within a prescribed distance of hog farms and prohibiting court challenges if the business meets such prescribed regulations.

Finally, option and existence values also are served by investments in science. Raising output per unit on safe land avoids expansion of crops on fragile land and helps to preserve biodiversity. Greater investment in gene banks and other measures to conserve genetic material along with the search for more environmentally benign pesticides and biological controls are helpful adaptations.

Non-renewable Resource Depletion

Conceptual Issues

Depletion of nonrenewable resources such as fossil fuel and phosphorus (or its agricultural application form, phosphate) poses other potential issues leading to market failure. The *rational expectations* presumption implies optimal rationing and use by markets of a nonrenewable stock resource over time — if market participants are informed, capital markets function well, and consumers are not risk averse. However, market participants may not be sufficiently informed to make sound decisions.

The Situation

The most limiting nonrenewable resources for a sustainable agriculture appear to be phosphorus and fossil fuels.

Rock phosphate. Some 11,225 million metric tons (mmt) of rock phosphate reserves are available at a cost of $40 per ton (f.o.b. mine) and 34,045 mmt are available at a cost of $100 per ton (Bureau of Mines, 1993, p. 830). Only the latter, higher, estimate is used below in estimating the remaining life of reserves. This 34,045 mmt "reserve base" includes resources that are currently economic, marginally economic, and some of those that are currently uneconomic. This reserve base also is sometimes called the "geological reserve".

World rock phosphate production increased on average by 4.0 percent annually from 1950 to 1990, but decreased from 166 mmt in 1989 to 134 mmt in 1993 (see Bureau of Mines, 1993, p. 831 and earlier issues). The drop after 1989 is transitory, a response to factors such as recognition of excessive buildup of phosphate in many soils, the fall of the Soviet Union, and increasing awareness of environmental problems from excessive fertilization. Global phosphate fertilizer use will resume its upward trend, probably at a rate near 2 percent annually. This projection is consistent with an expected global 1990-2020 population growth rate of 1.4 percent per year (Rosegrant et al., 1995) plus a 0.4 percent per year increase in per capita food use due to income growth, plus increased fertilizer intensity per acre of 0.2 percent annually. The 2.0 percent rate is also consistent with world food production trends estimated by the Food and Agriculture Organization (FAO, 1994, pp. 39, 41) and with the world demand growth in rock phosphate forecast by the World Bank (1995, p. 22).

A 2 percent phosphate growth trajectory makes sense for the next two decades but does not make sense for the long term. Global population, currently 5.8 billion people, has slowed its growth rate to 1.6 percent annually. Although approximately 80 million people will be added to global population per year for a decade, the International Institute of Applied Systems Analysis (Lutz, 1996) predicts that world population will stabilize at 11 billion persons by year 2100. However, food consumption is predicted to triple before population and food demand stabilize. Assuming world population will double and food demand triple before stabilization as noted earlier, we assume a 2 percent growth rate of phosphate use until year 2050 when use reaches 450 mmt (triple normalized current phosphate consumption in *keeping with food use triple that of 1995)*, then assuming that phosphate demand will remain stable. Under this scenario, rock phosphate reserves are adequate to year 2076 (81 years).

Current base reserves surely are underestimated. Actual reserves in North and West Africa and in the Middle East may be several times estimated present reserves. Large phosphate resources have been identified in the Atlantic and Pacific Oceans. Higher phosphate prices that would attend depletion of current reserves would result in successful searches for new deposits. Marginal deposits become economic to exploit at higher prices. The schedule of depletion under various scenarios is summarized in Table 2.

In a separate analysis, Paul Barton (1996) estimated global reserves of phosphorus (3,400 mmt) relative to 1992 use (14 mmt). The 1992 consumption continued for 242 years would exhaust reserves, implying a reserve to steady-state use ratio similar to scenario 5 shown in Table 2 for rock phosphate. The comparable result is not surprising given that estimates are from similar sources.

Table 2. Rock phosphate depletion under various scenarios

	Scenario[*]	Years to depletion from 1995 base	Year of depletion
1.	Historic 1950-90 rate of increased use, 4 percent/yr.	55	2050
2.	The 1995-2030 expected rate of increased use, 2 percent/yr. Projected until supplies are exhausted	76	2071
3.	2 percent rock phosphate use growth to year 2030, then steady consumption of 450 mmt/yr.	81	2076
4.	Scenario 3 but double reserves	157	2152
5.	Scenario 3 but triple reserves	233	2228

[*]Assume rock phosphate normalized consumption of 150 mmt in 1995 and base reserves in the same year of 34,045 mmt.

Other Nonrenewables. Nitrogen and potassium are also major elements of commercial fertilizers. Potash reserves dwarf those of phosphate and will last for hundreds of years (see CAST, 1988, p. 28).

Nitrogen is abundant in the air but currently is combined with petroleum and natural gas feedstocks processed for commercial fertilizer. Petroleum also is used for farm fuel. The economic life of petroleum reserves and rock phosphate reserves will be extended by reduced consumption and by utilization of currently unrecognized reserves as shortages emerge and prices rise. But petroleum use is less problematic for agriculture for several reasons. One reason is that more energy can be drawn from renewable resources such as the sun and wind. Another is that petroleum has substitutes such as coal reserves which are adequate for hundreds of years although not without environmental problems. Barton (1996) estimated steady-state use life of reserves to be 50 years for oil, 69 years for natural gas, and 258 years for coal. Also, some plants can fix their own nitrogen or may be bioengineered to do so. In contrast, phosphate, a basic biological building block, has no substitutes.

Agriculture is a small player in the petroleum industry. In the U.S., agriculture accounts for less than 3 percent of energy use. Much of the petroleum used in agriculture has high value. The industry will be able to compete for reserves to maintain food production as other sectors cut back energy use in response to higher energy prices. Finally, new technology such as nuclear fusion may provide a safe, clean, low cost, and abundant source of energy before fossil energy reserves are exhausted.

Policies

Most decisions regarding nonrenewable natural resources can best be left to markets, but some government role seems justified.

• In the case of phosphate, one role for government is to provide more complete information on future reserves so as to help markets work better. Also, genes influencing phosphorus use efficiency in plants have been identified; thus science may devise plant varieties and cropping systems making more efficient use of phosphorus.

• In the case of fossil fuels, policy issues extend well beyond agriculture. Because of the need to reduce air pollution (smog at ground level and greenhouse gases at higher altitudes), conserve reserves, and reduce reliance on petroleum imports, additional taxes on fossil fuels could bring private marginal cost in line with social marginal cost and closer to prices in other industrial countries.

Conclusions

Modern agriculture is and will continue to be a model of sustainable growth and productivity because it is adaptable. The sustainability of American and world agricultural growth depends on (1) a first-class scientific establishment continually improving plants and animals to more efficiently turn resources into food and fiber, (2) a well functioning market that will ensure having efficient farms and agribusiness firms continually developing and adopting new technology and management practices, and (3) competent government providing a secure macroeconomic environment, supplying public goods, and correcting externalities so as to serve the public interest.

These three requirements are interrelated and have priorities. The most critical policy decision is for a competent government (3 above). The market will make most decisions of when, where, what, and how to produce and account for at least two-thirds of all output, but a well functioning market (2 above) will take care of itself if government provides a supportive framework. And a first class scientific effort and technology development and diffusion (1 above) will be possible only with a supportive government and private sector supplying an economic base. Although government need not be large, it must perform a few tasks well to provide sustainable economic and environmental climate.

Reliance on markets as in (2) helps to ration rival and exclusionary goods, including renewable and nonrenewable resources. Science and technology can continue to raise farming productivity, thereby saving nonrenewable resources such as phosphate, water, and land. Improved productivity of land from better technology frees land from crops to be used instead for biodiversity, wildlife, forest, and recreational purposes.

Regarding item (3), government policies for a sustainable agriculture could benefit from greater targeting, complementary technologies, and focused research (Ervin and Graffy, 1996, p. 33). Targeting would focus limited public environmental funds more narrowly on high priority environmental problems and public goods, emphasize public investment to encourage complementary technologies such as conservation tillage and precision farming that serve both production efficiency and the environment, and direct public research to environmental improvement as well as to production efficiency.

Notes

1. Current tests do not distinguish between carcinogens that are mutagens at low doses relevant to people and carcinogens at massive doses tested on rodents where cell damage and repeated repair growth eventually result in cancer. Few of the many rodent "carcinogens" cause cancer in humans at dosages ordinarily consumed.

2. "Taking" can be a violation of the 5th Amendment to the Constitution, defined as "taking private property for public use without just compensation" (Goldstein, 1996, p. 6). The courts have required a near total loss of property value before compensation is due, rejecting the view that property owners are entitled to *maximum* potential return on their

property, and do not call for compensation to people required to stop doing "bad things" to us (Goldstein, 1996, p. 5). We use the term "taking" more broadly, herein, not requiring a near total loss of property value.

Acknowledgements

The comments of Jeff Hopkins are appreciated.

References

Ames, Bruce and Lois Gold. 1989. "Pesticides, Risk, and Apple Sauce". *Science* 244:755-757.

Barton, Paul. 1996. "Renewable and Nonrenewable Resources". Presented to the American Association for the Advancement of Science meeting in Baltimore, Maryland, Feb. 10, 1996. Washington, DC: U.S. Department of the Interior.

Blaine, Thomas. 1997. "Does Residential Development in Rural Areas Pay Its Own Way?" Wooster, OH: Ohio State University Extension.

Brown, David and Kenneth Deavers. 1987. "Rural Change and the Rural Economic Policy Agenda for the 1980s". Chapter 1 in *Rural Economic Development in the 1980s: Preparing for the Future*. ERS Staff Report No. AGES870724. Washington, DC: Agriculture and Rural Economic Division, ERS, USDA.

Bureau of Mines. 1993. "Minerals". Volume I in *Minerals Yearbook*. Washington, DC: U.S. Department of Interior.

CAST (Council for Agricultural Science and Technology). June 1988. *Long-Term Viability of U.S. Agriculture*. Report No. 114. Ames, IA: CAST.

Clark, E., J. Haverkamp, and W. Chapman. 1985. *Eroding Soils: The Off-Farm Impact*. Washington, DC: Conservation Foundation.

Colacicco, Daniel, Tim Osborn, and Klaus Alt. 1989. "Economic Damage from Soil Erosion". *Journal of Soil and Water Conservation* 44: 35-39.

Committee on Long-Range Soil and Water Conservation. 1993. *Soil and Water Quality*. National Research Council. Washington, DC: National Academy Press.

Conway, G. R. 1987. "The Properties of Agroecosystems". *Agr. Systems* 24: 95-117.

Council of Economics Advisors. *Economic Report of the President*. 1973 and later issues. Washington, DC: United States Government Printing Office.

Crosson, P. 1992. "Cropland and Soil: Past Performance and Policy Challenges". Chapter 5 in *America's Renewable Resources*, Kenneth Frederick and

Roger Sedjo, eds. Washington, DC: Resources for the Future.

Dicks, Michael and John Coombs. 1994. "Evaluating the CRP using the 1992 National Resources Inventory". Pp. 50-69 in 1992 *National Resources Inventory Environmental and Resource Assessment Symposium Proceedings*. Washington, DC: NRCS, U.S. Department of Agriculture.

EPA (Environmental Protection Agency). 1990. *National Pesticide Survey: Summary Results*. Washington, DC: Office of Water and Office of Pesticides and Toxic Substances, Environmental Protection Agency.

Ervin, David and Elisabeth Graffy. Fourth Quarter, 1996. "Leaner Environmental Policies for Agriculture". Pp. 27-33 in *Choices*.

FAO (Food and Agriculture Organization of the United Nations). 1994 and earlier issues. *FAO Production Yearbook*. Volume 48. Rome: FAO.

Goldstein, Jon. 1996. "Whose Land Is It Anyway? Private Property Rights and the Endangered Species Act". Washington, DC: U.S. Department of the Interior.

Hopkins, Jeffrey, Gary Schnitkey, and Luther Tweeten. Sept. 1996. "Impacts of Nitrogen Control Policies on Crop and Livestock Farms at Two Alternative Farm Sites". *Review of Agricultural Economics* 18:311-324.

Ladd, H. 1992. *Effects of Population Growth on Local Spending and Taxes*. Cambridge, MA: Lincoln Institute of Land Policy.

Lutz, Wolfgang. 1996. "Global versus Local Approaches to Population, Development, and Environmental Analysis". Presented to American Association for the Advancement of Science meeting in Baltimore, Maryland, Feb. 10, 1996. Laxemburg, Austria: International Institute for Applied Systems Analysis.

Magleby, Richard, William Crosswhite, Carmen Sandretto, and C. Tim Osborn. 1995. "Soil Erosion and Conservation in the United States: An Overview". Agricultural Information Bulletin. Washington, DC: Economic Research Service, USDA.

Markandya, A. 1992. "Criteria for Sustainable Agricultural Development". In *Environmental Economics: A Reader*, eds., A Markandya and J. Richardson. New York: St. Martin's Press.

Napier, Ted. 1994. "Regulatory Approaches for Soil and Water Conservation". Ch. 15 in Louis Swanson and Frank Clearfield, eds., *Agricultural Policy and the Environment*. Ankeny, IA: Soil and Water Conservation Society.

Padgitt, Merritt. September, 1990. "Production, Resource Use, and Operating Characteristics of Participants and Nonparticipants in Farm Programs". Pp. 48-54 in *Agricultural Resources*. AR-19. Washington, DC: Economic Research Service, USDA.

Pierce, Francis and Peter Nowak. 1994. "Soil and Soil Quality: Status and Trends". pp. 1–23 in *1992 Resources Inventory Environmental and Resource Assessment Symposium Proceedings*. Washington, DC: NRCS, U.S. Department of Agriculture.

Ribaudo, Marc O., Daniel Colacicco, Alex Barbarika, and C. Edwin Young. 1989. "The Economic Efficiency of Voluntary Soil Conservation Programs". *Journal of Soil Conservation* 44(1): 40–43.

Rosegrant, Marc, Mercedita Agcaoili-Sombilla, and Nicostrato Perez. 1995. "Global Food Projections to 2020: Implications for Investment". Food, Agriculture, and the Environment Discussion Paper 5. Washington, DC: International Food Policy Research Institute.

Sanders, John, Douglas Southgate, and John G. Lee. 1995. *The Economics of Soil Degradation*. SMSS Tech. Monograph No. 22. Washington, DC: NRCS, U.S. Department of Agriculture.

Sanders, John H., Joseph G. Hagy, and Sunder Ramaswamy. 1990. "Developing New Agricultural Technologies for the Sahelian Countries: The Burkina Faso Case". *Economic Development and Cultural Change* 39(1): 1–22.

Tweeten, Luther. 1992. "The Economics of an Environmentally Sound Agriculture". Pp. 39-83 in Ray Goldberg, ed., *Research in Domestic and International Agribusiness Management*, Vol. 10. Greewich, CT: JAI Press.

Tweeten, Luther. July-August 1995. "The Structure of Agriculture: Implications for Soil and Water Conservation". *Journal of Soil and Water Conservation* 50(4):347-351.

Tweeten, Luther and Lynn Forster. Fourth Quarter, 1993. "Looking Forward to Choices for the Twenty-First Century". *Choices.* Pp. 26-31.

Tweeten, Luther and Carl Zulauf. 1997. "Public Policy for Agriculture After Commodity Programs". *Review of Agricultural Economics* (forthcoming).

U.S. Department of Agriculture. 1938. *Yearbook of Agriculture.* Washington, DC: U.S. Government Printing Office.

U.S. Department of Agriculture. September 1990. "Agricultural Resources: Cropland, Water, and Conservation". AR-19. Washington, DC: Economic Research Service, USDA.

U.S. Department of Agriculture. 1997. "Total Cropland by Region and States, United States, 1945-1992". Table 4. http://www.manlib.cornell.edu/data-sets/land/89003. Washington, DC: National Agricultural Statistical Service, USDA.

World Bank. 1995. "World and Regional Supply and Demand Balances for Nitrogen, Phosphate, and Potash, 1993/94-1999/2000". Technical Paper No. 309. Washington, DC: Fertilizer Working Group, World Bank.

World Resources Institute. 1994. "Biodiversity". Chapter 8 in *World Resources 1994-95.* New York: Oxford University Press.

4 Sustainability and Production Technology: Measuring Sustainability for Agricultural Production Systems

Susan M. Capalbo and John M. Antle

Introduction

In the 1980s, the goal of promoting sustainable agricultural practices gained prominence and reflected public concerns about the long-term social, economic, and environmental impacts of agricultural production technologies. The low input sustainable agriculture (LISA) program is an example of how sustainability became institutionalized within the USDA. The 1990 Farm bill relabeled the LISA program the Sustainable Agricultural Research and Education Program, or SAREP. Under current legislation, sustainability is still an important criterion for evaluating the impact of agricultural production technologies on the environment and the natural resource base.

From an economic perspective there are tradeoffs associated with alternative technologies because there are few technologies that provide improvements in all of the social, economic, and environmental dimensions. Thus using sustainability criteria to guide policy analysis requires measuring and valuing the tradeoffs among different dimensions and outcomes. In this chapter we report on a general approach to assess quantitatively the economic, environmental, and health tradeoffs associated with the use of agricultural production technologies, and provide two case studies to illustrate the methodology. The approach accounts for key measurement issues that arise in addressing sustainability concerns including spatial variability of the impacts, the need to integrate disciplinary models and data at a small scale or level of aggregation, and the need to assess impacts at a larger scale for purposes of policy analysis.

Both of the case studies emphasize the need to quantify the tradeoffs associated with specific agricultural production practices as opposed to measuring sustainability per se. The first case study is dryland grain production system in Montana, which is characterized by differing levels of

67

land use intensities and management/tillage practices. The issues raised in this case study include the multidimensional nature of the environmental impacts, and the site-specific variations in the tradeoff relationships. The second case study is the potato-pasture production system in the Andean highlands of Ecuador. The physical heterogeneity of the landscape in this region, the intensive use of pesticides for commercial potato production, and the potential for farm worker exposure to pesticides, provide an opportunity to investigate the impacts of spatial variability on estimates of the environmental and health tradeoffs.

A Conceptual Framework for Quantifying Tradeoffs in Agricultural Production Systems

The motivation for the development of this approach is the recognition that it is not possible to conduct environmental impact analysis with the regional or national units of analysis typically used by economists. The approach is to disaggregate the economic analysis in a manner compatible with the soil science analysis, estimate economic, environmental, and health impacts at that disaggregate scale of analysis, and then statistically aggregate impacts to the regional level needed for policy analysis (see Antle and Just, 1991; Antle, Crissman, Hutson and Wagenet, 1996; Antle 1996).

Market prices, policies, and the physical attributes of land affect farmers' management decisions in terms of both land use and input use. These decisions affect agricultural production, but also may affect the environment through two distinct but interrelated mechanisms. Land use decisions determine which particular acres of crop land are put into production and which crops are grown, land management decisions determine the application rates of chemicals, water use, and tillage practices. Physical relationships between the environmental attributes of the land in production and management practices then jointly determine the agricultural output and environmental impacts associated with a particular unit of land in production. The distribution of farm and environmental characteristics induces a joint distribution of input use, outputs, and environmental impacts. This joint distribution provides the basis for aggregation of the field-specific impacts to the regional level for policy analysis.

The construction of the disaggregate model begins by defining a population of land units (fields) in relation to an environmentally meaningful geographical unit, such as an aquifer or watershed. A vector ω^i represents the

i^{th} field's physical characteristics (e.g., soil types, climate) that affect both crop productivity and environmental impact. Environmental impact is represented with a stylized physical model $z^i = z(x^i, \omega^i)$, where x^i is a vector of management actions taken on the ith field measured per unit area and z^i is the scalar environmental impact, such as a change in water quality. The function $z(x, \omega)$ is a static representation of a reduced-form process model of the type that is developed by physical and biological scientists to quantify environmental processes on a site-specific basis (Wagenet and Rao, 1990).

Note that z could also be interpreted as an indicator of health status. In this case $z(x, \omega)$ would be a health production function (see, e.g., Cropper and Freeman, 1991) and ω would represent the characteristics of an individual exposed to a health risk. More generally, there could be multiple outcomes in both the environmental and health dimensions, and z could accordingly be interpreted as a vector of environmental or health outcomes. In the first case study, multiple environmental indicators are analyzed, while the second case study addresses both environmental and health outcomes. Alternatively, multiple environmental or health outcomes could be aggregated to a single indicator or index if an appropriate aggregation method were available.

The economic model is based on the allocation of land and other inputs to maximize expected economic returns. Crop production on the ith field, measured per unit area, is defined by the production function $q^i = q(x^i, \omega^i, \tau^i)$, where x^i is a vector of inputs measured per unit area. For simplicity, the production process with technology τ^i is represented as static and deterministic. If the crop is produced, the farmer's management problem is to maximize expected returns. The solution to this problem is represented by the profit function $\pi(p, \omega^i, \tau^i)$ and input demand functions $x(p, \omega^i, \tau^i) = -\partial\pi(p, \omega^i, \tau^i)/\partial w^i$, where p is a vector of input prices normalized by the output price. Farmers allocate each field between crop and non-crop uses at the beginning of each production period according to its highest valued use. Letting c^i be the return to the non-crop use, farmers make land-use decisions to solve:

$$\max_{\delta^i} \quad \{\delta^i\pi(p, \omega^i, \tau^i) + (1-\delta^i)c^i\}.$$

The land-use decision is therefore a step function of the form $\delta^i = 1$ if $\pi^i > c^i$ and $\delta^i = 0$ otherwise, implying that the land allocation decision is a function of p, ω^i and c^i.

This model implies that the environmental and health impacts of agriculture are determined by two fundamental factors. First, farmers' land use decisions determine which parcels of land are in crop production. This decision determines the environmental characteristics of the land in production, and the characteristics of the farm population who work on the land and thus could be exposed to health risks. Second, farmers' input use decisions on the land in production, combined with the land's environmental characteristics, determine the environmental and health outcomes z^i on each parcel of land.

Assume that the physical characteristics ω^i of fields are distributed in the population according to a distribution $f(\omega|\Omega)$, and production technologies are distributed according to $g(\tau|T)$. These distributions induce a joint distribution of input use, land use, crop production, and environmental impact through the input demand functions, the production function, and the physical process model.

Given the sustainability goals of balancing agricultural production against environmental impacts, the joint distribution of crop production and environmental impact is of particular interest. This joint distribution provides two basic types of information. First, it is possible to assess tradeoffs between crop production and environmental outcomes as prices are varied and physical characteristics of land in production and the production technology are held constant. Second, it is possible to estimate the shifts in the output-environment tradeoff that occurs when either the resource base (land attributes) or the production technology changes. This shift is analogous to a shift in the production possibilities frontier that occurs in response to changes in resource endowments or production technology.

Formally, for a given price vector p faced by all farmers in the region, farm output and environmental or health impacts are jointly distributed random variables. For example, the mean crop output and mean environmental impact can be derived as:

$$\mu_q(p,\Omega,T) = \int\int q(x(p,\omega,\tau),\omega,\tau)\, f(\omega|\Omega)\, g(\tau|T)\, d\omega d\tau$$

$$\mu_z(p,\Omega,T) = \int\int z(x(p,\omega,\tau),\omega)\, f(\omega|\Omega)\, g(\tau|T)\, d\omega d\tau.$$

Under the assumption that q and z are increasing in x, it follows that changes in p induce changes in mean output and mean environmental impact so as to trace out a positive relationship between the two as in Figure 1. For some technologies, there may be a negative relationship between a specific environmental indicator and net returns. The first case study illustrates that there are both positive and negative tradeoffs.

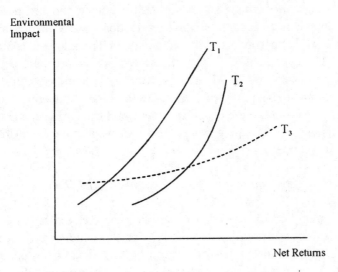

Figure 1. Output-environment tradeoffs associated with alternative technologies

Moreover, a change in either the distribution of physical characteristics of land in the region, or a change in the technology used in production will cause a shift in this tradeoff relationship. Figure 1 shows that a technology T_1 causes more environmental impact than technology T_2 while technology T_3 causes more impact at low output levels but less impact at high levels.

Assessing Sustainability Dimensions for Dryland Cropping Systems in Montana

In this section we briefly describe the methodology and empirical results for assessing the tradeoffs associated with alternative cropping systems in the dryland areas of Montana which is characteristic of the Northern Great Plains area of the United States. A full description of the data collection, model development and empirical results are found in Antle et al, 1996. This case study provides an example of the tradeoffs among the net returns and environmental indicators for alternative production systems in three subareas: the Northeast(NE) part of the state, the Southern Triangle area (ST) and the Northern Triangle area(NT). The latter two areas are part of what is commonly referred to as Montana's Golden Triangle, because of the productivity and the importance of grains to the state's economy. The major findings are that the economic and environmental tradeoffs depend upon the physical setting and the management or tillage decisions taken in relation to the production systems.

Description of the Production Technology and Model Overview

Existing dryland cropping systems may be characterized by cropland use intensity, rotation, and tillage method. For this study we defined three categories of land use intensity: crop/fallow, flexible cropping, and continuous cropping systems. A flexible cropping system usually represents an intermediary to the crop/fallow and the continuous cropping systems. In a flexible cropping system the decision to recrop or fallow is based on an inventory of soil moisture and expected growing season precipitation. The expected percentage of fallow would usually be 40 to 50 percent of total cropland.

The rotation involves primarily wheat (both winter and spring), barley, and fallow; tillage methods are differentiated by how the fallowed acres are managed. Some producers use three to four mechanical tillage passes, while others use herbicides in combination with one or two mechanical passes. This latter method is referred to as minimum tillage. Each fallow method implies different chemical applications and different amounts of soil disturbance, thus providing a tradeoff among the environmental indicators of erosion, leaching, and runoff.

The integrated simulation model is composed of an economic model and an environmental model. In the simulation model for this case study, the economic and physical models are simulated independently, and the outputs from both models are combined to infer environmental impacts. The only feedback that we have incorporated is to utilize the estimated yields that are output from the physical simulation models into the net revenues calculations.

The Erosion-Productivity Impact Calculator (EPIC) was used to determine the effects of alternative production practices. Each of the rotation/tillage systems analyzed was simulated thirty times by EPIC for a thirty year period. Crop yield observations for a given system were computed as the mean yield for those years that a given crop was produced in the thirty year cycle. The EPIC model outputs numerous environmental variables along with estimates of annual yields. The environmental variables include measures of water and wind erosion, pesticide and nitrate movement, and leaching of chemicals through the root zone.

An on-farm survey was administered to representative groups of producers to obtain the basic economic information regarding input use, machinery complement, typical rotations, and enterprise mix necessary to generate enterprise budgets. Budgets were generated for each production system in each of the three subareas, and for two representative farm sizes. Because of the lack of a statistically representative sample of producers, we did not econometrically estimate factor demands for the inputs, but rather relied on crop budgets to generate the needed economic information to assess net returns for each production system.

Empirical Results

Using the framework described above, comparisons of the economic returns across cropping systems were generated as well as the tradeoffs between economic and environmental outcomes. The primary conclusions drawn from the results of the economic analysis is that within a given area a farm manager would be indifferent between the use of mechanical tillage or minimum tillage to manage the fallowed acres. Based on comparisons of the cropping systems in use, all with similar land use intensities and crop rotations, there was no appreciable difference in the profitability of those systems in the three areas. Therefore, it seems reasonable to conclude that farm managers make their decisions on tillage methods according to other criteria such as previous investments in equipment or their long-term soil management strategy.

For this study the environmental-economic tradeoffs are calculated in terms of each environmental indicator since values needed to aggregate the specific environmental indicators into a single index of environmental damage are not available. To illustrate the findings, Figures 2 and 3 present the tradeoff relationships between soil erosion (USLE) and net returns (above variable costs), and between nitrate leaching and net returns for selected tillage and input use simulations in the NE and ST areas. Each point represents a mean value for both the environmental measure and net returns based on thirty year simulations.

Based on the information in Figure 2, three conclusions are drawn: first, for a given area and input use, net returns do not vary substantially by tillage practices. Net returns above operating costs are nearly the same for the two tillage methods considered in this study, and thus a manager should be indifferent in the use of mechanical tillage and minimum tillage from a short run economic perspective. The decision to utilize mechanical or minimum tillage is not necessarily driven by net returns considerations. Second, within a given area, erosion is not very sensitive to changes in fertilizer use or tillage practices. For the NE area, the soil erosion-net returns tradeoff is slightly negative, indicating a possible win-win situation in both the environmental and economic dimensions as input use increases. For the ST area, the tradeoff curve is flat for mechanical tillage practices indicating no tradeoff betwen erosion and net returns, and slightly positive for minimum tillage practices. And third, both the magnitude of the erosion and the direction of tradeoffs depend upon site-specific environmental and economic characteristics.

For nitrate leaching, the results are somewhat reversed. In figure 3, for the NE the quantity of nitrate leaching does not depend upon tillage practice and is positively related to net returns. This differs from the erosion tradeoff, since as net returns increase, so too does the amount of nitrate leaching. For the ST area, there is a strong tradeoff between net returns and nitrate leaching, for both tillage methods.

Taken together, Figures 2 and 3 are useful in addressing sustainability concerns and highlight the site-specific as well as dimension-specific nature of the analysis (incidentally, Chapter 2 also alludes to some of these tradeoffs, although more so in the hypothetical sense). Whether higher input use or alternative tillage practicies are damaging to the environment in an aggregate sense depends upon the relative weights attached to erosion and nitrate leaching, and upon the spatial dimensions of the production technologies. Cross-area comparisons indicate that the specific tradeoffs depend upon the physical setting and management decisions.

The EPIC model was also used to predict relative changes in concentrations of organic carbon in the soil at the end of each thirty year simulation. While the predicted concentrations of organic carbon declined for all production systems, the rate of decline was less when tillage was reduced, and cropping intensity increased. Thus, the increases in some of the environmental indicators were also accompanied by a decrease in the inherent productivity of the soil. This brings into question the long term tradeoff between improvements in specific environmental dimensions and changes in soil productivity.

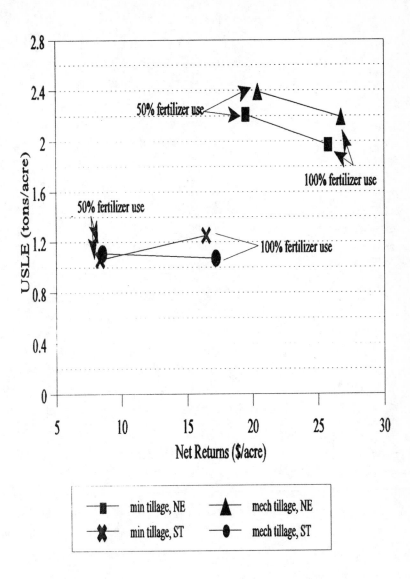

Figure 2. USLE vs net returns tradeoffs, by area and tillage

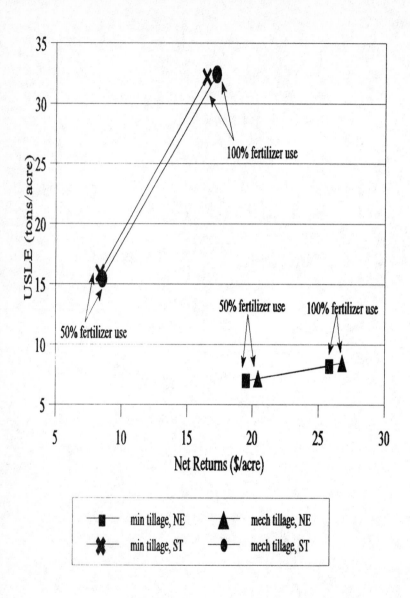

Figure 3. Leaching vs net returns tradeoffs by area and tillage

This case study illustrates that it is not obvious that a sustainable production technology can be identified or defined for a given area, even for a system as relatively homogeneous as dryland grain production in Montana. Most of the production technologies that are winners in some environmental dimensions are often time losers in other environmental or long term productivity dimensions. Furthermore, the tradeoffs shift as physical conditions and production technologies change.

An Assessment of Tradeoffs in the Potato-Pasture Production System in Ecuador

In this section we illustrate the tradeoffs between economic and environmental impacts, and between economic and health impacts for the potato-pasture production system in the Andean highlands of Ecuador. A complete description of this research is found in Crissman, Antle, and Capalbo (1997). Several factors make the tradeoffs potentially important in this setting. Potato production is management intensive and potatoes are a high-value, high-risk crop for farmers. Much of the production risk is associated with late blight fungus (*Phytophthora infestans*)which is the principal disease and the tuber boring Andean weevil (*Premnotrypes vorax*) and several foliage damaging insects are the principal insect pests affecting production. Farmers apply as many as 12 applications of fungicide and/or insecticides during the growing season to control these pests. Combined with the continuous production of the crop, the risk to the environment and to human health is potentially high.

The Economic, Environment, and Health Models

The economic models include decisions made with respect to land use, and decisions made with respect to input (pesticide) use. For each field for each production cycle, a land use decision is made based on the comparison of net returns to the two competing uses (potato and pasture). These net return distributions are based on an econometrically estimated profit function. Pesticides are not used on pasture in this study area. For potato production, pesticides are classified as fungicides, insecticides used to treat the Andean weevil, and insecticides used to treat foliage pests. For each type of pesticide, a pair of reduced-form, dynamic factor demand equations representing both the quantity and timing of pesticide applications was estimated econometrically, following the procedures described in Antle, Capalbo and Crissman (1994).

This econometric model represents both the quantity-of-an-input decision as well as the time-interval-between-application decision. This information is needed as an input into the physical process models that estimate environmental impact, because the timing of application decisions in relation to rainfall plays an important role in determining the environmental impact.

At the end of the production cycle, the input realizations and physical characteristics of the field are combined to estimate the value of crop production on the field. Output is generated with an econometrically estimated Cobb-Douglas revenue function.

Based on field observations, the principal environmental impact of pesticide use would be through leaching of pesticide through the root zone into ground water and through return flows. An existing pesticide leaching model, LEACHA, adapted to Andean conditions generates outputs in the form of loadings into the environment (the total mass leached into ground water), water concentrations leached below the root zone, and estimates of the risk of loadings or concentrations exceeding critical values (Hutson and Wagenet 1993). The LEACHA simulations model (Hutson and Wagenet, 1993) was parameterized with data measurements made in each zone to represent both the mass of chemical leached below the crop root zone and the chemical concentration in water leaving the crop root zone. The simulations were run using historical weather data.

To facilitate integration of the economic and physical simulations models, a statistical meta-model was estimated to represent the simulation outcomes of the LEACHA model runs. The LEACHA model was executed multiple times for each month of the year for each agroecological zone, for standardized applications of each type of pesticide. Output from the economic model indicating the date and the quantity of pesticide applied was input into the physical simulation model. The physical simulation model then determined, for each field and for each pesticide application, whether a positive leaching event occurred, and if so, how much pesticide mass and what concentration of pesticide leached beyond the root zone.

To examine the health impacts of this pesticide use, a survey of the farm population and an age- and education-matched referent group not exposed to pesticides was conducted. All participants answered questions on pesticide use and medical problems, received a clinical examination by a field physician, completed a series of tests of nervous system function and underwent blood tests. The health component of the simulation model is based on an econometrically estimated health production function that specifies health (measured as an individual's mean neurobehavioral score) as a function of the total number of applications and total quantity applied of neurotoxic substances that the individual was exposed to, the total quantity of potatoes consumed by the individual during the period (to control for possible exposure through the consumption of potatoes by farm workers), and the individual's verbal intelligence scores (to control for individual differences in neurobehavioral function not associated with pesticide use). Estimation of these health production functions is described in Cole *et al.* (1997). The estimates of the health production function indicate that pesticide use was statistically significant in explaining the neurobehavioral health of the farm population.

Tradeoffs in the Potato-Pasture Production System

Using the simulation model described in the preceding section, tradeoffs between economic, environmental and health outcomes were generated by varying output and input prices. For each price setting, 30 fields were drawn and simulated for five production cycles, and the resulting output, chemical leaching, and health outcomes were aggregated for these 30 fields. To generate a distribution of these aggregate outcomes, each of these 30 field simulations was replicated 30 times. For each price setting, a total of 30x5x30 = 4,500 crop cycles was simulated for the 30 sample fields. The crop rotation averages two potato crops (cycles) for each pasture cycle, and there are an average of about 9 pesticide applications in each potato cycle. Thus, for each set of 4,500 simulations, there are about 3,000 potato crop cycles simulated and about 3,000x9=27,000 pesticide applications simulated.

Figure 4 presents the scatter plot of aggregate outcomes for output and carbofuran leaching, using the base technology and the other price scenarios. Carbofuran is the principal pesticide used by these farmers to control Andean weevil and accounts for 47 percent of the total active ingredient of insecticides applied. Most people living in the watershed obtain their drinking water from higher in the watershed, so the main risk is from return flows of water that leach below the crop root zone and then return to surface water which, in turn, is drained from the watershed and is used as a source of drinking water. As production moves progressively up slope onto higher land the potential for drinking water supplies in the watershed to be contaminated also increases.

The horizontal axis in Figure 4 measures the total value of production on the 30 simulated fields for the 5-crop cycle simulation; the vertical axis measures the cumulative mass of active ingredient of carbofuran leached beyond the one meter depth over a five-year time horizon after the pesticide is

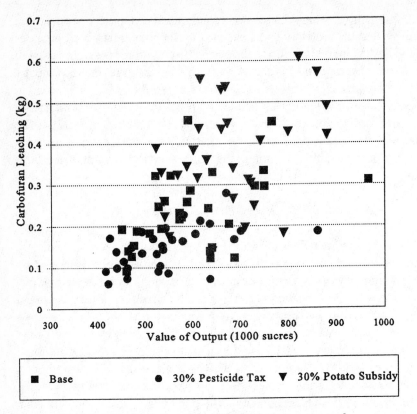

Figure 4. Pesticide-output tradeoffs, Ecuador case study

applied (simulations showed that virtually all leaching below the one meter depth occurs within a five-year period after an application). This scatter plot represents the stochastic simulation of a curve like T_1 in Figure 1.

The variability in Figure 4 represents the combined effects of variation in management decisions, weather, and soil properties on crop production and leaching. Key features of this scatter plot are the positive slope of the tradeoff between output and environmental impact, and the increase in the dispersion of leaching outcomes as output increases. This increased dispersion in leaching is explained by the interaction of management and weather. As prices change so as to increase the incentive to grow potatoes, i.e., a potato subsidy, farmers shift the crop rotation towards potatoes and they intensify pesticide use on potato crops. The combination of these changes in management means that whenever weather is favorable to leaching (high amount of rainfall immediately after chemical application), there is an increased likelihood that there will be a leachable amount of chemical on the potato plant or on the soil to be transformed to soluble form and transported through the soil profile and into ground water.

The US Environmental Protection Agency (EPA) established a Maximum Contaminant Level (MCL) for carbofuran in ground water of 40 parts per billion. When the data of Figure 4 are converted into concentration units, we find that all of the simulated concentrations are more than an order of magnitude below the MCL, indicating that by EPA standards carbofuran would not pose a human health risk in drinking water drawn from ground water. Recall that contamination of ground water is only one of the possible pathways of pesticides into the environment. Thus, it is unclear whether this MCL is an adequate indicator of environmental impact, because it considers only human cancer risk, and it does not account for the total loadings into the environment and the possible bioaccumulation of compounds at critical points in the food chain which may have important human health or environmental impact. For these reasons, it may still be considered important to know whether technologies are increasing or decreasing loadings into the environment, especially when those loadings vary substantially over the landscape or with policy or technology choices.

To investigate the effects of spatial heterogeneity on environmental impact, the study watershed was disaggregated into four zones characterized by different soil and climate types. These zones represent changes in these features as field locations move up slope in the watershed. The results indicate that the mean output-leaching tradeoff is near zero for zones with lower rainfall levels and less steep slopes, and much higher for zones with higher rainfall and elevation, i.e., almost all of the contributions to total environmental loadings were due to production activities in less than half of the land area. From a methodological perspective, these results show how the use of a representative farm for the region could be misleading. For example, if researchers based their analysis on a representative farm from lower elevation zones they would incorrectly conclude that chemical loadings into the environment are virtually nil, and that the slope of the output-environment tradeoff—the environmental opportunity cost of increasing output—is zero. On the other hand, if the representative farm were parameterized with data from higher elevation zones, total environmental loadings would be overestimated by almost 100 percent.

Figure 5 shows the scatter plots for output-health tradeoffs obtained for the base technology and two policy scenerios. In Figure 5 the vertical axis

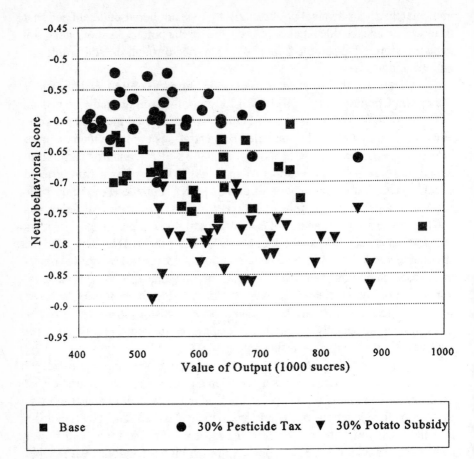

Figure 5. Health-output tradeoffs, Ecuador case study

measures the mean neurobehavioral score simulated for the farm population, the more negative the score the more damaging is the health effect. As pesticide use increases, farm workers and other members of the farm population are exposed more times to pesticides, thus increasing the mean level of exposure and the mean impact on the farm population's health. This figure also shows that there is an increase in the dispersion of health outcomes as the value of crop output increases. The increase in dispersion reflects the differing vulnerabilities of individuals to higher exposure levels of pesticides.

Conclusions and Implications

This paper presents a general approach to quantitatively assess the tradeoffs between output, environmental quality and human health associated with the use of agricultural technologies, and how those tradeoffs may change with the introduction of new technologies or policies. The derivation of tradeoffs is presented in static terms. But in the analysis of sustainability of agricultural production systems, long-run dynamics of the system are often the critical concern. In dealing with concerns such as the long-term sustainability of the soil resource, the physical characteristics of land in the region may evolve over time as a function of farmers' land use and management decisions. Also climate change may impact the land in production over long periods of time. By explicitly incorporating these dynamic elements into the model, the long-term issues of sustaining productivity and environmental quality can be addressed.

The two case studies illustrate the importance of key measurement issues, such as the need to account for the spatial variability of agriculture-environment interactions in measuring sustainability of alternative technologies, and the use of tradeoff curves as a policy analysis tool and as a means for *ex-ante* assessment of changes in technology. Both case studies also imply that defining a sustainable production technology for a given area may be misleading since most technologies have both positive and negative impacts on the environment or human health. The site-specific nature of the environmental and health effects, and the difficulty in creating a single enviromental indicator index, are the principal reasons for this finding.

References

Antle, J.M. 1996. "Methodological Issues in Assessing Potential Impacts of Climate Change on Agriculture". *Agricultural and Forest Meteorology* 80:67-85.

Antle, J. M., S.M. Capalbo, J.B. Johnson, and W.E. Zidack.1996. "Economics and Sustainability of Crop and Livestock Agriculutre in the Northern Plains and Foothill Mountain Environments", unpublished project report, submitted to USDA/ERS/RTD, May.

Antle, J.M., S. M. Capalbo, and C.C. Crissman.1994. "Econometric Production Models with Endogenous Input Timing: An Application to Ecuadorian Potato Production", *Journal of Agricultural and Resource Economics*, vol. 19, no.1: 1-18.

Antle, J.M., C.C. Crissman, R.J. Wagenet, and J.L. Hutson. 1996. "Empirical

Foundations of Environment-Trade Linkages: Evidence from an Andean Study". M.E. Bredahl, N. Ballenger, J.C. Dunmore, and T.L. Roe, eds., in *Agriculture, Trade and the Environment: Discovering and Measuring the Critical Linkages.* Boulder, Co: Westview Press.

Antle, J.M. and R.E. Just. 1991. "Effects of Commodity Program Structure of Resource Use and the Environment", in *Commodity and Resource Policy in Agricultural Systems.* N. Bockstael and R.E. Just, eds. New York: Springer-Verlag. pp. 97-127.

Bouma, J., and M.R. Hoosbeek.1966 "The Contribution and Importance of Soil Scientists in Interdisciplinary Studies Dealing with Land" in *The Role Of Soil Science in Interdisciplinary Research.* SSA Special Publication 45. Madison, WI: American Society of Agronomy and Soil Science Society of America,pp1-15.

Bouma, J., A. Kuyvenhoven, B.A. M. Bouman, J.C. Luyten, and H.G. Zandstra. 1995. *Eco-Regional Approaches for Sustainable Land Use and Food Production.* Kluwer Academic Publishers in cooperation with International Potato Center, Dordrecht, The Netherlands.

Cole, D.C., F. Carpio, J. Julian, N. Leon, R. Carbotte, H. de Almeida.1997. "Neurological Outcomes among Farm and Non-Farm Rural Ecuadorians". *Neurotoxicology and Teratology* : in press.

Crissman, C.C., J.M. Antle and S.M. Capalbo.1997. *Economic, Environmental, and Health Tradeoffs in Agriculture: Pesticides and the Sustainability of Andean Potato Production.* Boston: Kluwer Academic Publishers (in press).

Crissman, C.C., D.C. Cole, and F. Carpio.1994. "Pesticide Use and Farm Worker Health in Ecuadorian Potato Production". *American Journal of Agricultural Economics* 76 (August):593-597.

Cropper, M.L., and A.M. Freeman, III.1991. "Environmental Health Effects". J.B. Braden and C.D. Kolstad, eds. *Measuring the Demand for Environmental Quality.* Amsterdam: North-Holland.

FAO. *1982. Guidelines: Land Evaluation for Rainfed Agriculture.* FAO Soils Bulletin 52 (Rome: FAO).

Forget, G.. T. Goodman. and A. de Villiers.1993. *Impact of Pesticide Use on Health in Developing Countries.* Ottawa: International Development Research Center.

Hutson, J.L. and R.J. Wagenet. 1993. "A Pragmatic Field-Scale Approach for Modeling Pesticides". *Journal of Environmental Quality* 22 :494-499.

Pingali, P.L. and P.A. Roger. *1995. Impact of Pesticides on Farmer Health and the Rice Environment.* Kluwer Academic Publishers, Norwell, MA.

Wagenet, R.J and P.S.C. Rao.1990. "Modeling Pesticide Fate in Soils", in H.H Cheng et al., ed. *Pesticides in the Environment: Processes, Impacts and Modeling.* Soil Science Book Series No. 2. American Society of Agronomy, Madison, Wisconsin.

5 Family, Community and Sustainability in Agriculture

Sonya Salamon, Richard L. Farnsworth and Donald G. Bullock

Introduction

Agricultural systems that do not sustain soil productivity nor take into account the surrounding ecosystem are hardly unique to the modern era. The archaeological record is replete with agrarian societies that flourished, sustained large populations, and then fell into decline after soil erosion, monocrop dependence, deforestation, over-grazing, or siltation related to irrigation degraded their environments. The vanished Cahokians from the banks of the Mississippi, the ancient Mayans from the lowland forests of Central America, and the past kingdoms from the Mesopotamian Fertile Crescent are examples of civilizations with agricultural systems that were not sustainable (Salamon, 1996).

Advocates of sustainable farming argue that agricultural systems exist world wide, however, that have maintained high productivity over centuries and sustained large populations while being efficient and preserving the environment. Found, for example, in the wet-rice systems of Japan, China and elsewhere in Southeast Asia and the Swiss mountains, these small-holder systems are an adaptation to great population pressure and scarce land resources. In these places farmers work small plots intensively with family labor and cannot afford to degrade the soils (Netting, 1993). They rotate crops, intercrop, manure fields, avoid soil erosion with winter cover-crops or structures such as terraces, raise animals, and use part-time or full-time off-farm work to supplement incomes. Critical to such systems is a culture that assures farm families permanent tenure to their land, thus making worthwhile intensive labor and capital investment. Farmers in industrialized societies adopting sustainable farming have looked to these smallholder systems cross-culturally for inspiration. Because we know from the cross-cultural record that highly productive systems can be sustainable, it is evident that adoption of sustainable systems is more a social issue than it is a technological one.

Our understanding of how agricultural innovations are adopted derives from locales typified by family farmers, but the family is rarely examined as a context for the adoption process. Recent studies persist in focusing on a single male farmer as the actor making adoption decisions (Bird, Bultena, and Gardner, 1995; Lockeretz, 1990; Rogers et al., 1988). The transition from conventional to alternative farming systems literature likewise ignores relevant social barriers to adoption other than profitability (National Research Council, 1989).

Whether all family members are relevant to adoption, does adoption involve a paradigm shift, do adopters differ fundamentally from conventional farmers, all remain unanswered questions about the social context for adoption. It is our argument that broadening the adoption context to the farm-family and the community in which the decision-making takes place casts light on how adoption of sustainable farming systems is accepted or rejected.

The Social Context for Adoption of Innovation

Research has identified numerous ecologic, economic, and agronomic factors that influence alternative farming-systems adoption. Far less attention has been paid to the social context of adoption for what is widely acknowledged as a paradigm shift associated with the transition from conventional to sustainable systems (Beus and Dunlap, 1990). We know this shift involves social issues because farmers point to an information scarcity, community criticism, or local traditions in addition to agronomic and economic factors as crucial (Lockeretz et al., 1984; National Research Council, 1989). Furthermore, the most obvious social context affecting adoption is the family because family-farm persistence is dependent on the flexible household production form; a unit highly compatible with the varied and seasonal demands of agriculture (Netting, 1993; Reinhardt and Barlett, 1989).

How do family members affect the adoption or continuation of sustainable farming systems? Because the farm family merges kinship and production functions this interdependence is central to a whole-farm analysis (Salamon, 1992). Thus, the farm family—its history, its kinship network and its community—shape the context for adoption. Household studies, as an example, indicate that differing lifecourse and gender agendas inevitably bring family members into conflict (Laslett, 1984; Broderick, 1993).

Farming ordinarily carries many risks; the weather, commodity markets, health and safety are issues capable of damaging the operation economically (Rosenblatt 1990). Farm families consider these hazards as givens for the occupation. Widely accepted technologies and practices, however, tend to be viewed as reliable, though this can be a false assumption. Sustainable farming practices are seen as potentially increasing family stress because more complex management, more information, trained labor, experimentation, and more risk are involved (Bird, Bultena, and Gardner, 1995; National Research Council, 1989; Pfeffer, 1992). Furthermore, the tendency for adopters to constantly tweak the system means that repeated experimentation can create persistent stress. Adopting sustainable systems therefore may produce different stresses for families than do conventional farming systems.

Much of what is known about chronic stress among farmers derives from a recent comprehensive study of Iowa families who, as a consequence of the 1980s farm crisis, suffered a sense of household jeopardy that lasted over many years (Conger and Elder, Jr., 1994). Chronic stress had a significant and lasting impact on individual well-being and family ties, particularly for children's development and marital relationships (Conger and Elder, 1994; Rosenblatt, 1990). Transition to the complex management that sustainable systems require is described as an incremental rather than a wholesale conversion process (Flora, 1990). An incremental transition seems associated with farm-family concerns about risk and stress (Buttel and Swanson, 1986). Adopting sustainable farming systems does not inevitably produce financial decline. The transition, however, has the potential to build chronic stress for those family members (wives or children) who consider the risks greater than those incurred with conventional systems. We need to explore whether family stress constitutes a barrier to adoption, or the persistence of adoption through an inter-generational transfer.

Family life-course phase, labor supply, land tenure status, debt level, attitudes toward the future and resources, or beliefs about an agrarian way of life and ecological concerns all shape farm-household decision-making (Bennett and Kohl, 1982). Deciding to pursue a particular farming-strategy is also influenced by cultural priorities shaping family goals (Salamon, 1992). Research shows that operators of all sized farms express considerable interest in sustainable practices, but do not actually adopt. Why rank-and-file farmers do not adopt is perplexing and points to the value of expanding analyses with social factors (Buttel, Gillespie, and Power, 1990).

In summary, we know little about why some families adopt sustainable systems and why their neighbors who share many social, cultural and environmental traits, do not. These fundamental questions and whether the family or its community context erects barriers to adopting sustainable farming systems, drove our research agenda.

Sample Selection and Methods

We chose to select a representative, rather than random, sample of 60 Illinois farm families (30 using sustainable systems and 30 using conventional systems) due to classification variability and small numbers of sustainable families. Sets of 10 such pairs were interviewed from three zones of the state each characterized by distinctive soils, weather, and operation-structure representative of Illinois and the Midwest region: northern Illinois/ livestock and grain; central Illinois/ grain; and southern Illinois/ livestock and grain.

The Illinois Sustainable Agricultural Network (ISAN) membership, augmented by recommendations from local Natural Resources Conservation Service personnel, were used to identify families involved with sustainable farming systems. Families were first contacted by telephone. Those who met the social criteria of being an active, full-time farm family with children were preferred. What defined a sustainable farming system was revised during our selection process, prior to data collection. Those families who raised livestock, planted cover crops, used fertility and IPM programs to reduce inputs, or no-tilled farmed were judged to be moving toward sustainability.

Once selected each sustainable family was asked to identify another family in the same community using conventional systems, whose lifecourse phase and farming operation were similar. Farm sizes of the conventional group fall within the acreage range for commercial farms reported by the Illinois-based Farm Business Farm Management (FBFM) Association (FBFM, 1995). Furthermore, characteristics of the conventional group such as family size, age, and education almost duplicate a 1992 FBFM family study. Corn and soybean yields tend to be higher in our sample, but that is to be expected because of the inclusion of smaller, part-time farms in the FBFM sample (FBFM, 1993). Thus, our conventional family sample closely resembles full-time, commercial farmers in Illinois. By holding as many family and farm factors constant as possible the controlled comparison design aimed to throw into sharp relief those cultural and social factors that differ in association with adoption or rejection of sustainable farming systems.

The 60 families were each interviewed and observed on-farm for approximately two days using in-depth and semi-structured questionnaires designed by the team of an anthropologist, a natural resources economist and an agronomist. The on-farm interviews were followed by two waves of phone interviews to flesh out the data central to social issues of adoption and to obtain comparable production data. The combined interviews, observations, and telephone calls produced a data base composed of four parts: 1) social and cultural characteristics of the families (life-course phase, labor supply, attitudes toward the future and resources, beliefs about farming, ecological concerns, and goals for farm and family); 2) a physical description of the farm (e.g. soil type, slope, and drainage); 3) detailed production information (e.g. yields, crop rotation, chemical inputs, and practices); and 4) economic information including production costs, assets and debts for the present and previous years.

Characteristics of the Families

When the whole-farm system was taken into account no two operations were identical. We obtained great diversity in the mix of machinery, rotations, inputs, cultivation, and other practices among families in both the sustainable and conventional groups. The summary data that follow provide a general overview of sample families and farms.

The two groups are similar according to age (44 years for husbands and slightly younger for wives), education (14 years), and occupation. More sustainable farmers held another job. For both groups, the second job almost always related directly to farming (e.g. selling seed and fertilizer, building or repairing farm machinery). In both groups more than 50 percent of wives worked off-the-farm; her income and health insurance directly benefitted the farming operation (for details see Salamon, Farnsworth, Bullock and Yusuf, 1997).

Family size of the sustainable group was significantly larger (4.9 versus 4.3 people per family). Out of 60 families only two lacked children and in only two cases (one from each group) was a wife absent (due to divorce or death). Husbands in the sustainable sample are slightly more German in ethnicity and the conventional sample slightly more "Yankee", as predicted by Salamon's previous research focusing on the farming as a way of life versus farming as a business, cultural distinctions of these Illinois ethnic groups (1992). Generally, both groups actively participated in religious activities, and, to a much lesser degree in farm, educational, and Cooperative Extension Service, community service or other activities.

Characteristics of the Farms

Consistent with other studies though not statistically significant, the sustainable group's average farm size of 941 acres is smaller than the conventional group's average size of 1147 acres (Bird, Bultena and Gardner, 1995). The sustainable group, however, owns slightly more of its land (394 acres to 359 acres) and rents fewer acres (537 acres to 788 acres).

Accepted wisdom is that families adopting sustainable farming systems do so because the land they farm is intrinsically less productive. When the soils of the two groups were compared (using a representative field selected by the operator) no significant differences in the inherent productivity at either the basic or the high management levels were found between the conventional and sustainable fields. There were significant differences for both basic and high management level between regions. For each crop, land in the north and central regions has similar expected production levels and both are greater than those of farms in the south region.

Specific soil parameters such as P, K, pH and organic matter also did not differ significantly between the sustainable and conventional fields within a region. Again, the region of Illinois in which a farm is located, is important. In particular, the north zone has significantly greater soil P level than either the central or south zones. The large number of livestock (hogs) in the north and subsequent manuring of fields probably explains the higher P level. Manuring also probably contributed to the large organic matter content of the north zone farms, but native vegetation would have led to the difference between north and south.

Information collected about crop production (comparison of same crop in same year) was also similar between the two groups. The sustainable group's soybean yields (45, 48, and 45 bushels per acre for 1991-3) from their representative fields and the conventional group's yields (49, 47, and 47 bushels per acre for 1991-3) from their representative fields were not significantly different. The sustainable group's corn yields (141, 137, and 133 bushels per acre for 1991-3) tended to be a little lower than the conventional group's yields (150, 167, and 132 bushels per acre for 1991-3). Only 1992 corn yields, however, proved to be significantly different.

During the past ten years sustainable farmers changed the way they farmed compared to conventional farmers, and those changes were statistically significant. Slightly more than half of sustainable farmers diversified their crop mix while only 3 percent of conventional farmers had. Over half of the sustainable group reduced herbicides compared with only 3 percent of the conventional group. Almost two-thirds of the sustainable group reduced its use of synthetic fertilizer compared with only 20 percent of conventional farmers.

Sustainable farm families worked fewer total hours than the conventional farm families (4333 to 5129 hours), but spent more time per acre (6.2 hours to 5.3 hours). Both groups allocated their time among fieldwork (51 versus 52 percent), management (29 versus 30 percent), bookkeeping (11 versus 10 percent), and miscellaneous activities (9 versus 8 percent) along the same lines. Differences between hours worked per acre and how the time was allocated among activities were not statistically significant.

On average sustainable farmers used tractors with significantly smaller horsepower (122 to 156), and that were significantly older (1974 to 1980) than their conventional counterparts. Average horsepower per acre did not differ significantly between the sustainable and conventional groups (.24 to .22 hp per acre), thus suggesting similar power use per acre.

Each group acknowledged contrasts between themselves and their opposite. Asked to place themselves on a continuum from conventional (1) to sustainable (10) each group chose a position consistent (and statistically significant) with how we designated them. That is, the sustainable group placed themselves toward the sustainable end of the continuum (7.4) and the conventional group placed themselves toward the conventional end (3.9). Dissatisfaction with current achievements accounts for few sustainable farmers placing themselves at the extreme of the continuum. One who placed himself midpoint (e.g. 7.5) on the sustainable end of the continuum explained: "I'm not there yet, but I know what it takes to get there". That is, sustainable adopters are striving toward a goal that is continually refined, so that full achievement is rarely admitted.

All the families preferred a self-sufficient farm. Self-sufficiency, however, was defined according to agronomic and financial factors by the sustainable group and according to financial factors by the conventional group. These statistically significant distinctions reveal that each group thinks about farming differently, although for sustainables the contrasts do not represent a paradigm shift. We will show that how sustainable families approach farming resonates with other dimensions of their lives (Bell, 1994).

In summary, the sustainable and conventional groups look similar. Our sample design contributed partly to these findings. Some contrasts, however, echoed larger studies (Bird, Bultena, and Gardner, 1995) such as sustainable families having more children and significantly changing their pesticide and fertility practices. There is sufficient similarity, however, to allow our focus on the cultural and social factors that differ in association with adoption or rejection of sustainable farming systems.

Why Farm Families Adopt Sustainable Farming Systems

In this section we describe a set of social characteristics identified inductively for the sustainable group that are associated with adoption: family traditions; critical family events with environmental or health consequences; and family resource conservation and frugality patterns. Together these characteristics point to the sustainable families as a group as being distinctively different people than those families farming conventionally. At the cursory level, the frequency for behaviors provided here for the two groups looks similar. What is important is not the magnitude of the numbers, but the substance of the quotations that illustrate contrasting family cultures and processes.

Family Innovative Tradition Over half (60 percent) of the 30 sustainable families compared with about half (48 percent) of conventionals reported a kin-mentor as crucial to how they farmed. Typically it was a father, but fathers-in-law or siblings were also cited. The kin-mentor relationship was substantively different, however, for sustainables. Their role-models were described as the community's earliest adopter of environmentally sensitive practices or as a prudent person. For example, a northern Illinois farmer maintains practices initiated by his father. "My dad's philosophy was to sell as least as possible off your soil. You sell the grain, but not the hay or straw. He liked to have that [hay or straw] back out on the land...We feed the hay to the livestock or cut hay and leave it lay as residue." Another man credits his grandfather as being prescient. "My grandfather always said 'We need to go back to the way we used to do it. We're using too many chemicals.'" A farm woman lauded her father-in-law as a mentor: "His father is one of the most innovative and open to change people I've ever seen. ...He'll say 'Let's try this and see what happens'".

Families expressed great pride about being first adopters of sustainable practices in the area, just as did conventional farmers about being early adopters of new equipment. A retired widow, partners with her son reported, "We were the first ones [in the community] to do no-till beans in the fall, and about the second to use the chisel plow". A retired father bragged "I had the first soil conservation plan in the county...I did contour farming and built terraces and waterways on my land". A farmer lauded his father's innovation: "I started farming full-time in 1984... We had been using the moldboard plow until then. Dad decided that was not where it was at. We had to make changes. In 1985 or so, we went to ridge till... because of soil conservation". Thus, adoption of sustainable practices was associated with a family's traditions rather than representing a sudden paradigm switch, for over half the group.

Adoption of sustainable farming systems by the operators we interviewed has also influenced the decision of sons, now reaching maturity, to become farmers. In four cases among the sustainable group parents remarked that a son's commitment to ecological concerns brought them back to farming after college. In one case the son never showed much interest in the farm, but as a college senior became attracted to the ecological aspects of his dad's endeavors. "Most other professions just don't present the same kind of challenge that farming does for me", said the son about what his father is doing.

Finally, a statistically significant 83 percent of sustainable parents felt positively enough about the occupation to want their children to continue farming, in contrast to only 47 percent of conventional parents. It may be that a family's farming sustainably obtains greater satisfaction for families than does farming conventionally.

Environmental or Health Trigger Two-thirds of sustainable families (67 percent) cited an environmental or health event that triggered changes in how they farmed. A typical account was a northern Illinois farmer's conversion experience. "In 1965 a neighbor fall and spring plowed his ground next to our alfalfa field. Then a bad windstorm came.... so much of his field blew that it piled up high enough to cover the bottom wire of the 4-strand barb-wire fence... the dust was so bad on our crop that it ruined our engines...At that point my dad said, 'I don't want to fall or spring plow again', and we began to chisel plow...the neighbors thought we were crazy and called it trash farming, but that never bothered my dad." Another change came after their spraying for grasshoppers precipitated a bad bird kill. "My dad said, I'm not going to use chemicals like that anymore. It's not worth it.' We decided there was enough there for everybody and we made sure we raised enough for us both."
A father's contracting a rare form of cancer caused a southern Illinois man to suspect their use of a herbicide subsequently taken off the market. "When we applied that stuff it was just horrible; it even killed dogs." This family now farms organically because as he explains, "I hate chemicals".

Systematic On-farm Experimentation Associated with adopting alternative farming practices is a family pattern of experimentation. Most sustainable farmers (84 percent) volunteered that they had test plots primarily used to judge the viability of different crops and production systems. Test plots were a taken-for-granted practice. Commented a northern Illinois sustainable farmer: "I've been curious what the effects are of my different practices on the land. So I've been keeping these plots out here comparing my practices with conventional practices". Test plots are evidence that adopters consistently experiment with the system. A farmer prominent in the ISAN has tried so many different practices that his wife says, "We ought to call this [Family name]'s Experimental Farm".

Conventional farmers only occasionally mentioned use of test plots (17 percent) as a standard operating procedure. The percentage difference between the two groups may reflect more accurately a divergence in the type of test plots, however, than a lack of experimentation. Conventional farmers, for example, mentioned variety, fertility, and chemical comparison plots, but rarely mentioned the types of test plots used by the sustainable group.

Prudence with Resources As a whole, sustainable families tend to be judicious or frugal consumers of all resources. That is, concerns about reducing chemical inputs or preserving soil are aspects of a family culture. Family aphorisms justify frugality. A farmer recalled his father saying, "If you can't pay for it, don't buy it". He typifies his farming as "conservative". "I buy farm equipment at auction sales or otherwise second hand". He shares equipment, "I have a combine-partnership with my nephews". Sustainable families not only farm modestly, but live modestly. Sustainable farm families are significantly less likely to have central air conditioning (47 percent) than conventional families (67 percent). Lack of central air-conditioning indicates an older home or a reluctance to invest in such equipment. Each group had a comparable 3.7 average number of tractors. For the sustainable group as seen previously, however, the average age of their tractors was 1974 compared with the average of 1980 for the conventional group. These contrasts are indicative of a distinctive resource-use pattern by sustainable families.

A northern Illinois hog, cattle, and grain farm family (900 full owned acres) represents an extreme frugality case. Everything is recycled. No equipment is purchased new including the family cars. Their equipment is all eight-row based. His son-in-law commented, "This is a LISA farm...We use everything until it falls apart". They bed their hogs on shredded paper from the local bank, the school system, and their mail. "We've got the best educated hogs around." The semi-retired patriarch of the three-family operation says, "I never sold a bushel of corn in my life". All grain produced on the farm is fed to the cattle and hogs and "this saves on transport and produces something [manure] that can be returned to the soil.... I believe a farm should be self-sufficient... I would like to see the time when we don't buy anything...possibly this is my goal". A central Illinois farmer proudly cites his frugal management as explaining his successful competition in an aggressive cash-rent land market. He uses so little fuel for their 1200 mostly rental acres: "My gas man asked me if I farmed 600 acres....I can out bid the others because I use less chemicals".

Male Adopters and the Community

Certain traits characterize the early male-adopters, whose wives and children may be enthusiastic or reluctant collaborators, and whose community is watching. A central Illinois farmer portrayed himself as: "I'm out here on my lonesome". An oft heard self-characterization by such men was: "I don't care what anybody thinks", about their farming. Few farmers from either group owned up to being regular coffee-shop participants (less than 20 percent). A sustainable adopter, however, was apt to cite a community reason as one did: "If I went to the coffee shop I wouldn't be using no-till. Everyone would have shamed me into not using it". A southern Illinois farmer with an on-farm business had a similar story: "A customer of ours was talking to a seed salesman and asked 'What's [farmer] doing these days?' The seed salesman said, 'Oh, don't talk to him; he's crazy'". He, as other early adopters take pleasure in being ornery and are self-described as "crazy" or "radical". He commented, "I don't care what my neighbors think. They don't pay my bills or see my net". As early adopters they occasionally receive encouragement from conventional neighbors, like one who confessed: "If I had enough guts, I'd do it just like you do [no herbicides]", or as another said "Don't worry [about a weed-setback], you're ten years ahead of your time".

Our original research design targeted a single county in each zone. This plan quickly changed when it was impossible to find county clusters of 10 adopter-families. Despite the relative rarity of like-minded neighbors adopters are not actually isolated. Men typically cited other earlier adopters who "mentored" them, and others they mentored. Farmers counseled new adopters by telephone even while being interviewed. It became evident that innovators were also supported by organizations such as the ISANs member groups. Male adopters join state or regional organizations and are brought into contact with like-minded farmers in other counties. Only recently has ISAN begun reaching out to wives who lack the substantial support their husbands do, as we will show. As a consequence, women are more "out there on their lonesome", receiving the brunt of community criticism.

The independence, tinkering, and innovativeness of the adopters of sustainable farming systems indicates an openness to new practices. This openness may originate from the shape of their careers. About half (47 percent) the sustainable farmers had varied occupational experiences excluding college (from several to 10 or more years) before returning to farming. In contrast, only 27 percent, but not a statistically significant number of conventional farmers had done anything other than attend college or farm. Sustainable farmers' work experiences run the gamut from banks or insurance to the armed forces or the Peace Corps.   Alternative occupations mean a variety of perspectives, experiences, and training brought to the business of farming.

Barriers to Adoption

Lack of Family Consensus Family members from sustainable farms may disagree about the wisdom of this management pathway. In particular wives, whose farm background included a father-role model dedicated to conventional farming systems, were critical of a husband's management (17 percent). Typically weedy fields were a bone of contention for sustainable couples. An example is a central Illinois woman who: "learned farming from my dad [and]...he never tolerated weeds...I guess I feel about weeds like having them in a garden; they don't belong". Pointing out her kitchen window to some smartweed in a field of corn she said, "Either [husband] does something about it or I will...I don't care if it's 2,4D or Roundup, I'll use anything, it doesn't bother me". Some couples farming sustainably have no conflict about weeds because they agree on using chemicals judiciously. "I would not have the land I do [rented] if I had a weed problem...the landlords don't like to see weeds even if I'm doing cash rent and it's none of their business", commented a central Illinois farmer.

If the sustainable farm is dependent on rental acreage, critical wives believe that weed problems eventually threaten viability of the operation. One such wife is nervous that weedy fields reflect poorly on her husband's farming skills. "Last year everything [husband] did backfired with his weed control program....I think it keeps him from getting more ground... landlords don't like to see the weeds." Although she admits, "We probably came out the same financially as a conventional farmer because we paid less for inputs". Aesthetics count nonetheless she believes, for example, in preventing their expansion by renting a farm from a relative near retirement. Husbands say their wife's anxiety about financial security results from unrelenting community criticism. Her sister tells one: "He's going broke. He's crazy". Such community pressures, say men, cause unrealistic fears for wives that sustainable systems will destroy the farm they built together. Sustainable families who own all their land can most easily operate without regard for community gossip. "I suppose our neighbors think we're lazy...but I'm reluctant to mow when it will kill off wildlife.. I only mow when I have a bad, a serious weed appear... though I know it don't look good", said one full-owner.

Critical women think the conventional systems used by kin or neighbors are more reliable and acceptable to the community. Furthermore, conventional farming appears to make more predictable management demands. Faultfinding wives argue that sustainable systems produce more family stress. "With this sustainable, there's a lot of work. We never get the maintenance done.....We are working harder, making less money, and it doesn't look good", commented an unhappy wife. Another woman agreed: "I think the system [husband] uses now is more stressful than conventional farming.. it's a more timely system". Perpetual experimentation also accounts for family tensions. A woman whose husband recently shifted to a fully organic operation finds constant change stressful. "Why can't we let someone else do the experiments? [He's] like a mad scientist....We've done every field we own....If you had a million dollars, would you bet every thing you had"?

About the same percentage (17 percent) of conventional couples also disagree about farming. It is interesting that for conventional couples, her environmental concerns about the chemicals a husband employs or his reluctance to adopt practices such as no-till, creates conflict. Financial consequences of his management are not an issue. In contrast, sustainable wives' concerns are about financial stability and management and the couples' disputes focus on using chemicals to achieve the wives' goals.

Community Pressures Sustainable farmers are more respectful about their conventional pair's management than vice versa. Traits viewed positively by sustainable adopters—diversification, flexibility, and environmentally sound practices—are negatively branded by unimpressed conventionals. Almost half the conventional farmers (40 percent) judged sustainable farmers poorly. For example, flexibility according to a conventional farmer symbolizes uncertainty: "I'm watching my [sustainable] neighbors.... I see them changing their practices every year. What that tells me is that they're not sure what they are doing. If they're not sure about it, I don't see why I should adopt what they are doing." Weeds, a temporary setback for a sustainable farmer represent poor management, according to a conventional one: "I've got nothing against sustainable farmers... [neighbor] is a nice man. But I just don't see how farmers are going to respect a farmer who keeps his farm that way".

Conventional farmers regard sustainable farmers' work habits as lazy or as busy-work generators. That is, sustainable management seems flawed to them. To one his neighbor's no-till system means less work, "He just thinks he's busy". A conventional farmer labels no-till as, "no-skill farming". He said disparagingly, "It doesn't take much talent to do...we like.... a nice level seed bed...When I was at [chemical dealer] we tore up lots of equipment going over some guy's no-till ground...full of hills and gullies".

A criticism leveled by conventional farmers is that sustainable systems are adopted out of financial desperation. "I'm wondering if people didn't go to sustainable if costs weren't driving 'em to it", said a conventional operator. Conversely sustainable farming is "for the very rich farmer who can afford to dabble". An aggressive conventional farmer sees sustainable practices as bringing eventual ruin: "I'll tell you I'm worried about [sustainable pair]...I think that in 5 years only one of us will be farming and I don't think it will be [pair]...Maybe he'll be alright if we have good crops and good years".

Conventional farmers watch the fields, yields, evidence of finances, and farm size of sustainable adopters and judge them poor managers based on these criteria. A central Illinois farmer wondered about his neighbor and friend: "Now you tell me why when we farm so close together, have about the same soils and get the same weather did [sustainable pair] have so many bad years, and I've never had a bad year". His neighbor, he thinks, adopted new methods precipitously and spent too much on equipment. The conventional farmer characterizes himself as a "semi-perfectionist", in contrast to his sustainable pair. "I'm picky about how I plant...you could shoot a bullet down my corn rows and knock off every one".

When a sustainable family sells land the community is likely to attribute it to management problems, regardless of facts. Explained a central Illinois conventional farmer: "I heard [sustainable neighbor] lost some ground and I expect the neighbors would say it was because of how he farms". Finally, a conventional operator commented on his sustainable pair, "I was a seed representative ...I concluded that farmers who didn't have a clucked-up farmstead were much more successful at getting rental land". The above remarks are indicative of social judgements influencing perceptions about sustainable systems.

Finally, conventional farmers resent being a target for the missionary zeal of those they judge as dubious managers. One conventional farmer, whose neighbor relentlessly tries to convert him, said, "Sustainable farmers ought to shut their mouths, get to work, and let us do our work". A couple farming conventionally resent a certain preachiness: "You get this moral thing. They say . . . Chemicals are bad...and when you see their field, you see a field full of weeds". The husband says like many conventional farmers, "I'm not going to poison my family". The "holier than thou" stance of some sustainable proselytizers is difficult to take for religious families farming conventionally. A Mennonite farming conventionally explained resentfully that their religion enjoins them to "be stewards of the land...if someone says he's a sustainable farmer he is saying he's a better steward of the soil and a better, religious person than I". Born of personal observation, these issues in all probability constitute substantial barriers to adoption.

Conclusion

A perceptive sustainable farmer reflected on the distinctive style of his group versus conventional farmers: "I think all farmers divide into two types. Either you have power-genes or soil-genes. A power-gene guy likes machines, buys new the latest and most powerful he can. A soil-gene guy uses less horsepower, has old or used equipment, and does anything not to use as much horsepower. A soil-gene guy looks under the soil while the power-gene guy only cares about what going-on on top". Accepted wisdom is that a transition to sustainable farming systems necessitates a fundamental paradigm shift regarding nature and the environment beliefs (Beus and Dunlap 1990). Our findings indicate that rather than a deep philosophical shift to environmentally sensitive farming (although not excluding it) sustainable families share both a family history of adoption and a predisposition to use resources prudently in every dimension of their lives. Cutting back on chemicals according to a prudent world-view is as much for efficiency or economics as it is for environmental motives (Bell 1994). A grand paradigm shift, therefore, did not occur among our sample in association with adoption. Similarly, conventional families categorizing themselves at the extreme are unlikely to take a dramatic shift in their management practices.

Our findings show that perceptual differences about the same practices are barriers to adoption. Conventional families reject what sustainable adopters culturally value. Sustainables are proud of the older machinery they repair; conventionals view old equipment as proof of financial stress. Sustainables are dedicated experimenters; conventionals view annually altering practices as confused or poor management. Sustainables consider weedy fields as a temporarily ugly setback; conventionals view weeds as a sign of poor practices. Each group views the same phenomena as reinforcing their particular beliefs about farming. Sustainables and conventionals are marching to different drummers.

To be sustainable, that is long lasting, a family farming system must socially survive an intergenerational transfer. Our research highlights that a family consensus, that includes a wife or a successor is crucial to whether social issues hinder continuity of an established sustainable operation. Similarly, whether the family rents rather than owns farmland is potentially a barrier to social sustainability, because the landlord and possibly the community are variables critical to continuity of the chosen farming system.

Current understandings about how families function tells us if all family members are not committed a farming system is unlikely to be socially sustainable. In the long term social sustainability may rank in importance equal to achieving the critical initial adoption of sustainable farming systems. In addition to ecological sustainability met by farming in environmentally sensitive ways, concern must be focused on social sustainability that preserves decisions made by one generation when the next generation takes over. This will help ensure that future generations do not repeat the mistakes of now long lost civilizations such as the Mesopotamians and Cahokians who vanished in part because their agricultural systems were not sustainable.

Acknowledgments

An earlier version of this paper was published in the July/August 1997 issue of the *Journal of Soil and Water Conservation*. This research was carried out with the support from the Sustainable Agriculture Research and Education Program, Grant Number LWF 62-061-03113, the Illinois Agricultural Experiment Station, the University of Illinois Research Board, and the University of Illinois Cooperative Extension Service. We wish to thank the research assistants who contributed to the project: Cathey Huddelston, Raji Yusuf, Paul Benjamin, and Viju Ipe. The authors also wish to thank the Illinois Sustainable Agricultural Network, and Deborah

Cavanaugh-Grant, Director, for their cooperation, and the 60 farm families who were so generous with their time. In addition the paper benefitted from discussions with members of the Economic Research Service, U.S. Department of Agriculture, Washington, D.C. and the Henry Wallace Institute for Alternative Agriculture, Greenbelt, MD where Salamon gave talks in 1996.

References

Bell, M. M. 1994. *Childerley: Nature and morality in a country village*. Chicago: University of Chicago Press,

Bennett, J. W. and S. B. Kohl. 1982. "The agrifamily system". Pp. 128-147, In J. W. Bennett, *Of time and the enterprise*. Minneapolis: University of Minnesota Press.

Beus, C. E. and R. E. Dunlap. 1990. "Conventional versus alternative agriculture: the paradigmatic roots of the debate". *Rural Sociology* 55: 590-616.

Bird, E.A.R., G.L. Bultena, and J.C. Gardner. 1995. *Planting the future: Developing an agriculture that sustains land and community*. Ames: Iowa State University Press.

Broderick, C. B. 1993. *Understanding family process: Basics of family systems theory*. Newbury Park: Sage Publications.

Buttel, F.H., G.W. Gillespie, Jr., and A. Power. 1990. "Sociological aspects of agricultural sustainability in the United States: a New York case study". Pp. 515-532, In C.A. Edwards, R.Lal, P.Madden, R.H. Miller and G. House, eds. *Sustainable agricultural systems*. Ankeny: Soil and Water Conservation Society.

Buttel, F.H. and L.E. Swanson. 1986. "Soil and water conservation: a farm structural and public policy context". Pp. 26-39, In S.B. Lovejoy and T.L. Napier, eds. *Conserving soil*. Ankeny: Soil Conservation Society of America.

Conger. R.D. and G.H. Elder. Jr. 1994. *Families in troubled times: Adapting to change in rural America*. New York: Aldine De Gruyter.

FBFM. 1993. 1992 *Summary of farm and family sources and uses of dollars*. Department of Agricultural Economics. University of Illinois at Urbana-Champaign.

FBFM. 1995. 1994 *Summary of Illinois farm business records*. Circular 1341. Department of Agricultural and Consumer Economics. University of Illinois at Urbana-Champaign.

Flora, C.B. 1990. "Sustainability of agriculture and rural communities". Pp. 343-359. In C. A. Francis, C. B. Flora, and L. D. King, (eds.) *Sustainable agriculture in temperate zones*. New York: John Wiley and Sons.

Laslett, P.1984. "The family as a knot of individual interests". Pp. 353-379. In R. McC. Netting, R. R. Wilk, and E.J. Arnould, eds. *Households*. Berkeley:

University of California Press.

Lockeretz, W. 1990. "What have we learned about who conserves soil?" *Journal of Soil and Water Conservation* 45: 517-523.

National Research Council. 1989. *Alternative agriculture*. Washington, D.C.: National Academy Press.

Netting, R.McC. 1993. *Smallholders, householders: Farm families and the ecology of intensive, sustainable agriculture*. Stanford: Stanford University Press.

Pfeffer, M. J. 1992. Labor and production barriers to the reduction of agricultural chemical inputs. *Rural Sociology* 57: 347-362.

Reinhardt, N. and P. Barlett. 1989. The persistence of family farms in United States agriculture. *Sociologia Ruralis* 29: 203-225.

Rogers, E.M., R.J. Burdge, P.F. Korsching, and J.F. Donnermeyer. 1988. *Social change in rural societies*. Englewood Cliffs: Prentice Hall.

Rosenblatt, P.C. 1990. *Farming is in our blood: Farm families in economic crisis*. Ames: Iowa State University Press.

Salamon, S. 1992. *Prairie patrimony: Family, farming, and community in the Midwest*. Chapel Hill: University of North Carolina Press.

Salamon, S. 1996. "Sustainable agriculture". Pp. 1272-1274, in D. Levinson and M.Ember, eds. *Encyclopedia of cultural anthropology*. New York: Henry Holt and Company.

Salamon, S., R.L. Farnsworth, D. G. Bullock, and R. Yusuf. 1997. "Family factors affecting adoption of sustainable farming systems". *Journal of Soil and Water Conservation* 52:265-271.

6   Gender and Sustainable Development

Cornelia Butler Flora and Margaret Kroma

Introduction

Sustainability has been raised to an international goal through the discussion of Vision 21 and in the rhetoric of national governments and multinational development organizations. Action toward sustainability is highly dependent on the material and cultural context in which actors are situated.

Sustainability has been framed in terms of a broad range of objectives: meeting basic human needs while maintaining ecological processes and life-support systems, preserving genetic diversity, and ensuring sustainable utilization of species and ecosystems (IUCN/UNEP/WWF, 1980).

While the definition seems straight forward, in fact the meaning and indicators of each objective: "basic human needs", "ecological processes", "life-support systems", and "genetic diversity" are a function of *location*. Location is both physical and socio-economic. Thus, different ethnic groups may define basic human needs quite differently. Different social classes may focus on different ecological processes. And different places on the globe may identify different aspects of genetic diversity. Each position, in addressing sustainability as a systems property rather than "maximum sustainable yield" of a particular resource, "does not discount the future and embodies three imperatives":

1.   Environmental: living within ecological means,
2.   Economic: meeting basic material needs, and
3.   Social: meeting basic social needs and cultural sustainability (Holling, et al., 1997: 352).

If we are to move toward more sustainable agriculture and rural development, it is critical to incorporate how actors in different locations define and react toward these imperatives. Gender is an important determinant of location, although it never acts independently of other "locators", such as ethnicity, social class, and geographic location.

103

Ideology, or superstructure[1], influences how the imperatives of sustainability are gendered. (Gender is a social construct, linking sex, a biological variable, to expected characteristics and behavior.) Women are often viewed as uniquely suited for domestic, reproductive activities, such as food preparation, washing and cleaning, health maintenance, and child care, based on the uniquely female potential to bear children. Men in a number of cultural settings are viewed as innately incapable of such nurturing activity, with their inability to give birth offered as evidence. Men are often vested by law and custom with property rights as well as the control of the labor of household members. Women are sometimes viewed as too weak or too emotional to have such control. Those viewpoints are shared through cultural norms and codified through law.

Material conditions influence gender locations in a variety of ways. Because women seldom have direct access to and control of privately held resources, they are more often than men attuned to common resources and their condition. Women's responsibilities in the domestic sphere give them a different point of view of sustainability and an awareness of when it is threatened. Women's access and control over resources – financial, manufactured, human, social and environmental – often limits their ability to act effectively to put their values into practice. Shields, et al. (1996) found in parts of the Philippines that women were much more inclined to protect common resources than men, because those resources represented the base for their domestic and market activities. But because men's goals were viewed as more important, women's common resources were consistently destroyed in areas of high external market penetration.

Material conditions and ideology come together in interaction among human beings for mutual support. Those interactions create communities of interest and of place. The interactions, trust, and collective action generated have been termed *social capital* (Coleman, 1988; Putnam, 1993, 1994; J. Flora, et al., 1998). Social capital is relatively vulnerable, in part because it is difficult to quantify and therefore often ignored. It is also gendered, as men and women often have different networks and different ways of building and generating trust, due to their different material and cultural positions.

Following Rocheleau, et al. (1996), we see the importance of gender differences in experiences of, responsibilities for, and interests in environmental imperatives, but that these differences are not rooted in biology *per se*. These gender differences result in gendered knowledge, resource rights and organizations which all determine definition of and action toward sustainability.

System sustainability is challenged by rapid change. The changes that different ecosystems are now facing are very rapid, exacerbated by the increased mobility of financial capital and human capital (Flora, 1990). The care needed to move social capital and the impossibility of moving environmental capital makes ecosystems vulnerable – and threatens sustainability – at the turn of the 21st century.

Gendered Resources

Resources can be consumed, stored or invested. When they are invested to create more resources, we refer to them as "capital". Investing resources, rather than consuming them, is critical for sustainability. Forms of capital conventionally viewed as important include financial capital, manufactured capital, and human capital. When looking at system sustainability, it is also important to analyze environmental capital and social capital.

Interactions of Different Forms of Capital[2]

Each form of capital can enhance the productivity of other forms of capital. Increasing social capital greatly cuts transaction costs, making other resource use more efficient. A number of scholars have found that social capital has an independent effect on the functioning of economic systems (Granovetter, 1985; Lincoln, et al., 1996; Putnam, 1993a, Portes and Sessenbrenner, 1993; Robison and Hanson, 1995, among others). That literature also demonstrates that male networks dominate the control of corporate capital, and the social capital they represent is critical to cutting transaction costs in capital flows. Nowhere does the literature suggest that these investments are influenced by concerns with sustainability of anything but that same social capital, and, presumably financial capital.

Overemphasizing the value of a single form of capital can reduce sustainability. For example, focusing on increasing short term financial and manufactured capital without regard to the pollutants generated can reduce the value of human capital through negative impacts on health, on environmental capital through destruction of soil and water quality, and on social capital through by-passing local networks and replacing them with impersonal bureaucratic structures with top-down mandates.

Financial Capital

Financial capital consists of money or instruments of credit for investment and speculation and can be public or private. Futures, stocks, bonds, derivatives, mutual funds and mortgages are all forms of financial capital. Financial capital is controlled by men in most ecosystems, particularly the forms of financial capital which move globally.

Individuals generate financial capital through salary and wages, and earnings on investments, including lending. Firms generate financial capital through earnings, investments, and debt offerings such as stocks and bonds. Governments generate financial capital through fees, taxes and borrowing (e.g., bonds and other government debt instruments).

The public sector transfers resources to the private sector through loans, grants, tax abatements and other tax advantages. This form of financial capital is increasingly used as a development tool with little consideration of its impact on other forms of capital within the community.

Financial capital is the most mobile of all forms of capital which can be invested in a community. These capital transfers are much more likely to go to men and male-controlled firms than to women. In turn, the way that financial capital is turned into manufactured capital will define certain aspects of other forms of capital as important, privileging the location of those making the decisions, usually upper class men from the urban centers of industrialized countries.

The international flow of financial capital has increased markedly over the last 25 years. As the *Financial Times of London* (September 30, 1994) explained, international financial markets are governed by the principles of fear and greed — neither one conducive to sustainable agriculture or rural development.

Manufactured Capital

Manufactured capital is composed of physical infrastructure such as machinery, chemical fertilizers, pesticides, housing, office buildings, schools, roads, sewers, factories and water systems. Financial capital is turned into manufactured capital by either the private or public sector. The choices of investment in manufactured capital are highly gendered, which in turn have real implications for long-term sustainability. For example, choosing to increase agricultural productivity led to construction of large-scale irrigation in West Bengal, India, using ground water. Irrigation greatly increased the wheat production in the area, although with some concern about increased social stratification as land ownership and water access are relatively concentrated compared to before the irrigation schemes. An increasing number of arsenic-related cancers among the population led to testing the local population for arsenic concentration in their bodies – and it was found to be alarmingly high. The arsenic was ubiquitous in all the wells in the irrigated area – a relatively untreatable water contamination problem. Arsenic is a normal part of the soil in that part of India, but the fast withdrawal of water for irrigation leached it from the soil. Because there was little monitoring of human health or drinking water quality (two areas of traditional concern for women), the problem was discovered at a point where the provision of drinkable water is extremely difficult and expensive (Bagala and Kaiser, 1996). And meanwhile, despite extensive testing by WHO and the government of India (Subramanian, 1996), people continue to get sick and to die of arsenic poisoning and arsenic-generated cancers. The sustainability of the entire region is endangered – certainly in terms of its role as human habitat.

Human Capital

Human capital includes individual capacity, training, human health, values and leadership. Economists use the term labor, consisting of the skills, abilities, education and training which workers possess and bring to their jobs. Human capital includes non-formal skills associated with experience carrying out a particular task and indigenous knowledge about an area. Women's knowledge is often different than men's knowledge, and systems for knowledge and skill transfer are also different.

Health status and commitment are aspects of human capital important for sustainability. Women's traditional responsibility for human health care, particularly in poor families, gives them a different perspective on the use of other forms of capital. It also means that they may be the first to notice health problems associated with shifts in environmental quality. Women and men can be committed to sustainability, but to different aspects of sustainability (Meares, 1997; Chiappe and Flora, 1998).

Environmental Capital

Environmental capital consists of air quality, water (its quality and quantity), soil (its quality and quantity), biodiversity (plants and animals) and landscape. The components of environmental capital are highly interrelated and tend to enhance one another. Attention to biodiversity helps maintain soil cover, which decreases soil erosion and enhances soil quality in terms of organic materials and biological communities within the soil. This in turn contributes to water quality.

Environmental capital creates fresh air, clean water, food and fiber, and scenery. Men and women in different contexts may value and act toward different elements of environmental capital. Men are often concerned with soil quality, while women may focus on biodiversity, based on their specific material responsibilities within the household and control over and access to different resources. Land is often controlled by men, and women depend on men for their access to it. Women have access to common areas, or specific garden areas, where biodiversity contributes to household as well as environmental sustainability. Often investments are made in soil quality (soil amendments) that define soil quality in terms of chemistry, and can be detrimental to biodiversity by favoring monoculture.

Social Capital

Putnam (1993b) describes social capital as "features of social organization, such as networks, norms, and trust, that facilitate coordination and cooperation for mutual benefit. Social capital enhances the benefits of investment in physical and human capital".

Social capital for sustainability depends on strengthening communities of interest and communities of place. Social capital in both these types of communities is often gender-based and has implications for environmental capital.

The SANREM CRSP (Sustainable Agriculture and Natural Resource Management Collaborative Research Support Program) in Mindanao in the Philippines focuses on increasing long term sustainability. The Manupali watershed, the project site, degrades greatly from the top (cloud forest) to the bottom (Pulangi IV River Reservoir). Further, there is ethnic diversity, with indigenous people living in the higher, less degraded part of the watershed. A SANREM-sponsored non-government organization (NGO) was formed to monitor water quality of the river. That organization, while open to both men and women, was initially made up primarily of men.

In assessing perceptions of the environment, particularly the degree to which the various parts of the environment are interconnected, Gabriela Flora (1997) found no difference by ethnic group or location on the watershed. There was a significant difference by gender, but the greatest difference was between those who were members of the water-monitoring organization and those who were not. Further, membership in the water monitoring team made a very large difference for men—and no difference for women. Using that knowledge, women were recruited to the existing organizations, instituting mechanisms to make sure that women's water quality concerns are addressed in the water monitoring activity (which has begun, as the women requested specifically that e-coli concentrations be measured, because of their immediate impact on the health of their children), and women-only water monitoring teams were formed. Attention to the gendered nature of social capital can have important environmental implications.

A study of pastoral women in milk processing and marketing in Zonkwa, Central Nigeria suggests the gendered nature of social capital and how shifting control of manufactured capital can destroy it, leading to declining community sustainability (Waters-Bayer, 1994). The central government invested millions of dollars into modernization of dairying in the region, although the bulk of milk production remained largely controlled by Fulani women in the informal sector. That network of production and distribution served to form important inter-tribal reciprocal exchange.

Their distribution system linked producers directly to consumers rather than going through intermediaries. By choosing to deal directly with customers, women in the region had sustained a critical web of relations with their customers in which reciprocity and mutual support constituted the mainframe. For example, they receive the occasional bundle of wheat at harvest time, whilst they in turn make occasional gifts of butter or milk to their customers when they have special occasions. Through such networks, the Fulanis were able to acquire land use from the indigenous Kaje and Kamantan ethnic group, the traditional holders of land rights in the region. These traditional mechanisms of exchange and reciprocity helped to keep the peace and reduced tensions between the different ethnic groups (Waters-Bayer, 1994).

The failures of the dairy production program in the region, present a lucid picture of the real consequences of neglecting to explore the more subtle dynamics of community social organization as a basis for implementing sustainable community interventions. Those planning the rural development had failed to explore a *priori* the complex web of relations sustaining the traditional milk processing and marketing enterprise. As a consequence, they focused instead on male household members, not recognizing the gender-related division of responsibility and control within the households and the traditional dairy enterprise. Extractive interventions often weaken complex networks built on horizontal linkages of reciprocity and mutual support, such as existed in the Fulani community. The recognition of the differential access and control over resources by gender – and a recognition of the importance of female social capital – would have made a big difference in both social and economic sustainability.

Where gender balance is destroyed by ignoring what women actually do, landscape sustainability declines. In a case study account of an agroforestry research project in the semi-arid farm and rangeland in Machakos District, Kenya, Rocheleau (1991) systematically demonstrates the pervasiveness of gender in community organization for the management of natural resources. The study evidences the presence of women's self help groups as important signals of community sustainability, because of their potential to address equity issues, a critical aspect of both economic and social sustainability.

These groups were largely reciprocal work groups and mutual aid networks where each member contributes to labor and other forms of productive activity of any member of the group. The range of activities include reciprocal weeding and terrace repair on each other's cropland to sharing of food and household supplies during social functions and periods of scarcity.

It has been suggested that community groups and associations function as more viable vehicles for implementing programs geared towards community development because of the greater degree of participation of women and the equity their participation enhances (Rocheleau, 1989; Moser, 1993). It has also been posited that these community groups and associations foster a greater degree of effectiveness and accountability of programs. The presence of community self help groups is an indicator of social capital within the community.

Thrupp's (1984) work suggests that availability of cooking fuel is an important gendered indicator of sustainability. Drawing evidence from a rural community study in Kenya, she argues that the related problem of wood scarcity and fuel shortage are tied into women's poverty—and thus how sustainably they judge a landscape—because of the cultural restrictions that constrain women's access to or control of land. The widespread introduction of community woodlot and agroforestry projects do not necessarily translate into enhanced opportunities for women, which therefore compromises the long term sustainability of such interventions. While a male might assess a forest as sustainable as long as timber cutting was constant, women would assess the landscape's sustainability quite differently.

The Gendered Nature of Reliance on Social Capital

Both men and women rely on social capital to enhance the productivity of other forms of capital. But reliance on social capital—and the impacts of its absence—are more visible at lower social strata. Relying on social capital is part of a survival strategy which, though not exclusively, is frequently gendered due to the multiple roles that women play in the private sphere of the household and the public sphere of the community. Survival strategies can either enhance or decrease long term sustainability.

Careful consideration of how communities and households are organized by gender, class and race—how they are stratified—can reveal systems of reliance on social capital as a livelihood or survival strategy. Social inequalities are sometimes embedded in social capital.

Men tend to play a greater role in community politics (where they draw heavily on social capital), while women are responsible for community management as a "natural extension of their domestic work" (Moser 1993: 35). Community management, according to Moser, consists of "work undertaken at the community level, around the allocation, provisioning and managing of items of collective consumption" (1993: 34). These items include water, health care, education, garbage collection, community gardens, playground construction, Christmas bazaars, altar guild, etc. Anglin (1993) tells how women in a small, poor community in North Carolina extended their history of sharing resources in their reproductive and productive labor efforts to struggle against power and job insecurity in the male-dominated mica industry, where their wages were kept lower than men's and work opportunity fluctuated with the seasons. In interviews women described how they took up collections to pay for health care when a co-worker fell ill, since health benefits were not provided by the factory, and extended illness could result in job loss. When there were new job openings, they informed their sisters and female cousins first. Those women who were unemployed became a part of the social network by looking out for the children of mica factory workers. Anglin describes this exchange of resources as qualitatively different from the experience of male community members who were employed in the factory. Women, she said, recognized and used the strength of kin and community networks to undermine the control that industry owners had over their lives.

Examples of reliance on social capital can be found in resource-scarce communities and regions in the industrialized and developing worlds. (Although it is not always present and is frequently undermined by many social and economic policies.) Dill and Williams (1992) compare their research in rural Tennessee and Mississippi to research on women and poverty in developing countries. "As in the third world, low wages and underemployment in the South are made possible by laborers' reproductive costs being born by subsistence enclaves made up primarily of kin and informal sector work—work that is disproportionately the burden of women" (1992: 105). They conclude that poor black women in the United States depend on informal kinship networks for child care and pooling and exchange of financial and other resources. As part of sustainability is resiliency in the face of rapid change, rural development that ignores the importance of informal social capital—and therefore undermines it through creating new dependencies—are unsustainable.

Stack (1996) reveals the adaptive strategies that women predominantly create in a black rural community in the U.S. to cope with economic crisis. She calls them "cooperative networks" or "women's kin networks" through which the exchange of goods and services is channeled. Poverty, she says, creates a necessity for reliance on this type of social capital. Women care for one another's children, share clothing and income among households, challenging the notion of the household as an insular economic unit. And return migrants, bringing with them the human capital resources acquired in the north of the United States, created strong formal women's organization to provide—and insist that the state provide—mechanisms for women to gain access to resources.

Research in Agbanga in the Philippines parallels this widespread reliance on social capital among women – and the potential impact community social capital that is hierarchical and reinforces patterns of stratification can have on environmental degradation (Buenavista et al., 1994; Shields, et al., 1996). A complex web of social relations based on an age-old system of resource exchange can be linked to specific resource management strategies which ensure villagers' survival. Although all members of this rural community play a role in the exchange network, class and gender emerge as important variables which differentiate reliance on the network and place along the succession of exchanges. Agbangans employ diverse livelihood strategies to ensure their survival, frequently relying on more than one strategy per household. Neighbors share their harvest, catch, products and even labor with one another allowing households to diversify their income and subsistence resources. Despite the encroachment of modernization and privatization of property, social capital is still a measurement of one's assets. It is particularly important to women, who tend to be involved in more subsidiary or sideline occupations (which fluctuate frequently and have historically been relied upon and cultivated when natural disasters wiped out male sources of income such as the fishing industry), like hog raising or selling dried fish. Resource exchange makes up the safety net for villagers as an important means of income diversification which allows households to mitigate the risks associated with agriculture and fishing—two important male occupations.

However, that social capital has led to local dynamite fishing, which destroys the coral reef and decreases future catches. The members of the community—men and women—are aware of the negative impacts of such action. Women in particular voiced the hope that an outside authority would force compliance to the law breaking which destroyed natural resources—including dynamite fishing. And women were greatly concerned over the decline in biodiversity (which meant that they could not continue generating their own income streams through home-based value-added enterprises which used indigenous species) due to the free grazing of water buffalo, the source of much of male income. Social capital was hierarchical in Agbanga (as opposed to other villages studied with less external market penetration) and so community-based solutions were not addressed.

Conclusions

Location determines both perceptions of sustainability and ability to act to achieve it. Women and men have very different relations to different types of resources, which influences both their definition of sustainability and the actions they take to achieve it. Gender alone does not automatically mean that women (or men) will perceive sustainability more broadly or act toward it more responsibly. Gender is only a partial determinant of location – but in many contexts it is an important one. Sustainable agriculture and rural development can best be achieved when women's voices from a variety of locations are heard and responded to. And they are more likely to be responded to when development activities do not cut off their control of and access to key resources, including financial, manufactured, human, environmental and social capital.

Further, the superstructure which relegates women's voices to background noise must be seriously addressed. This occurs through implementing policies which do not disadvantage women, and through fostering the creation and strengthening of women's participation in groups – formal and informal – which allow them to collectively leverage the various forms of capital inside and outside their community.

Notes

1.   The model linking superstructure and base to actions impacting sustainability is based on Eide (1982).
2.   This section is based on Flora (1997).

Acknowlegements

The research which serves as a base for this chapter was supported by the SANREM CRSP (Sustainable Agriculture and Natural Resource Collaborative Research Support Program), USAID (United States Agency for International Development).

References

Altieri, M., A. Yurjevic, J. M. Von der Weid, and J. Sanchez. 1994. "Assessing the sustainability of NGO-led agroecological interventions in Latin America". *Proceeding of the indicators of sustainability conference and workshop.* SANREM Research Report No. 1-95: 121-130.

Anglin, M. K. 1993. "Engendering the struggle: women's labor and traditions of resistance in rural southern Appalachia". *Fighting back in Appalachia*, Stephen L. Fisher, ed. Philadelphia: Temple University Press: 263-282.

Bagala, P. and J. Kaiser. 1996. "India's Spreading Health Crisis Draws Global Arsenic Experts". *Science* 274: 174-175.

Buenavista, G., C. B. Flora and A. Meares. *Surviving natural resource decline: exploring gender, class and social capital in Agbanga, Philippines.* Blacksburg, VA : An ECOGEN Case Study, Office of International Research and Development, Virginia Polytechnic Institute and State University.

Chiappe, M. B. and C. B. Flora. "Gendered dimensions of the alternative agriculture paradigm". *Rural Sociology.* 1998 (forthcoming).

Coleman, J. C. 1988. "Social capital in the creation of human capital". *American Journal of Sociology 94* (Supplement S95-S120):95-119.

Dill, B. T. and B. B. Williams. "Race, Gender, and Poverty in the Rural South: African American Single Mothers". *Rural Poverty in America*, C. M. Duncan, ed. New York: Auburn House, 1992: 97-110.

Eide, W. B. 1982. "The nutrition educator's role in access to food: from individual orientation to social orientation". *Journal of Nutrition Education*. 14: 14-18.

Flora, C. B. 1990. "Rural peoples in a global economy". *Rural Sociology*:157-177.

_____. 1997. "Enhancing community capitals: the optimization equation". *Rural Development News* 21: 1-3.

Flora, G. C. 1997. "Do geographic location, ethnicity, group membership and gender impact perceptions of environmental connection? a case study from the Philippines". *Bifurcation* 4 (1): 9-12.

Flora, J.L., J.S. Sharp, C. B. Flora, B. Newlon, and T. Bailey. 1998 "Entrepreneurial Social Infrastructure and Locally-Initiated Economic Development". *Sociological Quarterly* (forthcoming).

Granovetter, M. 1985. "Economic Action, Social Structure and Imbeddedness". *American Journal of Sociology* 91: 481-510.

Holling, C.S., F. Berkes, and C. Folke. 1997. "Science, sustainability and resource management". *Linking social and ecological systems: institutional learning for resilience.* F. Berkes and C. Folke (eds.) Cambridge, England: Cambridge University Press: 346-366.

IUCN/UNEP/WWF 1980. *World conservation strategy: living resource conservation for sustainable development.* Gland, Switzerland: IUCN.

Lincoln, J. R., M. L. Gerlach, and C. L. Ahmadjian. 1996. "Keiretsu networks and corporate performance in Japan". *American Sociological Review* 61: 67-88.

Meares, A. C. 1997. "Making the transition from conventional to sustainable agriculture: gender, social movement participation, and quality of life on the family farm". *Rural Sociology* 62:21-47.

Moser, C. O. N. 1993. *Gender planning and development.* London and New York: Routledge,

Portes, A. and J. Sensenbrenner. 1993. "Embeddedness and Immigration: Notes on the Social Determinants of Economic Action". *American Journal of Sociology* 98(6):1320-1350.

Putnam, R. D. 1993a. *Making democracy work: civic traditions in modern Italy.* Princeton, NJ: Princeton University Press.

Putnam, R. D. 1993b. "The prosperous community: social capital and public life". *The American Prospect*, 13 : 35-42.

Robison, L. J. and S. D. Hanson. 1995. "Social capital and economic cooperation". *J. Agr. and Applied Econ.* 27: 43-58.

Rocheleau, D. 1989. "The gendered division of work, resources and rewards in agroforestry systems". A.E. Kilewe, K.M. Kealey, and K.K. Kebaara, eds. *Agroforestry development in Kenya.* ICRAF: Nairobi:228-245.

Rocheleau, D. 1991. "Gender, ecology and the science of survival: stories and lessons from Kenya". *Agriculture and Human Values*: 8(1/2):156-165.

Rocheleau, D., B. Thomas-Slayter, and E. Wangari. 1996. "Gender and environment: a feminist political ecology perspective". *Feminist political ecology: global issues and local experiences.* London: Routledge: 3-26.

Rowbotham, S. and S. Mitter (eds.) *Dignity and daily bread: new forms of economic organizing among poor women in the third world and the first.* London and New York: Routledge, 1994.

Shields, M. D., C. B. Flora, B. Thomas-Slayer, and G. Buenavista. "Developing and dismantling social capital: gender and resource management in the Philippines". *Feminist political ecology: global issues and local experiences.* London: Routledge: 155-179.

Stack, C. B. 1996. "Call to home: African Americans reclaim the rural South". New York : Basic Books.

Subramanian, K.S. 1996. Letter to the editor. *Science* 274: 1285.

Thrupp, L. A. 1984. "Women, wood and work in Kenya and beyond". *Unasylva (FAO)* 36: 37-43.

Waters-Bayer, A.. 1994. "Studying pastoral women's knowledge in milk processing and marketing for whose empowerment". *Agriculture and Human Values.* 11: 85-95.

7 Population and Sustainability: Understanding Population, Environment and Development Linkages

Daniel C. Clay and Thomas Reardon

Introduction

The challenge of achieving economic and environmental sustainability in the face of the most explosive population growth the world has ever known is daunting to developing country governments and to members of the donor community. What makes this challenge so formidable is that sustainability and population growth are not independent problems. They are intimately related. They cannot be isolated from one another and they cannot be addressed individually. Their solution is simultaneous and requires an understanding not of how they are unique, but of how they are linked.

Throughout the developing world, population growth is putting more pressure on farmland. Farmers with access to affordable inputs and in areas where agriculture is profitable are intensifying sustainably. That is, they are farming more on the same land but making appropriate land improvements and using inputs to maintain or enhance soil fertility. But far more common are the farmers who push their land to the limit without using enough fertilizer, manure and compost, or without protecting the land with terraces and bunds, or those who push their farming out into the commons to survive.[1] If they can foot the migration costs, they move to the cities and to the mines and plantations for work.

In turn, the degradation is reducing land productivity and increasing food insecurity. This growing poverty then results in higher birth rates, and the cycle is perpetuated. The policy and economic context has in some cases exacerbated this vicious circle by undermining the public agricultural support system. That system, in past decades (although in a costly and fiscally unsustainable way) helped make farm inputs affordable. Moreover, the reigning instability of prices and climate makes farming risky, which reduces the incentive to make the kinds of investments that would reduce the environment-agricultural tradeoff.

In short, the links in this system form a cycle as depicted in Figure 1. This figure draws our attention to population growth and its effects on how farming is practiced. In turn, the links are strong between the farm, the environment, and the rest of the economy, and these economic and physical outcomes in turn affect population growth. What happens to agriculture affects the farm environment, as well as the environment off-farm in forests, hillsides and wetlands. And what happens to forests then affects food security strategies (wood and wild flora/fauna gathering and use of commons resources as inputs into service and small-scale manufacturing activities of rural families). It also affects the biodiversity of the ecosystem which is important to farming through species provision, and is often important culturally and socially. What happens in the cities and the off-farm rural economy affects the alternatives farmers have to farming, as well as the means they can employ to buy inputs and hire labor to sustainably intensify farming. And, coming full circle, what happens to

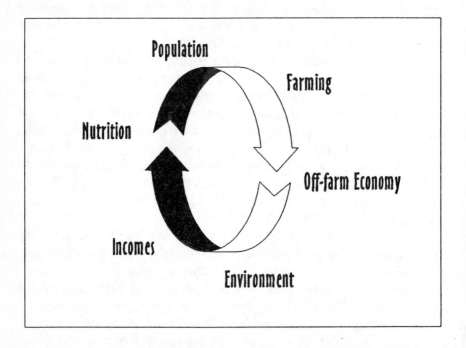

Figure 1. Dynamic links from farming practices to population growth

the rural households' food security and incomes influences their health and decisions about childbearing.

In section 2 of this chapter we briefly describe our household livelihood strategies approach to the subject of sustainability and population growth. Section 3 reviews the cornerstones of the population-environment-development debate and some of the research literature that has fueled this debate. Section 4 summarizes what we have learned that will help inform the debate and lessons learned for development programming. We conclude in section 5 with a brief review of program and strategic implications.

Approach: Household Livelihood Strategies

Farm households and their livelihood strategies are at the core of the intersectoral linkages described above and depicted in Figure 1.[2] We take as our starting point the farm household surrounded by these conditions, and now pervasive in much of the developing world, particularly in sub-Saharan Africa: growing population pressure, declining agricultural productivity, and growing poverty. The approach focuses on the behavioral alternatives to demographic pressure, resource degradation, and poverty. The alternative paths, and the dynamic linkages among them, are far and away the farm households' most worrisome concern. As such, they must also constitute the top priority of the development planner, and figure prominently in major program decisions.

The above constellation of household-level paths and alternatives is depicted in the lower half of Figure 2. Farm/rural households can adopt a mix of activities in the farm and nonfarm sectors. To undertake these activities, they use family or hired labor, land they own or rent, and capital equipment and other inputs. Based on their "means of production" (family size and wealth in terms of land, money, and equipment), their short-term problem is to pursue activities that meet the income and food needs of the household. These choices, both in the short and the longer term, affect their health and nutrition, the quality of their land, and the forests, wetlands, and hillsides around them. In the longer run, choosing to invest in the "means of production" will affect household welfare. How many children they have, health care and education they invest in, and their migration patterns will affect labor availability for farm and nonfarm activities. Investment in farm capital or purchase of fertilizer and animals will affect their ability to intensify production sustainably on the land they have. Their capacity to make investments will

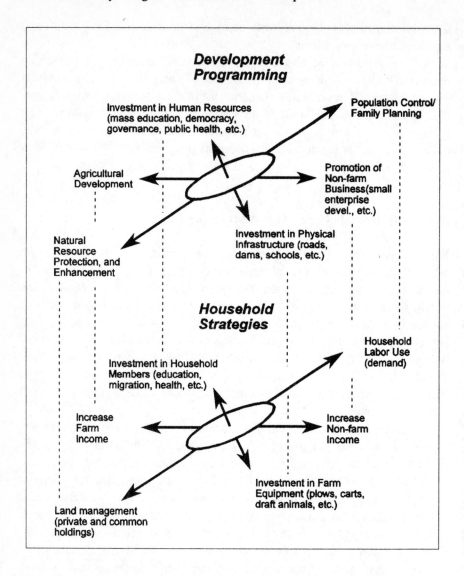

Figure 2. Links among natural resources, human resources and farm/non-farm activities

Note: Linking natural resources, human resources and farm/non-farm activities is as important for development programmers as for farm households.   Investments in human and physical capital cross-cut these linkages at both levels.

be conditioned by credit markets, but also by the wealth available from livestock husbandry, cash cropping and nonfarm activity. The latter is often of special importance both as a source of cash to make farm investments, or, alternatively, as an "escape valve" to relieve growing demographic pressure.

Hence, the farm household sees that what it does in the nonfarm sector affects what it can do in the farm sector, what education investments it can make, and how reliant it is on the land. It also sees that its childbearing and education decisions affect what chances it has to work off-farm (and at what wage), and how much family labor it will have to meet farming and land improvement needs. In short, the household must engage in cross-sectoral strategic planning to meet its needs. It can combine complementary sectoral choices, or choose between alternative paths.

We argue here that governments and donor missions face very similar sets of choices and opportunities, but at an aggregate level. We posit further that these actors, unlike households, are less likely to recognize the links among these choices and take them into account in their strategic planning, much to their detriment. The top half of Figure 2 shows the interrelated challenges to development programming, and one can see that they parallel those faced by rural households. Where the household weighs investments in human capital (in education, in health, in numbers) and in "social capital" (in connections to local governments, in social status, in links to other households), governments and donors weigh investments in education, public health, democracy and governance structures, and so on. Where households make decisions about household members and labor (childbearing, training, time allocation, etc.), governments and donors weigh the relative merits of family planning programs, worker training, extension service funding, and so on. Where households make choices about farm and off-farm capital investments, governments and donors weigh the hard and soft infrastructure alternatives such as roads, dams, dikes, irrigation systems, agricultural research institutions, communications, and so on. Where households strike a balance between farm and off-farm income generation, governments and donors strike a similar balance in their support for agricultural development and nonfarm small business promotion. Finally, where households struggle with erosion and degradation of their farm lands, as more and more time is spent searching for grazing land or fuelwood or clean water, governments and donors struggle with the aggregate consequences of peasant survival strategies, of logging, mining, and plantation land-use, and of profit-making strategies on the land and its water and biodiversity resources, both on-farm and in the commons.

Hence, the parallels are striking between what the household must decide in a "multisectoral world", and what the government and donor face. But where the household sees naturally the links because it must (for instance, it knows it must start an off-farm business to generate the cash to buy a plow), very different thinking and strategizing prevails in many governments and donor missions. For instance, rarely does a ministry of agriculture meet with a ministry of industry to confer on complementary strategies for rural development to make the links and create "virtuous spirals" of growth in the two sectors. Rarely would a small business promotion unit in a donor mission mesh its strategy with that of the agricultural development office; rarely would the population unit take into close account the rural household's economic survival strategies on and off the farm, and how these relate to their fertility, migration, health care, and education decisions.

This lack of strategic linkage can be dangerous, not only because it means stopping short of finding the best possible complementary solutions, but because a seemingly well-conceived "sectoral" strategy can be easily undermined by factors developing outside that sector, factors that need to be spotted and dealt with as part of the larger program strategy. For example, a program designed to protect a biodiversity-rich forest in Madagascar must also take into account the possibility that such a program could have adverse effects on the farm sector. To survive, demographically-squeezed farmers will relentlessly push farming up the hillsides and into the forest. If fertilizer becomes too expensive, or roads too poor, or farmland too degraded, farming is undermined and desperate extensification ensues. A good farm strategy can thus be at least as important as a good forest strategy or population control strategy in saving those forests.

Knowledge Gaps in the Population-Environment-Development Debate

The population-environment-development debate is important to us because it provides a framework for understanding intersectoral linkages, and because it helps us define the context and very nature of the individual linkages. In turn, policy and development programming can be improved by taking into account what we know about the compatibilities and inconsistencies among strategic objectives in key sectors. This section provides an overview of the ongoing debate and identifies shortcomings in previous research and associated gaps in the literature. We begin with a short review of the defining parameters of the debate.

Ecological theory tells us that, over the long term, there are two interrelated sets of responses that populations will muster in adapting to greater population pressure and resource scarcity (Gibbs and Martin 1959, Bilsborrow 1987). They are systemic adaptations that occur gradually, usually over periods of one or more decades, that can profoundly change the structure of rural life. The first response is to change the population's size through lower fertility, higher mortality, and/or emigration. The second is to change the productive economy of the population toward more diversified and specialized use of labor, and using more productive technologies (Cohen, 1968). We note that the economic response often entails a demographic change when household members are obliged to migrate to cities and mines and other places where more diversified and specialized jobs can be found.

These two adaptive responses, one largely demographic and the other economic, have received considerable research attention over the years, and their relative importance to understanding present day development issues has been hotly debated. Our objective in this section is not to review the many twists and turns in this great volume of literature.[3] Rather, we briefly discuss some of the cornerstone positions and research directions that define the debate.

Cornerstones of the Population-Environment-Development Debate

The demographic response has been a focal point of the debate since the time of Malthus, whose writings depicted the dangers of population growth—notably higher mortality through disease, war, famine, and other "positive checks" that populations endure as they readjust to the carrying capacity of their resource base (Malthus, 1798). To Malthus, and to his latter-day disciples (e.g., Meadows et al., 1972, Demeny, 1981, Ehrlich and Ehrlich, 1991), demographic change is necessary to avert continued resource degradation and a declining standard of living.

Yet a main, perhaps *the* main, place where environment, population, and development interact is *on* the farm itself, and this is important because farmers constitute the vast majority of the Third World population. What happens on the farm affects whether and how much farmers need to rely on the commons for new farm land to extensify, or for alternative income through selling wood or herding. Hence, whether farmers can derive greater output from their landholdings—through sustainable intensification—is the crucial issue.

Boserup (1965, 1981), Ruthenburg (1980) and others have focused the debate on the economic (income generating) response (intensification) with the hypothesis that demographic pressure causes populations to intensify their systems of agricultural production with more labor, improved inputs, etc. Boserup (1965) outlines a number of technology and investment paths to agricultural intensification that farmers follow in the wake of increased land constraints—conditions that result from population growth, increased demand for agricultural products, or reduced transportation costs (Boserup, 1965; Pingali et al., 1987). To set the stage for our subsequent discussion, we distill and stylize from her work two broad paths.

The first we refer to as *capital-led* intensification, which entails, in addition to the use of farm labor and land, the use of "capital", the latter broadly defined to include nonlabor variable inputs that enhance soil fertility (such as fertilizer) and quasi-fixed capital that protects the land. The second path makes little or no use of "capital" (as defined above), so we refer to it as *labor-led* or *labor-only* intensification. Farmers merely add (unaugmented) labor to the production process on a given unit of land, allowing them to crop more densely, weed and harvest more assiduously, and so on.

Empirical research on agricultural intensification in developing countries has illustrated the two intensification paths initially described by Boserup, and here labeled the capital-led and labor-led paths. In the African context, several studies have categorized the agricultural systems in certain regions where demographic pressure has pushed farmers to intensify along these paths. For example, Matlon and Spencer (1984) note that the capital-led path is more sustainable and productive in fragile, resource-poor areas. Lele and Stone (1989) categorize a variety of agroclimatic and policy settings in terms of these two paths, focusing especially on the need for the capital-led path (which they term "policy-led"). They maintain that the labor-led path (the "autonomous model" in their words) has not led to land productivity growth in sub-Saharan Africa, and that policy-led intensification is needed so that land quality and productivity will be maintained and even enhanced as cropping is intensified.

In much of the tropics, the labor-led path to intensification is unsustainable, and leads to land degradation and stagnation of land productivity (Matlon and Spencer 1984). This danger is at its maximum in the East African highland tropics and other highland areas in Asia and Latin America, which are characterized by heavy rainfall and steep slopes. In the latter setting, the capital-led path of intensification that incorporates land conservation investments with the use of organic matter and fertilizer is much more sustainable. By contrast, areas that follow only the labor-led path in that setting are on course for long-run ecological degradation and poverty.

Hence, the question of what determines the particular technology and investment paths that households follow in response to growing demographic pressure is of critical importance in the current debate on sustainable development. The following two research gaps are areas we believe to be germane to advancing the population-environment-development debate in general and to understanding household livelihood strategies in particular.

First, household strategies as the behavioral basis of population-environment-development links have not been adequately explored. We need to know how households integrate demographic, income, and resource use strategies, and how opportunities in one sector reinforce those in another. Understanding the interactions between households' employment off-farm, for example, and their incentive and capacity to invest in sustainable intensification, food purchases, education of their children, and so on, is instrumental to strategic thinking and the way we approach development programming. The same is true for household decisions about childbearing, decisions that are intimately linked to both income and sustainable land management strategies.

Second, though sustainable agricultural intensification has become necessary and common in densely populated regions throughout the developing world, the "classical model" (Boserup 1965) of the context and characteristics of intensification is conditioned by three factors that subsequent macro-level analysis and debate have not taken into account.[4] The household strategies approach adopted here draws the three factors into clear view and provides a framework for examining alternative intensification paths. These conditioning factors include: the growing importance of non-farm employment/income diversification (Reardon et al., 1994), growing participation in the market economy, and the recognition that peasant strategies that promote intensification may require labor—an incentive for higher childbearing, which in turn increases the need for intensification, diversification and cash cropping.

Informing the Debate: Observations and Conclusions

Based on our work in Rwanda, Madagascar and elsewhere in Africa, we derive three key sets of observations and conclusions that we believe help inform population-sustainability dimensions of the debate described above. The first of these observations leads to the conclusion that inconsistencies between public (official) and individual household (couples) behavior regarding childbearing and family planning constitute a veritable "demographic tragedy of the commons". The second addresses the tendency of development frameworks to conceptualize population variables as "unmanageable", and exogenous to environmental and economic change. The third targets land markets and land tenure as critical population-sustainability policy issues. We return to each of these observations and conclusions in greater detail below.

Government and Donor Attempts to Slow Population Growth (via Family Planning) Are Not Always Seen by Households as Complementary to Their Income Strategies

Nearly all countries of the Third World are under considerable ecological stress due in large measure to decades of unprecedented demographic growth. Reports from the Population Reference Bureau (PRB, 1997) conclude that the governments of the vast majority of these countries are committed to relieving the pressure of population growth through lower birth rates.

However, even though policy-makers and public opinion in these countries recognize the importance of slowing high birth rates, fertility behavior at the household level often runs counter to this antinatalist position. Particularly among farm households, having *more* children increases family "success" and continuity through greater household wealth, security, and social standing. More hands mean more land is farmed and more food is grown; a larger family helps diversify income sources and manage risk; some land improvement and intensification practices are labor intensive and require a larger pool of household and/or hired labor; a large family is a sign of household standing in the community, and can help ensure that parents are cared for in their old age. Research in Rwanda (Clay and Reardon, 1996) illustrates the importance of increased fertility to household success. Evidence from Madagascar (Shaikh et al., 1995), and many other parts of sub-Saharan Africa shows a similar pattern.

Thus, we conclude that at the household level, the level at which fertility and family planning decisions are made, the classic demographic response discussed earlier is flawed. Reducing fertility, for households in sub-Saharan Africa facing land constraints, is *not* perceived to be an alternative to other strategies such as income diversification, cash cropping, and intensification. Indeed, to make these income strategies work, households often see the need for even greater household labor through higher birth rates.

What factors account for these incongruous views? We posit that the contradiction between public (national and community) and private (households) fertility goals is tied to the notion of intergenerational wealth flows. In rural settings across the developing world, the net flow of wealth moves from the younger generation to the older generation—from children to parents.[5] Despite the initial costs of raising and feeding children (among the Z-good costs)[6], their labor, beginning as early as six years of age and continuing through the parents' lifetime, will far surpass these initial outlays to raise them. Labor provided by the younger generation can take a number of forms, from herding cattle, gathering wood, and looking after younger siblings as children, to adult tasks such as tilling the fields and caring for parents in their old age. On balance, parents see children as a net asset to the household economy, not as a liability (Caldwell, 1976, p. 343). Thus, more children are better than fewer, and this is true even for poor households whose access to land and other opportunities are limited.

Yet, the entry barriers to eventually finding employment off-farm are high and often insurmountable, especially for children of landless and near-landless households. These include school fees and related costs, the expense of sending migrant adolescent children to the city and maintaining them during their search for work, and the on-farm opportunity costs of their schooling and/or migration. Thus, when asked about what children will need to do to survive in the absence of sufficient land, we found that the Rwandan parents in our study sample responded overwhelmingly that their children will just have to "make do on their own".[7]

This response reflects the peasant farmer's preoccupation with the survival of the household and extended family group, even if it means that some of its members may be marginalized and left to their own devices. Focusing on what's best for the household is what has ensured household success in the past.[8] High fertility and a large pool of household labor is what's best for households in which wealth flows upward.

As a result, many of these children fall short of parental aspirations. More often than not, the social costs associated with their failure to find productive employment falls on the shoulders of the larger population, and not on those of the parental household. But therein lies the dilemma—it is a veritable "demographic tragedy of the commons" (Clay and Reardon 1996). While households maximize their fertility to enhance their own station in life, those landless and unskilled children who are unable to find ways to contribute to the household economy are left to fend for themselves. Often they make their way to the city or to labor-deficit rural areas (Clay and Ngenzi 1990). The fortunate ones find employment as occasional wage laborers, but many others do not. Their costs in terms of schooling, housing, medical care, crime prevention, criminal justice, and social instability are borne by the larger community.

Indeed, we contend that the perception of "population pressure" is unknown to households where wealth flows from the younger to the older generation. The smallholder does not "feel" demographic pressure any more than the largeholder does. The two face the very same challenge: to keep the *household* out of poverty—which can be hard work and fraught with uncertainty even for those with resources. To be sure, those with little access to land are closer to the margin and more uncertain since their strategies for employing household labor are not as simple as for those with plenty of land to till. But in either case, a larger family is more likely to secure the future of the household than is a smaller family, since only those children who manage to contribute to the household economy count toward household success. Those who do not or cannot contribute are not viewed as a sign of failure where wealth flows from children to parents.

Thus, from the household's point of view, the challenge is one of working out a livelihood strategy that maximizes the use of household labor vis-à-vis available land and capital. Our research shows that the challenge is greater and the linkages among strategies are stronger among households with the least land. The pressure is to find employment, either on the farm or off, for all able household members. All else equal, prosperity accrues to households that are large in number and that manage their numbers effectively. Failure to do so is a missed opportunity for the household; it is a tragedy for the child who faces a potential lifetime of poverty, and for the community that shares this cost.

Even though fertility rates in many Third World countries have begun to decline in recent years, resistance to fertility control measures will remain strong in these countries because of the importance of household labor to the success of intensification and income diversification strategies. Until the intergenerational flow of wealth reverses direction, as it has already throughout the West and other parts of the developed world, the tragedy will play on. Other research has shown that reversing the direction of wealth flows is closely linked to investments in human capital, notably the education and autonomy of women (Caldwell 1980, 1982).

Population Changes Are Not Independent of Changes in Household Strategies, Environmental Degradation, and Income Growth

The separation of strategic planning in the population domain from that in the environment, agriculture, and enterprise development domains is unfortunate for the reasons described in section 2. Conventional NRM and economic development frameworks and literature have tended to reinforce sectoral thinking and sectoral boundaries by characterizing population variables (fertility, mortality, and migration) as "unmanageable", i.e., as an immutable force that lies outside of the "influenceable" realm. The treatment of population in the U.S. Agency for International Development (AID) Natural Resource Management (NRM) framework (Shaikh and McGahvey, 1995) is illustrative of this limitation. It groups population with agro-ecological conditions (such as rainfall and soil type) and other non-behavioral, exogenous variables.

One factor that has contributed to the practice of treating the demographic side of the population-environment-development nexus as exogenous to the others is the notion of "population momentum", i.e., that even if children alive today reduced their own childbearing to replacement-fertility levels, because of their sheer numbers, it would take 30 years or more for the population to actually stop growing. While this is fundamentally true, we must note that the adverse impact of population growth would decline steadily to zero during these 30 years.

Not often recognized is the fact that environmental changes and improvements in household incomes can be equally slow in coming, and generally require far greater human and physical capital investment by households, governments, and donors. For example, land lost to poor land management practices (e.g., lack of conservation investments in Rwanda, hillside and forest slash-and-burn *(tavy)* production in Madagascar, bush-cover removal and desertification in Niger) will take decades to turn around and make productive again. And changes that have led to a decline in livestock inventories, pasture, and knowledge of animal husbandry practices in Rwanda, Madagascar, and other parts of sub-Saharan Africa, coupled with low income levels, mean that development of more intensive livestock systems in these countries will now be doubly difficult to regenerate. There is an entire generation of young farmers in these countries who hold little or no experience in how to integrate livestock and cropping systems and it will take decades to rebuild this lost momentum.

Treating population as an exogenous variable is especially

problematic in that it obscures the fact that population-environment-development links are highly interactive. Fertility, mortality, and migration patterns can all influence income strategies and the ways in which households manage land and other resources, but these population variables are in turn affected by household income and resource management (i.e., reverse effects). As countless studies have shown, incomes and access to resources can be important determinants of household migration. Likewise fertility and mortality rates are known to vary with income levels and landholding. In Rwanda, for example, we show that access to land, resulting in higher incomes and better nutrition, has increased household labor through lower mortality (Clay and Johnson, 1992).

Labor availability and use are never taken for granted by households in their efforts to generate income and keep a step ahead of poverty. Governments and donor organizations can learn from this insight, and not treat the population variable as "given" in their approach to development programming.

Land Markets and Land Tenure Are Critical Policy Issues Mediating How Population Increase Translates into Problems for Agriculture and the Environment

The link between population pressure and land degradation is indirect. To address this link in terms of policy or program action we must focus on the intermediate mechanisms that connect the household's labor supply to its land management strategy (land use and investments in land conservation and fertility). Our research has demonstrated that the *structure of landholding* is central to on-farm population-environment interactions. The structure of landholding includes that set of bio-physical characteristics (size of holdings, fragmentation and dispersion, fragility, and years of cultivation, etc.) and economic/social characteristics (land tenure and profitability of land use) that define the farmer's incentive to invest in the long-term sustainability of his/her land.

Increasing population pressure and the ensuing competition for scarce land resources precipitates a restructuring of these physical and social attributes of landholding. Observations from our studies reveal some of these changes. More than ever before, farmers must rent the land they operate (shorter term use rights), family landholdings have radically diminished in size, and in highland areas farmers see little alternative to farming the steep and fragile slopes that once were held almost exclusively in pasture, woodlot and fallow.

How have these changes affected the long-term sustainability of farming? In Rwanda and Madagascar, for example, we found that traditional inputs such as compost, manure, and mulch invariably go on fields owned by the farmers and especially on those located nearer to the family compound. The same principle holds for field improvements such as the installation of terraces, hedgerows, grass strips, and drainage ditches—rented fields, distant fields, and the steep, fragile fields are largely ignored. Unless farmers can anticipate an economic return commensurate with their level of investment there will be little incentive for them to adopt such practices. As fields become more distant, steeper (less stable) and increasingly farmed under short-term lease agreements, cost-benefit ratios of conservation technologies will become even less favorable to the individual farmer—the net result being an acceleration of land degradation.

Thus, apart from the obvious need for political stability in countries like Rwanda and Madagascar, our focus on population-environment-development linkages shows that farmers need confidence in the longer term through secure land tenure. This means reducing the risk of appropriation and the right to transact land. Enhancing farmer access to the land market will require reform of existing and antiquated land laws prevalent throughout the developing world.

Conclusion

The challenges of achieving economically and environmentally sustainable development under conditions of surging population growth will require the right analytical tools and strategic approach. Government officials and development programmers must seek effective synergies and balance among "sectoral" program goals such as agricultural intensification, income diversification, and family planning. Government and donor strategic and program planning needs to mirror the same set of interactions that characterize poor rural households. Understanding how rural households behave, how they plan and how their strategies are formed and linked, is critical to understanding how programs and policies can best increase their welfare and reduce conflicts among goals.

Not too late, we think, there are moves afoot to start making these strategic links, in a practical way, in governments and donor missions. "Reengineering" at the U.S. Agency for International Development has that idea at its base, as did the Rio conference, the GREAN initiative,[9] and others. This chapter has provided grist and support for making these links—deeper and faster in donor and government strategizing and programs—and has provided examples of where links are important and action is called for. Though we have focused here on the demographic dimensions of sustainable development, we have also demonstrated that insights into the environmental and agricultural linkages are equally scarce and every bit as essential to the challenge. Other chapters in this volume will take up these complementary topics.

Notes

1. The "commons" here refers to land under collective stewardship. It includes unexploited, virgin territories as well as heavily used farm and range lands.

2. Support for the household strategies approach is gleaned from the recent conclusion by Falcon (1996) that the reformulation of the household as an economic entity is one of the most important research breakthroughs of the past decade, and that additional research on households and how they work is one of the most interesting analytical issues for the future.

3. See Weeks (1989) for a detailed review of the population-development debate.

4. These three factors were first described by Clay and Reardon (1996) in their discussion of population-environment-development linkages in Rwanda.

5. See Clay and Vander Harr (1993) for a review of intergenerational support and childbearing in the Third World.

6. Z-goods are household task outputs that are not monetized, such as child care, food preparation, and firewood collection.

7. Source: unpublished tables from the 1988 Rwanda Non-farm Strategies Survey conducted by the Rwanda Ministry of Agriculture.

8. Indeed, elevating the household/family group above individual needs is a cultural imperative, a universal cultural adaptation that has helped ensure the continuation of human populations through the course of time.

9. GREAN (Global Research on the Environmental and Agricultural Nexus for the 21st Century) is a strategy designed to promote and fund collaboration among U.S. scientific institutions, centers in the Consultative Group for International Agricultural Research (CGIAR), and the National Agricultural Research Systems (NARS). The goal of this three-way collaboration is to address simultaneously the triple global challenge of

environmental degradation, population increase in the world's poorest nations, and declining agricultural productivity (GREAN 1995).

Acknowledgements

We thank USAID/SD/PSGE/NRM for support for research on which this chapter is based via the Environment and Natural Resources Policy and Training project—EPAT/MUCIA-Research and Training, implemented by the Midwest Universities Consortium for International Activities, Inc. We also thank the Division of Agricultural Statistics of the Rwanda Ministry of Agriculture, USAID-Kigali, USAID/AFR/SD/PSGE/FSP, and AID/Global Bureau, Office of Agriculture and Food Security (via the Food Security II Cooperative Agreement) for provision of data, collaboration, and financial support during earlier stages of this research. Special thanks go to Tony Pryor, Mike McGahuey, Russ Misheloff, Ken Baum, and Nick Poulton for their insights on earlier sections of this research. The views, interpretations, and any errors are those of the authors and should not be attributed to USAID, MUCIA, their respective institutions, the United States Government, or anyone acting on their behalf.

References

Bilsborrow, Richard E. 1987. "Population Pressures and Agricultural Development in Developing Countries: A Conceptual Framework and Recent Evidence". *World Development*, 15:2, pp. 138-203.

Boserup, E. 1965. *The Conditions of Agricultural Growth: The Economics of Agrarian Change Under Population Pressure*. Chicago: Aldine.

———. 1981. *Population and Technological Change*. Oxford: Blackwell.

Caldwell, John C. 1976. "Toward a Restatement of Demographic Transition Theory". *Population and Development Review*, 2:321-366.

———. 1980. "Mass Education as a Determinant of the Timing of Fertility Decline". *Population and Development Review*. Vol. 6,2: 225-255.

———. 1982. *Theory of Fertility Decline*. London: Academic Press.

Clay, Daniel C. 1995. "Fighting an Uphill Battle: Population Pressure and Declining Land Productivity in Rwanda", in H.K. Schwarzweller and T.A. Lyson, eds., *Research in Rural Sociology and Development*, Vol. 6. Greenwich, Connecticut: JAI Press, Inc.

——— and Innocent Ngenzi. 1990. "Migration Temporaire dans les Ménages Agricoles au Rwanda". *Documents de Travail*, Division des Statistiques Agricoles, Ministère de l'Agriculture, de l'Elevage et des Forêts, Rwanda.

_____ and Nan Johnson. 1992. "Size of Farm or Size of Family: Which Comes First?" *Population Studies*, 46:491-505.

_____ and Thomas Reardon. 1996. "Linking Population, Development, and the Environment: How Households Confront Poverty and Demographic Pressure in Rwanda". Michigan State University Population Research Group. Research Paper Series. Paper 96-04.

_____ and Jane Vander Haar. 1993. "Patterns of Intergenerational Support and Childbearing in the Third World". *Population Studies*, 47.

Cohen., Y.A. 1968. *Man in Adaptation: The Cultural Present*. Chicago: Aldine Publishing Company.

Demeny, P. 1981. "The North-South Income Gap: A Demographic Perspective". *Population and Development Review*. 7(2):297-310.

Ehrlich, P.R. and A.H. Ehrlich. 1991. *The Population Explosion*. Simmons and Schuster Inc. New York.

Falcon, W. P. 1996. "Commentary: Food Policy Really Matters". *IFPRI Report*, Volume 18:1, International Food Policy Research Institute, Washington, D.C.

Gibbs, Jack P. and W.T. Martin. 1959. "Toward a Theoretical System of Human Ecology". *Pacific Sociological Review*, 2:1.

GREAN (Global Research on the Environmental and Agricultural Nexus for the 21st Century). 1995. "A Proposal for Collaborative Research Among U.S. Universities, CGIAR Centers and Developing Country Institutions". Report of the Taskforce on Research Innovations for Productivity and Sustainability. University of Florida and Cornell University.

Lele, U and S.W. Stone. 1989. *Population Pressure, the Environment and Agricultural Intensification: Variations on the Boserup Hypothesis*. MADIA Discussion Paper 4. The World Bank. Washington, D.C.

Malthus, T.R. 1798. *An Essay on the Principle of Population*. New York: August Kelley, Bookseller: reprinted in 1965.

Matlon, P. and D.S.C. Spencer. 1984. "Increasing Food Production in Sub-Saharan Africa: Environmental Problems and Inadequate Technological Solutions". *American Journal of Agricultural Economics*, 64 (Dec).

Meadows, D.H., D.L. Meadows, J. Randers, and W.W. Behrens III. 1972. "The Limits to Growth: A Report for the Club of Rome's Project on the Predicament of Mankind". London. Earth Island.

Pingali, P., Y. Bigot, and H.P. Binswanger. 1987. *Agricultural Mechanization and the Evolution of Farming Systems in Sub-Saharan Africa*. Johns Hopkins University Press, Baltimore.

PRB (Population Reference Bureau) 1997. *World Population Data Sheet*. Population Reference Bureau. Washington, D.C.

Reardon, T., A.A. Fall, V. Kelly, C. Delgado, P. Matlon, J.Hopkins, and O. Badiane. 1994. "Is Income Diversification Agriculture-led in the West African Semi-Arid Tropics? The Nature, Causes, Effects, Distribution, and

Production Linkages of Off-farm Activities", in A. Atsain, S. Wangwe, and A.G. Drabek (eds.), *Economic Policy Experience in Africa: What Have We Learned?* African Economic Research Consortium, Nairobi, Kenya.

Ruthenberg, H. 1980. *Farming Systems in the Tropics.* Third edition. Oxford: Clarendon Press

Shaikh, A. and M. McGahvey. 1995. *Capitalizing on Change: USAID's Contribution to Niger's Strategy for Sustainable Development.* International Resources Group, Ltd. Publication. Washington, D.C.

Shaikh, A., T. Reardon, D. Clay and P. DeCosse. 1995. *Dynamic Linkages Among Environment, Population, and Development in Madagascar.* Environment and Natural Resources Policy and Training Project (EPAT).

Weeks, John. 1989. *Population: An Introduction to Concepts and Issues.* Fourth Edition. Belmont California: Wadsworth Publishing Company.

8 Sustainability and Economics

Erik Lichtenberg

Introduction

The term "sustainability" has taken on a wide variety of meanings in public policy discussions. There is general agreement that sustainability has something to do with careful consideration of preserving environmental quality and stocks of natural resources. Beyond that, definitions of sustainability differ markedly. To some, sustainability implies the necessity of restoring environmental quality to a pristine state and eliminating any further drawdown of natural resource stocks, at least non-renewable ones—measures that require drastic changes in the world's economic systems (see for example Ehrlich and Ehrlich, 1996, or Daly, 1991). At the other end of the spectrum, some maintain that the world's current economic systems can deliver an increasingly high quality of life indefinitely, and that few if any institutional changes are needed to ensure sustainability (see for example Simon, 1996).

This chapter reviews economists' thinking on defining and measuring sustainability. The first section presents the standard definition of sustainability in economics. The second section discusses the use of net national product as a summary measure of sustainability. The third section discusses the relationship between property rights and the need for adjustments to net national product to account for natural resource depreciation. The fourth section discusses treatment of pollution control costs. The fifth section considers physical quantities of resource stocks as a measure of sustainability. The sixth section discusses issues relating to irreversibility and ecosystem resilience. The seventh section discusses the relationship between sustainability and policy reform in the environmental and resource sectors. The final section discusses the desirability of sustainability.

Sustainability and Society's Standard of Living

The consensus among economists is that sustainability should be evaluated in terms of the standard of living of humankind. Specifically, sustainable growth or sustainable development is a pattern of resource use that results in a non-declining potential standard of living over time. In other words, an economic system is sustainable if it has the capacity to provide at least as much of a livelihood in the future as it does at present.

This criterion is clearly human-centered, counting only human well-being. The well-being of other types of living organisms are given no consideration on their own account; rather, the welfare of non-human entities matter only insofar as it contributes to humans' standard of living. Contrary to this viewpoint, some have argued that evaluations of well-being should take into account the welfare of some (e.g., those capable of experiencing pain) or all non-human entities. One school of thought holds that non-human entities have rights on a par with those accorded to humans and that those rights should be taken into account in evaluating human actions. Another argues that actions should be evaluated relative to ecosystem health; what promotes ecosystem health and stability is good, what undermines ecosystem health and stability is wrong.

Neither of these alternatives can be justified rationally without recourse to human values, however (Schrader-Frechette, 1985). Non-human species cannot assert their rights against humans. They cannot adjudicate disputes over conflicting rights with members of their own or other species. They cannot express their own valuations of alternative actions. In short, they cannot participate in policy debates without human interpreters. Ecosystem health, too, is a matter of judgment in a world that evolves even in the absence of human action.

Economists define the standard of living in terms of human consumption, that is, use of goods and services. Natural resources and the environment are consumed in several distinct ways, which can be grouped into the three broad categories (1) raw materials, (2) direct consumption goods and services, and (3) waste disposal services.

Perhaps the most common use of natural resources is as raw materials in the production of consumer goods and services. Petroleum provides fuels, asphalt, and the raw material for plastics and other chemicals. Trees provide lumber, used as a raw material for building; pulp, used as a raw material for paper and similar products; fuel wood; and so on. Land provides a medium for growing food and fiber and for supporting housing, roads, and other structures. Ores are smelted into metals or refined into pure minerals. Genetic resources provide the raw material for the development of new pharmaceuticals and industrial chemicals.

Natural resources may also be direct sources of consumption goods. People eat fish and drink water. Scenic amenities and recreational opportunities (hunting, fishing, hiking, camping) are also consumption items that provide enjoyment even though they are not physically used up in the consumption process.

Human consumption produces waste as a by-product. These wastes are discharged into the air, water, and land, all of which serve as repositories. Biota in water and land degrade these wastes, as do photochemical processes in the atmosphere. In short, natural resources and the environment provide waste disposal services.

The economist's definition of consumption is thus less restrictive and, in principle, more environment-friendly than might seem at first glance. Consumption is construed broadly enough to include services such as scenic amenities, recreational uses of natural resources, and waste disposal services, all of which require maintenance of environmental quality. Human consumption and environmental quality are thus not inherently contradictory, even though some commercial interests may stand in opposition to environmental concerns.

Sustainability and Net National Product

Members of society consume a mix of goods and services. That mix of goods and services remains the same year after year in few, if any, societies. Thus, evaluating changes in a society's potential standard of living over time generally requires comparing different mixes of goods and services. In other words, evaluating sustainability requires the use of an aggregate index of consumption.

Net national product (NNP) has long been considered the appropriate aggregate index of consumption in cases where natural resources and the environment have not been taken into account. Recent research has demonstrated that NNP remains the appropriate index of consumption for evaluating sustainability once certain adjustments have been made.

NNP equals the value of all final goods and services less depreciation of capital assets. It is a linear index of consumption, specifically, a weighted average in which levels of consumption of different goods and services are weighted by their respective market prices. In an economy characterized by perfectly competitive markets, the market price of any good equals the monetary equivalent of the marginal satisfaction each consumer derives from the purchase of an additional unit, so that market prices are a monetary expression of consumer preferences for different goods and services.

Weitzman (1976) showed that NNP in any year is proportional to the annual income a society's capital assets can deliver over an indefinite period of time. In other words, NNP measures the standard of living that an economy has the productive capacity to sustain. An increase in NNP thus indicates a higher potential standard of living, while a decrease indicates the opposite. For this reason, NNP is an obvious indicator of sustainability. Increasing NNP indicates a level of productive capacity that is improving over time and thus a sustainable standard of living. Decreasing NNP indicates deteriorating productive capacity and thus an unsustainable standard of living. (A somewhat different rationale for the use of NNP is presented by Dasgupta, Kriström, and Mäler, 1997.)

Hartwick (1990) developed the appropriate adjustments to NNP for three types of resources: (1) exhaustible resources used as raw materials, (2) renewable resources consumed directly, and (3) pollution stocks, that is, in natural waste disposal capacity. All three involve stocks of natural resources and environmental amenities that function as capital assets, since they deliver flows of goods and services over time. Hartwick shows that NNP should include a depreciation charge for changes in exhaustible resource stocks equal to the change in stocks valued at the net marginal resource rent, that is, at the price of the extracted resource less the marginal cost of extraction. Net depreciation of renewable resources consumed directly should similarly equal the physical change in the resource stock times the marginal rent, equal to the price of the resource less the marginal cost of harvesting it. The physical change in the resource should equal the net natural increment due to growth less the amount of the resource harvested. Hartwick considers two adjustments for pollution. If the social value of environmental damage is a function of pollution, the per-unit value of net increments or decrements in pollution equals the marginal cost of pollution control measures, so that NNP should be adjusted by subtracting the marginal cost of pollution control times the change in pollution stocks. If the social value of environmental damage is a function of changes in pollution stocks (rather than the levels of the stocks themselves), the per-unit value of net increments or decrements in pollution equals the sum of (1) the social disutility of changes in pollution stocks and (2) the marginal cost of pollution control measures.

Property Rights and Adjustments to NNP

Natural resources and environmental amenities enter NNP in two ways, via direct consumption of resources and environmental amenities and via changes in resource stocks. The former are included in standard national income accounts as long as they are traded in markets. The latter are incorporated into national income accounts as long as they are exploited under private ownership. Natural resources and environmental amenities will be omitted from standard national income accounts when they are not allocated through markets. However, these omissions will only affect measurement of sustainability when stocks of resources and environmental amenities change over time, since NNP includes only the value of changes in stocks of capital assets, that is, net depreciation of all forms of capital.

When resources are owned privately, standard accounting procedures will include depreciation charges to measure changes in natural resource stocks. Depreciation of natural resource stocks will thus be incorporated into standard national income accounts. Hartwick notes that standard accounting procedures, which use average rather than marginal extraction costs, may actually overstate true depreciation of exhaustible resources. If extraction costs are rising rapidly, marginal extraction costs will be significantly higher than average extraction costs. In such cases, the true marginal rent earned by a unit of the resource will be smaller than the price of the resource less average extraction cost. As a result, standard national income accounting procedures may make economies appear less sustainable than they actually are.

Hartwick's framework can easily be extended to encompass amenities such as scenic amenities and recreational opportunities afforded by natural resource stocks. In cases where these amenities are privately owned, expenditures on them will be incorporated into standard national income accounts. Examples include hiking trails, boating facilities, and similar facilities in privately-owned resorts, privately-operated boating trips, horseback expeditions, and similar activities in publicly-owned park land, and the travel costs visitors incur to make use of these recreational opportunities. Significant shares of the value of amenities that are not privately owned may be captured in the values of nearby privately-owned properties. It is well-established that willingness to pay for scenic amenities is capitalized into the values of neighboring parcels of land for instance (see for example Palmquist, 1991). Changes in the stocks of such scenic amenities will cause changes in nearby land values that may be captured in standard national income accounts or that can be estimated separately using hedonic methods.

Many natural resources—both renewable and exhaustible—are publicly-owned and are thus exploited under conditions of open access or under government leasing arrangements. Resources typically characterized by open-access exploitation include fisheries, groundwater, oil (common pool problem), and tropical forests. Resources typically operated under government concession or leasing operations include logging and minerals. In either case, standard national income accounts will tend to omit charges for depreciation of natural assets. Under conditions of open access, this omission does not matter. Ignoring depreciation of resources extracted under government leasing arrangements may, however, bias measurement of sustainability significantly.

Under conditions of open access, resources are treated as having no intrinsic value. Because the resource is not privately owned, those wishing to extract or harvest it do not pay for the use of the resource itself; the only costs incurred are those directly associated with harvesting or extraction. In particular, the resource rent—the opportunity cost of harvesting the resource today in terms of reductions in future harvests—does not enter into harvesting decisions. In fact, the resource earns no rent under open access exploitation. Agents will harvest the resource until the marginal harvesting cost equals the market price of the resource. No agent will be able to realize increased future harvests by limiting harvests in the present because other agents will find it profitable to increase their harvests correspondingly. For example, if one fisherman reduces harvesting effort, resulting in increased stocks of fish, other fishermen will find harvesting cheaper due to larger stocks, and will thus increase effort until any cost savings have been exhausted. In general, agents will increase harvests as long as marginal rents are positive. As a result, in equilibrium, marginal resource rents will be zero. Since an open-access resource earns no marginal rent, the value of changes in open-access resource stocks is zero, that is, there is no economic depreciation of those resources even when there are positive or negative net changes in the physical stocks of the resource. Standard national income accounts, which ignore depreciation of open-access resource stocks, therefore give an accurate estimate of economic depreciation of these resource stocks.

Some resources are exploited under systems of incomplete or limited property rights rather than pure open access. In many societies, land is owned collectively by a village or extended family and is allocated annually among members. Those using land under such ownership systems may have inadequate incentives to invest in the land resource, for example, by undertaking erosion control measures or by manuring to increase soil fertility stocks. Since land is not traded in markets, depreciation of land resources is not reflected by changes in market land values and must be estimated independently for incorporation into national income accounts. These adjustments may be substantial. For example, Bishop and Allen (1989) estimate depreciation of agricultural land in Mali due to soil erosion at 1.5 percent of GDP. Depreciation of manufactured capital in Mali is only about 4 percent of GDP (Pearce and Atkinson, 1992), so that adding depreciation of agricultural land due to soil erosion by itself increases estimated depreciation by 38 percent.

Incomplete ownership rights do not necessarily lead to a lack of investment in resource stocks or to excessive depletion of those stocks. In many parts of sub-Saharan Africa, users of a particular parcel have security of tenure even if they do not own the land outright and cannot sell it. Security of tenure alone gives farmers an incentive to invest in erosion control and soil quality augmentation (Place and Hazell, 1993; Besley, 1995; Gavian and Fafchamps, 1996). Empirical studies from Central America and Asia suggest that the main effect of more complete property rights is to secure access to capital markets by giving farmers collateral, allowing them to undertake larger-scale investment projects (Feder and Onchan, 1987). It thus cannot be said *a priori* that incomplete property rights result in significant net depreciation of such resources. Crosson (1994), for example, argues that net depreciation of soil resources is typically of the same modest order as that estimated by Bishop and Allen (1989) for Mali. As a result, ignoring such depreciation may not bias national income accounts to any great extent.

Depreciation of government-owned resources is typically not included in standard NNP calculations. This omission can severely distort measurement of sustainability, albeit primarily in economies where extraction of government-owned resources makes up a significant share of economic activity. In the U.S., for example, agriculture and forestry together account for 1.8 percent of gross domestic product (GDP), while mining accounts for an additional 1.6 percent. Logging on government-owned forests accounts for 5.3 percent of U.S. timber production (U.S. Department of Agriculture, 1996), while oil and gas extraction from government-owned outer-continental shelf leases accounts for only 6.7 percent of total U.S. production (U.S. Bureau of the Census, 1997). Depreciation accounts for about 10 percent of GDP (Council of Economic Advisers, 1996). If government-owned forests and mineral deposits account for the same share of total depreciation as these sectors' share of GDP, then ignoring them completely will have negligible effects on NNP calculations. In Indonesia by contrast, oil and gas—which are state-owned—account for about 19 percent of GDP. Repetto et al. (1989)

have estimated that during the mid-1980s depreciation from government-owned oil and gas amounted to as much as 14 percent of Indonesia's estimated GDP. Pearce and Atkinson (1992) estimate depreciation of total natural capital (resource stocks, environmental amenities, and natural waste disposal capacity) in Indonesia at 17 percent of NNP.

Government-owned recreational opportunities, scenic amenities, and other environmental consumption items require different treatment. First, these forms of natural capital need not enter into national income accounts unless the stock changes, that is, unless stocks have either increased or decreased over time. The value of these stocks cannot be measured by the costs incurred in maintaining them or by access fees because government operations are not designed to maximize returns. In such cases, indirect methods must be used to value the flows of services provided by these stocks. The value of the stocks themselves can then be estimated by capitalizing the value of these service flows. As noted above, costs incurred traveling to and using publicly-owned recreational sites will be included in standard national income accounts. Contingent valuation methods, in which survey methods are used to elicit public valuations of environmental amenities, can also be used to adjust standard national income accounts for changes in stocks of these amenities.

Treatment of Pollution Control Costs

Some have argued that total pollution control costs should be subtracted from standard NNP as a practical means of adjusting for environmental damage (see for example Bartelmus, Stahmer, and van Tongeren, 1989). Hartwick's measure is somewhat different; in the case where pollution stocks affect welfare, then economic depreciation of natural waste disposal capacity equals the product of marginal control cost and the change in the stock of pollution. The two will be equal only if pollution control technologies exhibit constant returns to scale, which is not generally believed to be the case. If pollution control costs are increasing sharply, so that marginal cost exceeds average cost, then total pollution control costs will understate the true social value of depreciation of natural waste disposal capacity.

Hartwick's measure is itself an appropriate adjustment to NNP only when society has engaged in an efficient level of pollution control, that is, a level of pollution control that equates the value of marginal reductions in environmental damage with the marginal cost of pollution control. Determining the efficient level of pollution control is not easy. Environmental damage is difficult to measure. Polluters will tend to overstate pollution control costs as well. Political-economic considerations suggest that countries will tend to underinvest in pollution control. The benefits of pollution control tend to be diffuse while the costs tend to be concentrated, suggesting that polluters will be more effective in limiting the scope of environmental regulation than those suffering the effects of pollution are in expanding it (Stigler, 1971). In such cases, pollution control costs understate the true costs of pollution, so that NNP adjusted using Hartwick's method will overstate sustainability.

Should Changes in Resource Stocks be Used to Measure Sustainability?

Using NNP to measure sustainability implicitly assumes that tradeoffs among capital assets—including tradeoffs between manufactured capital and natural capital—are (1) possible and (2) adequately valued using current prices. Both of these assumptions have been challenged. Some have argued that manufactured capital and natural capital are complements, rather than substitutes, so that tradeoffs between natural and manufactured capital are infeasible (Costanza and Daly, 1992). Others have argued that current prices are based on the preferences of current members of society living and may well not reflect those of future generations (see for example Norgaard and Howarth, 1991). In particular, current prices may not reflect the long-run costs of irreversible changes in resource stocks (e.g., extinction of species or eradication of unique scenic amenities).

Proponents of these points of view generally argue that physical quantities of resource stocks are superior to NNP as indicators of sustainability. According to this view, sustainable development patterns are characterized by net increases in stocks of natural resources, environmental amenities, and natural waste disposal capacity. Net decreases in natural capital indicate unsustainable growth and development.

The notion that manufactured and natural capital are complements arises from the idea that production is, at bottom, a process of transforming raw materials into usable goods and services (for an exposition see Costanza and Daly, 1992). Natural resources and environmental services provide the raw materials. Moreover, it is asserted, manufactured capital is itself made from raw materials and thus cannot exist without natural resources.

The problem with this argument is that the conceptualization of production on which it is based is not particularly useful. One could just as easily note that the Earth has a finite endowment of matter that can be rearranged into different forms to serve different uses. From this perspective, there is little substantive difference between manufactured capital and natural resources. Both are no more than particular arrangements of matter, and these different forms of matter may substitute for one another. In truth, much of what manufactured capital does is allow the productive use of resources that were previously in unusable form. For example, synthetic fertilizers are a close substitute for nutrients fixed in soil from the atmosphere and from the decay of dead organic material. In this case, manufactured capital (a fertilizer factory) is a close substitute for natural capital (soil microbes).

The argument that current prices do not adequately take into account the preferences of future generations is also problematic. In most societies, current generations bequeath to their successors a complex portfolio of capital assets, including manufactured capital, human capital, and natural capital. The composition of that portfolio is determined by current prices operating through capital markets, which rearrange investments in capital assets to equalize rates of return on investment in all three kinds of capital. If the rate of return to standing timber is less than the rate of return to steel mills, for example, owners of forest land will harvest timber, effectively disinvesting in the forest resource, and reinvest the proceeds in steel mills or other opportunities offering higher rates of return. In particular, if current stocks of natural resources exceed long-run equilibrium stocks, it is efficient to harvest those resources at rates exceeding regeneration rates and reallocate the proceeds elsewhere in the economy. The result will be net physical reductions in resource stocks but net increases in NNP and in the value of the portfolio of capital assets passed on to future generations.

A portfolio of assets in which natural capital makes up a smaller share and other forms of capital make up a larger share will not necessarily favor present generations at the expense of future ones. Some of today's investment is in the form of human capital, embodied both in more highly-trained scientific and technical personnel, and in greater knowledge. For example, some of the proceeds earned by disinvesting in natural resources (that is, by increasing resource harvests and drawing down resource stocks) are reinvested in R&D by providing livelihoods and equipment for researchers. Much of this R&D will provide lasting benefits to future generations. Some will even pay off only in the long run, and hence be of direct benefit only to future generations. Similarly, proceeds of disinvesting in natural resources may be used to provide physical infrastructure such as roads, bridges, and communications systems. For example, a significant share of the physical infrastructure of the U.S. today dates back to the 1930s and earlier. Overall, then, it is by no means clear that future generations would be better off with higher levels of resource stocks and less human capital and physical infrastructure.

A further argument against using physical stocks of natural resources as sustainability indicators is the physical impossibility of conserving all resource stocks at current levels. Species evolve. Some currently existing species will become extinct at any point in time, and some would have become extinct even in the absence of human activity. Other new species will emerge. It is therefore impossible to hold constant the species composition existing at any given point in time. If a reduction in the physical stock of any species indicates a lack of sustainability, then sustainability is impossible because reductions in the physical stocks of at least some species are inevitable.

The fact of evolution implies the necessity of using an index of resource stocks in order to evaluate sustainability. Losses in some species must be balanced against preservation of or increases in other species. Even the apparently innocent use of aggregate measures (e.g., the extant number of species of tropical forest insects) is, in essence, a particular index. Once one accepts the necessity of indices for evaluating sustainability, use of NNP becomes quite attractive. Any other measure that allows balancing reductions in the physical stocks of some species against increases in the physical stocks of others is open to the same general criticisms as NNP without having the advantage of a sound conceptual basis.

Sustainability, Irreversibility, and Ecosystem Resilience

Another set of arguments against using NNP as a measure of sustainability arises from consideration of the prospect of irreversible change. Reallocation of a society's portfolio of assets may result in elimination of resource stocks that cannot be undone at later dates. For example, constructing a reservoir for hydroelectric power generation and augmentation of irrigation and drinking water supplies may result in destruction of a scenic canyon and the recreational amenities it supplies. Restoration of such scenic amenities may be so costly and take such a lengthy period of time that it is best treated as irreversible. Water resources development projects, drainage of wetlands, extension of agricultural land, conversion of tropical forest, and other human activities frequently result in elimination of critical habitat and thus ultimately in extinction of one or more species. Low levels of resource stocks that appear sustainable may turn out to allow irreversible losses in the event of random shocks such as severe storms or new diseases. For example, random shocks may reduce low populations of a particular species to levels below the minimum needed to guarantee reproduction, ultimately resulting in extinction. Similarly, random events may reduce populations of keystone species below levels needed to preserve the integrity of ecosystems, resulting in qualitative changes in ecosystem structure.

Two different approaches have been proposed for dealing with the prospect of irreversibility: the safe minimum standard and option value.

Some have argued that the prospect of irreversible change implies that stocks of all resources should be maintained at least at levels sufficiently large to guarantee continued existence. This minimum level is sometimes called a safe minimum standard. Bishop (1978) provides a rationale for it as the outcome of a minimax loss strategy in a game-theoretic context. The safe minimum standard is unattractive because it essentially attaches an infinite cost to the prospect of extinction—which, as discussed above, is a certainty for at least some species. Moreover, it is difficult to implement. The parameters needed for quantitative models of ecosystem dynamics are difficult to estimate. Yet accurate estimation may be critically important because of the potentially high cost associated with implementation of a safe minimum standard.

An alternative approach is to augment estimates of the value of a resource stock to take into account the possibility that new information may increase the return to the resource stock. For example, many important pharmaceuticals are derived from naturally occurring compounds found in plants. Tropical forests contain numerous plants that have yet to be assayed for potential pharmaceuticals. The potential value of pharmaceuticals derived from yet-to-be-discovered plant species should thus comprise part of the intrinsic value of tropical forests (see for example Fisher and Hanemann, 1997).

One might expect that the values of privately owned resource stocks will include such option values, at least insofar as possibilities of future discoveries are anticipated by agents currently living. Thus, adjustment of NNP to include such option values is likely to be important mainly in cases where property rights in resource stocks or environmental services are lacking or incomplete. For example, option values associated with tropical forest preservation are typically not included in standard national income accounts because tropical forest resources are exploited under conditions of open access or government ownership.

The importance of including such option values into national income accounts—and into policy making—has been debated in the economics literature. One case where option value is likely to be important is that of loss of biodiversity from tropical deforestation. Logging and conversion of forest to agricultural uses is thought to result in extinction of numerous species, the loss of which is typically ignored in standard national income accounts. Balick and Mendelsohn (1992) have claimed that the expected losses of potential new pharmaceuticals due to exploitation of tropical forests in certain biological "hot spots" are extremely high, in the order of $20 to $60 per hectare. But expected losses of this kind are almost certainly much lower because of redundancy and/or similarities in genetic resources that reduce the likelihood that loss of an individual species results in the loss of a unique potential pharmaceutical. Simpson, Sedjo, and Reid (1996) and Pearce and Puroshothaman (1995) both estimate values of tropical forest preservation for pharmaceutical prospecting between $0.01 and $20 per hectare.

NNP, Sustainability, and Policy Reform

The preceding discussions suggest that standard national income accounts fail to make an accurate assessment of sustainability primarily in cases where private markets fail to generate efficient resource management. Resources such as fisheries remain subject to open access exploitation, for example, because property rights in resource stocks are largely unenforceable. Those wishing to begin harvesting the resource can do so cheaply, since capital requirements are generally low. Restricting access tends to be expensive, because such resources are dispersed over wide areas with numerous points of access. In fisheries, for example, boats and gear are relatively inexpensive, while launches and landings are difficult to monitor effectively. Maintaining property rights over tropical forests is similarly difficult for the same reasons. Other resources remain under public management because they are the basis for natural monopolies. For example, a single hydroelectric power plant provides almost all of Costa Rica's electricity. Water supply projects tend to fall into this category, since only a few are generally needed to provide water and electricity for a given market. Still other resources remain under governmental control because they provide public goods, that is, goods or services that are non-rival (can be utilized simultaneously by many) and non-excludable (access to which cannot be restricted at reasonable cost). Many scenic amenities and the waste disposal capacity of the environment both fall into this latter category.

Increased sustainability in such cases is largely synonymous with increased efficiency of resource management. Improving an economy's capacity to provide a living for current generations by implementing policies that reduce waste of resources simultaneously improves that economy's capacity to provide for future generations. Policy reform can thus be viewed as essential for promoting sustainability.

Policy reform at the national level fails to address concerns over sustainability for global problems such as climate change, ozone depletion, preservation of biodiversity (global genetic resources), and management of ocean fisheries. These problems are transnational and thus may not be solvable by unilateral actions of individual countries. Some have suggested in fact that unilateral actions aimed at curbing global environmental damage may actually exacerbate problems as countries with more polluting technologies increase their share of production at the expense of countries whose costs have increased due to greater pollution control efforts (Hoel, 1991). However, it may be possible for countries to achieve self-enforcing unilateral strategies that perform almost as well as fully coordinated agreements for achieving efficient management of such problems (Dockner and Van Long, 1993).

Is Sustainability Desirable?

The literature on sustainability has helped broaden understanding of economic growth and development by highlighting the roles played by natural resources and environmental amenities in supporting a society's standard of living. But sustainable development cannot necessarily be said to be unambiguously better than unsustainable development. Economists evaluate changes in an economy using the strict criterion proposed by Pareto: A change is unambiguously good if it makes some better off without making anyone worse off. Some changes cause improvements that are sufficiently large to allow gainers to compensate losers fully and still be better off. These changes represent potential, rather than actual, improvements, unless the losers actually are compensated fully (for a discussion and some examples see Just, Schmitz, and Zilberman, 1979). Policies that promote sustainability cause potential Pareto improvements. An increase in sustainability means an increase in the standard of living a society is capable of supporting, but not necessarily an increase in the standard of living of each member of society. For example, assignment and enforcement of clearly-defined property rights may increase sustainability by improving management of a natural resource. But some of those previously exploiting those resources will likely be deprived of their traditional means of livelihood. Unless they are compensated (e.g., by retraining and placement into alternative employment yielding at least as much income), such an increase in sustainability will not constitute an unambiguous gain in welfare.

The issue of equity and the distribution of benefits and costs is particularly important in global environmental problems. Efficient management of these problems frequently requires poor countries to bear a large share of effort. For example, efforts to preserve biological diversity fall disproportionately on countries that were too poor in the past for economic activity to threaten numerous species with extinction. Species extinctions in richer countries are largely complete, since species remaining in those countries have had a century or more to adapt to life in modern industrial societies. Similarly, curbing carbon dioxide emissions tends to be more costly relative to income for poor countries relying on more pollution-intensive technologies than for rich ones that have already undertaken significant investments in pollution control. Efforts to improve sustainability at the global level may thus require mechanisms for compensating poor countries for costs they bear for the common global good.

A narrow focus on resource and environmental issues may also detract from other issues important in assessing and promoting economic development. Two stand out in particular: decision making within families and human capital formation.

Standard neoclassical economic theory treats individuals as autonomous decision making units. But in most societies, decisions are made collectively within households or larger aggregates whose members have unequal say. Adult women in particular frequently have lesser status. The economics literature indicates that changes in relations within households can have profound effects on general welfare and, indeed, on pressure on natural resources and the environment. Improvements in women's status typically leads to reductions in birth rates and therefore on resource degradation induced by population pressure (see for example Dasgupta, 1993).

A significant share of any individual's or household's standard of living is produced within the home and is thus omitted from national income accounts, whether adjusted for sustainability or not. Investment in human capital through public health measures (sanitation, preventive medicine) and education may change standards of living substantially, as reflected in such measures as reduced mortality or disability (Sen, 1993; Dasgupta, 1993). The relationship between human capital development and resource conservation is complex. For example, education may reduce resource degradation (e.g., by promoting the adoption of improved management techniques) or exacerbate it (e.g., by promoting production of pesticide-intensive export crops or use of other degradation-intensive technologies). Similarly, efforts to improve sustainability may complement human capital formation or undercut them (e.g., if privatization of natural resources reduces the financial base for funding education and public health measures).

In sum, sustainability is important, but it is by no means the only important factor in economic development or even, in many cases, the predominant one.

References

Balick, M. and R. Mendelsohn. 1992. "Assessing the economic value of traditional medicine from tropical forests". *Conservation Biology* 6:32-39.

Bartelmus, P., C. Stahmer, and J. van Tongeren. 1989. "SNA framework for integrated environmental and economic accounting". Presented at the International Association for Research in Income and Wealth, Lauhstein, Germany.

Besley, T. 1995. "Property rights and investment incentives: Theory and evidence from Ghana". *Journal of Political Economy* 103:903-937.

Bishop, J. and J. Allen. 1989. "The on-site costs of soil erosion in Mali". Environment Department Working Paper No. 21, World Bank, Washington, DC.

Bishop, R. 1978. "Endangered species and uncertainty: the economics of a safe minimum standard". *American Journal of Agricultural Economics* 60:10-13.

Costanza, R. and H.E. Daly. 1992. "Natural capital and sustainable development". *Conservation Biology* 6:37-46.

Council of Economic Advisers. 1997. "Economic Report of the President". U.S. Government Printing Office, Washington, DC.

Crosson, P. 1994. "Degradation of resources as a threat to sustainable agriculture". Presented at the First World Congress of Professionals, Santiago, Chile, September 5-8.

Daly, H.E. 1991. "Elements of environmental macroeconomics", in R. Costanza, ed., *Ecological economics: the science and management of sustainability*. New York: Columbia University Press.

Dasgupta, P. 1993. *An inquiry into well-being and destitution*. Oxford: Oxford University Press.

Dasgupta, P., B. Krist m, and K-G. M ler. 1997. "The environment and net national product", in P. Dagupta and K-G. M ler, ed., *The environment and emerging development issues, volume 1*. Oxford: Oxford University Press.

Dockner, E.J. and N. Van Long. 1993. "International pollution control: cooperative versus noncooperative strategies". *Journal of Environmental Economics and Management* 25:13-29.

Ehrlich P.R. and A.H. Ehrlich. 1996. "Betrayal of science and reason: how anti-environmental rhetoric threatens our future". Washington, DC: Island Press.

Feder, G. and T. Onchan. 1987. "Land ownership security and farm investment in Thailand". *American Journal of Agricultural Economics* 69:311-320.

Fisher, A.C. and M. Hanemann. 1997. "Valuation of tropical forests", in P. Dagupta and K-G. M ler, ed., *The environment and emerging development issues, volume 2*. Oxford: Oxford University Press.

Gavian, S. and M. Fafchamps. 1996. "Land tenure and allocative efficiency in Ghana". *American Journal of Agricultural Economics* 78:460-471.

Hartwick, J. 1990. "Natural resources, national accounting, and economic depreciation". *Journal of Public Economics* 43:291-304.

Hoel, M. 1991. "Global environmental problems: the effects of unilateral actions taken by one country". *Journal of Environmental Economics and Management* 20:55-70.

Just, R.E., A. Schmitz, and D. Zilberman. 1979. "Technological change in agriculture". *Science* 206:1277-1280.

Norgaard, R.B. and R.B. Howarth. 1991. "Sustainability and discounting the future", in R. Costanza, ed., *Ecological economics: the science and management of sustainability*. New York: Columbia University Press.

Palmquist, R.B. 1991. "Hedonic methods", in Braden, J.B. and C.D. Kolstad, eds., *Measuring the demand for environmental quality*. Amsterdam: North-Holland.

Pearce, D.W. and G. Atkinson. 1992. "Are national economies sustainable? Measuring sustainable development". CSERGE, University College, London.

Pearce, D. and S. Puroshothaman. 1995. "The economic value of plant-based pharmaceuticals", in T. Swanson, ed., *Intellectual property rights and biodiversity conservation: an interdisciplinary analysis of the values of medicinal plants*. Cambridge: Cambridge University Press.

Place, F. and P. Hazell. 1993. "Productivity effects of indigenous land tenure systems in sub-Saharan Africa". *American Journal of Agricultural Economics* 75:10-19.

Repetto, R., W. Magrath, M. Wells, C. Beer, and F. Rossini. 1989. *Wasting assets: natural resources in the national income accounts*. Washington: World Resources Institute.

Sen, A. 1993. "The economics of life and death". *Scientific American* 40-47.

Shrader-Frechette, K. 1985. "Environmental ethics and global imperatives", in R. Repetto, ed., *The global possible: Resources, development, and the new century*. New Haven: Yale University Press.

Simon, J.L. 1996. *The ultimate resource 2*. Princeton, NJ: Princeton University Press.

Simpson, D., R.A. Sedjo, and J.W. Reid. 1996. "Valuing biodiversity for use in pharmaceutical research". *Journal of Political Economy* 104:163-185.

Stigler, G.J. 1971. "The theory of economic regulation". *Bell Journal of Economics* 2:3-21.

U.S. Bureau of the Census. 1997. *Statistical abstract of the United States, 1996*. Washington: U.S. Government Printing Office.

U.S. Department of Agriculture. 1996. *U.S. agricultural statistics, 1995-96*. Washington: U.S. Government Printing Office.

Weitzman, M. 1976. "On the significance of national product in a dynamic economy". *Quarterly Journal of Economics* 90:156-162.

9 Sustainability and Public Policy

Neill Schaller

Introduction

The sustainability of agriculture, seldom considered a national concern a few decades ago, is now an important public policy issue.[1] Driving it is evidence that today's chemical- and capital-intensive, conventional agriculture cannot continue to provide abundant food in ways that will also satisfy desired environmental, health, economic, and social requirements.

For years now, visionaries, scholars, and writers have articulated the rationale for a sustainable agriculture, among them Leopold (1987), Schumacher (1973), Berry (1977), Youngberg (1978), Jackson (1980), and Rodale (1983). Each has inspired the public to realize that modern agriculture is not moving down a sustainable path, and outlined what might be done to guide it there.

Today, public policies in the U.S. and elsewhere recognize and partially support numerous requirements of sustainability, such as conservation of natural resources, environmental protection, assurance of safe and wholesome food, adequate farm prices and incomes, and supportive agricultural research and extension education. Although state and local policies affect the sustainability of agriculture, in the U.S., the most visible policies have been those of the federal government expressed largely through "farm bills" passed every five years or so. Farm bill provisions supporting sustainability have consisted mainly of measures that seek to correct, or prevent, the rewarding of intensive, monocultural, and potentially unsustainable farming practices.

Through most of this century, concerns about sustainability have been overshadowed by the increasing bounty of American agriculture. Gradually, however, more and more people have become aware of its unforeseen, undesirable side effects. The growing list of such effects includes loss of topsoil due to water and wind erosion, health risks due to expanding use of synthetic chemical pesticides and fertilizer, depletion of groundwater supplies, agriculture's growing dependence on nonrenewable energy sources, soil compaction, and loss of fish and wildlife. More recent concerns that conventional agriculture might not be sustainable include its heavy reliance on outside capital, growing resistance of weeds and insects to chemical pesticides, and the replacement of family farming by an increasingly industrialized agricultural system.

Before "sustainable agriculture" became a popular term, people spoke of organic, regenerative, alternative, low-input, biological, and ecological agriculture. In the late 1970s and early 1980s, legislative attempts were made to support research on organic farming (U. S. House of Representatives, 1982; U. S. Senate, 1982). But the idea was rejected by the conventional agricultural community as well as by agricultural scientists in the U.S. Department of Agriculture (USDA) and the land-grant colleges of agriculture (Youngberg, 1978). Organic farming, they argued, was fine for a few farmers who wanted to meet the needs of niche markets. But any thought that it might become mainstream agriculture was seen as a "guarantee" of lower total food production and higher food prices. One still hears that view expressed (Gallagher, 1997).

Policy Confrontations Past and Present

As undesirable side effects of conventional agriculture recurred, concerned citizens and dedicated organizations urged new policies to encourage alternative farming approaches. But defenders of conventional agriculture continued to believe that ways could and would be found to head off or correct its unforeseen, adverse side-effects. Their differences were certain to lead to policy confrontations.

The Organic Red Flag

One such confrontation came as a result of a landmark scientific study by the U.S. Department of Agriculture on the nature and feasibility of organic farming (USDA, 1980). The findings quietly challenged the assumption that chemical-intensive, mechanized farming was the only realistic approach to abundant food production. A popular spokesman for conventional agriculture and a U.S. secretary of agriculture in the 1970s had consistently pooh-poohed the idea, saying "We can go back to organic agriculture in this country if we must—we know how to do it. However, before we move in that direction, someone must decide which 50 million of our people will starve!" (Butz, 1971).

The political impasse created by the symbolism of organic farming slowly encouraged consideration of other approaches with different names. Sustainability gained appeal not only because it eluded the emotionalism of "organic", but also because it could be seen as a conceptual yardstick to measure the effectiveness of alternative farming approaches (which of course could include organic farming). Throughout the 1970s, however, attempts to introduce legislation supporting alternatives to conventional agriculture met with little or no success (Youngberg *et al.*, 1993).

Growing Conflict in the 1980s

The 1981 farm bill opened the door a crack by quietly reintroducing modest support for research on organic farming (U.S. Congress, 1981). Attempts to build on that accomplishment were unsuccessful (U.S. House of Representatives and U.S. Senate, 1982). But Subtitle C, Title XIV of the 1985 farm bill finally achieved modest success by calling for research on farming practices to conserve natural resources and to protect the environment (U.S. Congress, 1985).

That seemingly innocuous provision was ignored until 1988 when the Congress approved $3.9 million for the research it had authorized. With support from a handful of enthusiastic USDA staff members, the Department quietly launched what it first called the "Low-Input Sustainable Agriculture Research and Education" program, or LISA (Schaller, 1991). But overwhelmed by objections to the term "low input" from the conventional agriculture community and members of Congress, the USDA renamed it the "Sustainable Agriculture Research and Education" Program (SARE).

A slow but steady shift toward support for sustainability was also evident in other parts of the 1985 act. Not only did it tell farmers to curb soil erosion on their cropland or lose their eligibility for federal farm program benefits, but it also launched the still popular Conservation Reserve Program to reward farmers who took highly erodible land out of the production of corn, soybeans, cotton, and other highly erosive row crops. The legislation included "sodbuster" and "swampbuster" provisions denying farmers crop program benefits if they converted range and wetlands to crops without following approved soil conservation plans.

Uneasiness about the path conventional agriculture was taking and the growing interest in alternative approaches were heightened in 1989 by publication of a book, *Alternative Agriculture* (National Research Council, 1989). It detailed developments impairing the sustainability of agriculture and told how farmers in different parts of the country were successfully beginning to adopt alternative approaches.

Slow but Steady Gains in the Early 1990s

As the 1990s began, supporters of sustainable agriculture had become better organized and more vocal. A national Campaign for Sustainable Agriculture was established, bringing together representatives of a large number of like-minded organizations from across the country to work for sustainability in the public policy arena. But their success in fostering policies to enhance sustainability was often slowed by endless debate over how to describe the ideal agriculture or what to call it. If the term "alternative agriculture" seemed too vague to some, "sustainable agriculture" had other drawbacks. While avoiding the symbolism of "organic", it was, and still is, disappointingly silent on the question of exactly what characteristics of agriculture should be sustained, and for whom.

Growing acceptance of the concept, though a welcome change from the impasse of prior years, also exacerbated the practical problem of determining the most promising strategies for achieving a sustainable agriculture. As Youngberg *et al.* point out,

> ...the power of sustainability as a symbol has drawn virtually every agricultural interest within its embrace. Fertilizer and pesticide technologies, as well as the products of biotechnology, now reside under the sacred temple of sustainability. The same is true for best management practices, integrated management practices, reduced tillage, improved manure management, and even corn-soybean rotations....The symbolic power of sustainability is truly intoxicating....When virtually all proposals are justified on the grounds that they will contribute to agricultural sustainability, it becomes increasingly difficult for decisionmakers to distinguish among them. They cannot do so on objective grounds, because the agricultural community has yet to develop scientific criteria and indicators of sustainability. Moreover, given the powerful and positive emotional symbolism of sustainability, it is politically difficult for both elected and appointed officials to dismiss proposals and programs bearing the sustainable label, regardless of their content... (Youngberg *et al.*, 1993, p. 300).

Frustration accompanying the issue of sustainability peaked as the

Congress wrote the 1990 farm bill (U.S. Congress, 1990; Youngberg *et al.*, 1993). The debate was more visible and controversial. The conventional agriculture community fought vigorously anything it feared might restrict farmers' freedom to use synthetic chemical pesticides and fertilizers to produce food profitably. Stymied by the intensity of conflict, agriculture committees of the Congress sought the safest political route by carefully responding to both sides.

The 1990 farm bill favored the more "efficient" use of pesticides and fertilizers. It dropped "low input" from the name of the popular LISA program. But as if to even things out a bit, it added a requirement that all federally supported cooperative extension agents should be trained in sustainable agriculture. The bill authorized a program to pay farmers to protect or restore wetlands on their farms and enacted a new Integrated Farm Management Program allowing them to receive commodity price supports while shifting from monoculture to greater use of rotation crops. And, for the first time in history, it called for the development of national standards for organically grown food.

Post mortems of the 1990 legislative process revealed that, as one analyst observed, "The Federal policy interest in sustainable agriculture relates more to its hoped-for environmentally benign characteristics than to the inherent character of its internal management, resource use, or social characteristics" (Doering, 1992, p. 23). Another observer commented that the 1990 bill was "...so complicated and legalistic as to frustrate effective administration. It invites accidental as well as intentional violations, even fraud" (Breimyer, 1992, p. 7).

A New Look in 1996?

When it came time to write the 1996 farm bill, called the Federal Agriculture Improvement and Reform Act (FAIR), the Congress had become more interested in lowering federal deficits and reducing government regulations than in renewing the battles of 1990 (Ray, 1996, pp. 75-94). In effect, the sustainability debate has not ended, but for now it is muted by those new and politically appealing goals.

Not surprisingly, the conventional agriculture community applauds the "freedom to farm" philosophy of the bill. Phased out at last are the commodity price support programs, acreage allotments, and production quotas that have long governed what farmers across the country could grow in return for price and income protection. Farmers can now adjust their cropping patterns to changing market conditions. Moreover, the bill tends to make conservation and environmental programs more "farmer-friendly"—meaning that farmers are given more time and technical assistance to meet environmental requirements.

Proponents of sustainability can also see good points in the 1996 legislation. The "freedom to farm" concept, in theory, lets farmers plant crops that make sense for the land, rather than what they had to grow to stay eligible for farm program payments. It also provides a diversion from the tiring struggle to keep commodity programs from impeding sustainable farming.

Also on the plus side, the 1996 act extends the popular Conservation Reserve Program, which was about to expire, increasing its potential coverage to 36.4 million acres. It consolidates existing conservation programs into an Environmental Quality Incentives Program. And it encourages use of whole-farm planning. Finally, the bill authorizes a new $300-million Fund for Rural America to support rural development and research, thereby increasing potential support for new sustainable agriculture research.

Still, obstacles to sustainability remain. The 1996 act sends the signal that letting markets work is the way to achieve sustainability. However, because it does nothing to assure commodity reserves, farm prices and incomes may now vary more widely as markets and farmers adjust to each other. The swings could increase the economic risks which younger and economically vulnerable farmers are especially ill-prepared to assume. Another drawback is that it "...supports the continued concentration of agricultural assets into fewer hands and the corresponding decline of agriculturally dependent communities" (Hassebrook, 1996, p. 95).

Major Policy Challenges Remain

While many policy actions have been taken in support of a sustainable agriculture, on the whole they continue to neglect three fundamental barriers to such an agriculture; the increasing industrialization of agriculture, neglect of the social side of sustainability, and federal policy habits.

Industrialization of Agriculture

In many parts of the country, American agriculture is no longer one in which farms are owned and operated by diversified family farmers believed to be practitioners of sustainable agriculture. Mainstream agriculture is fast becoming monocultural and industrialized. In many places, farms look more like factories owned and operated by large corporations headquartered in distant cities.

These and related trends are now often referred to as the "industrialization" of American agriculture (Welsh, 1996; Hamilton, 1994). A recent report by the Henry A. Wallace Institute for Alternative Agriculture describes an industrialized agriculture as one that is *coordinated, concentrated*, and *globalized* (Welsh, 1996, pp. 5 - 6). Coordination refers to the linking of production, processing, and marketing of agricultural products, often by the same firm, using techniques such as contract production and vertical integration. Concentration means the ownership and control of agriculture by fewer and larger corporations and other organizations. Globalization is the process through which firms acquire control over production and marketing channels for their products in different parts of the world.

Industrialization is not necessarily a characteristic only of conventional agriculture. Some of its attributes might also be seen in what could otherwise be considered a sustainable agriculture. For example, a large scale organic farm whose products are marketed through a multinational corporation might take on characteristics of an industrialized firm.

Some of the faces and impacts of industrialization have been described in the following assessment by Merrigan (1997):

> Farms are getting larger, markets are becoming integrated, and the 'little guy' increasingly is finding himself out in the cold....Swine confinement facilities housing 3,000 or more, cattle herds numbering in the tens of thousands, and broiler operations of 500,000 birds are becoming the industry norm...Small operators find it difficult to secure the services of packing houses and distributors, either because they are dismissed as too small to bother with, or because such services are owned by their large competitors. The four largest firms in the meat packing industry control more than 80 percent of the steer, heifer, and boxed beef market, greatly reducing the flexibility farmers have in selling their herds. Large manure lagoons that accompany most large livestock operations create severe pollution problems. Rural communities are disrupted as small businesses close their doors when large operators bypass them in search of corporate-size traders to fill corporate-size orders. Concerns arise over the exposure of workers to toxic fumes and the exposure of communities to smells that extend miles from confinement facilities (pp. 161-62).

Even if local citizens successfully oppose a large-scale livestock feeding operation that has moved into their community, the owner may simply decide to relocate it elsewhere, perhaps even in another country. When that happens, the price tag for the community could include not only a loss of jobs but the discomfort and high cleanup costs of leftover pollution.

People who support industrialization contend that it meets growing consumer desires for an increasing variety of high quality and lower cost food throughout the year. Skeptics of the trend, including especially proponents of sustainable agriculture, see it as accelerating a process, underway for decades, through which farmers have been steadily losing control of farming.

Their fears are not unjustified. According to Stewart Smith, an economist who recently documented symptoms of the trend, between 1910 and 1990 the farming sector's share of the food dollar declined from 41 to 9 percent (Smith, 1992). The portion accruing to the input sector rose from 15 to 25 percent, while the marketing sector share rose from 44 to 67 percent.

Other farm and rural trends pose further obstacles to attainment of a sustainable agriculture. For instance, the number of farms in the U.S. has been declining for decades—from nearly 7 million in the 1930s to 2 million in 1996 (USDA, 1997). Another related example is the gradual decoupling of traditional ties between agriculture and rural communities. Even when surrounded by farms, growing numbers of communities are no longer connected to agriculture, economically or socially. According to an insightful book, *Sacred Cows and Hot Potatoes,*

> By 1986, only 516 nonmetropolitan counties were dependent on agriculture. An agriculturally dependent county gets only 20 percent of its earned income from farming. At the same time, 577 nonmetropolitan counties were dependent on manufacturing. And it is more difficult to be counted as a manufacturing county because at least 30 percent of income must come from this sector....While 516 agriculture-dependent counties may seem impressive, these counties accounted for less than 7 percent of the entire U.S. nonmetropolitan population. Manufacturing-dependent counties accounted for 32 percent of the total nonmetropolitan population. However the employment pie is sliced, few rural people are directly or indirectly dependent on farming (Browne et al., 1992, p. 25).

Combined, these developments suggest that obstacles to a sustainable agriculture are numerous and reflect the often subtle side effects of society's emphasis on goals such as growth, consumer satisfaction, efficiency, and faith in science and technology.

Neglect of the Social Side of Sustainability

Of all the characteristics of sustainable agriculture considered important by its proponents, those of a social nature seem to be the most difficult to illuminate and foster. While sustainable agriculture is commonly defined as one that will be socially just and equitable, in addition to providing abundant and wholesome food and protecting the environment, most people prefer to talk about the latter, hoping that the social side can be addressed simply by meeting those other requirements.

Advocates of sustainability who try to recognize social dimensions openly face two hurdles. First, by their very nature, social requirements lack the clarity and measurability of physical and biological requirements. The social side of sustainabilty has an inherent vagueness about it, including requirements that range from quality of rural life to equal rights for people regardless of sex, race, or nationality. Second, social requirements are inherently more politically sensitive than other requirements. So even proponents of sustainability are inclined to concentrate on the more traditional requirements of profitable farm production, resource conservation, and environmental protection.

Further, social criteria are awkward because they tend to imply that, if taken seriously, they will inevitably call for some redistribution of the benefits and costs of agriculture among different people. Nothing can cause more tension and anxiety. Therefore, even strong proponents of sustainability may find themselves wanting to redefine social barriers as technical problems to be solved using good science (Allen, 1993).

Neglecting the social side can be a mistake for a very practical reason. According to Allen, "Framing sustainable agriculture in a natural science discourse that excludes social relations not only ignores social problems, but leaves unexamined the degree to which environmental problems have social causes" (p. 10). Allen's plea is that efforts to assure sustainability take simultaneous account of its ecological and social dimensions.

Federal Policy Habits

Historically, U. S. public policies relating to food, agriculture, and natural resource have consisted mainly of federal policies conceived almost exclusively by the U. S. Congress and carried out by the U. S. Department of Agriculture (USDA). State and local policies serve largely to back up federal policies. They consist of measures to support profitable production and marketing of agricultural products.   They supplement federal conservation and food programs.[2] Throughout this century, state and county governments have also been partners with USDA in conducting research, teaching, and extension education programs.

The apparent dominance of the federal role has historical roots. When the nation was young, agriculture was seen as "the bullwark of democracy and the cradle of religion". No other sector could justify greater attention and support from the federal government. But times have changed. Agriculture is now viewed as another sector of the economy. To this writer's knowledge, no recent president has mentioned its sustainability in a State of the Union address.

Nonetheless, old habits persist, deterring wider policy attention to agricultural sustainability by the states, as well as by parts of the federal government other than USDA. Pesticide policy issues illustrate that tendency. While the Environmental Protection Agency has responsibilities concerning use of pesticides in agriculture, its role has often been muted by softer USDA positions defended by the agricultural chemical industry. A notable exception in recent years was the Clinton Administration's 1993 pledge to remove pesticides from the diets of infants and children (Henry A. Wallace Institute, 1993). In addition to encouraging greater education and monitoring of the risks of pesticides for infants and children, it proposed that, by the year 2000, "integrated pest management" practices should be used on 75 percent of the nation's farmland.

Federal interest did lead to the recent creation of a White House Council on Sustainable Development, which has since formed a Sustainable Agriculture Task Force. An initiative due perhaps more to the personal interests of Vice President Al Gore than to broader concerns of the federal establishment, its contribution has been largely window dressing. Moreover, White House leadership can be fleeting. Its interests are known to shift overnight in response to changing pressures or new national or international concerns. Despite those tendencies, USDA support for the sustainability of agriculture has been increasing. Lack of more tangible federal evidence is due mainly to the Department's organization and style, as well as to strong political ties to conventional agriculture.

USDA acts largely through separate conservation, environmental, production, and consumer-related programs administered by different parts of the Department headed by different leaders and scrutinized by different committees of the Congress. Moreover, many Department personnel are still accustomed to listening to spokespersons for traditional farm and commodity organizations, many of which remain skeptical of the implications of sustainable agriculture. USDA may not always agree with them, but it is more comfortable interacting with them than trying to understand and address the concerns of farm labor, low-income people, nonfarm residents of rural communities, and other groups with which it has had limited continuous contact.

Real or imagined pressure from the Congress can weaken USDA's resolve to reach out and expand its traditional ties. An important reason is the amount of time and effort USDA staff must spend responding to routine Congressional queries as to what the Department is doing, for whom, and why. Therefore, a sustainable agriculture mission at USDA, though not impossible, can at best be the result of administrative patchwork and genuine concerns and efforts of Departmental staff members.

Political pressure from established farm, commodity, and input industry organizations remains a deterrent. While the Campaign for Sustainable Agriculture is now a significant voice for sustainability in Washington, lobbyists for conventional agriculture organizations are still the dominant players with disproportionate resources and access to federal policymakers.

As a rule, USDA has been more open to sustainable agriculture when Democrats are in office. As an example, in 1979, Secretary of Agriculture Bob Bergland commissioned a major fact-finding study to identify critical problems and issues facing agriculture and rural America. He and Department staff talked openly about organic farming and what is now called sustainable agriculture. They asked questions. Findings published in a major report entitled *A Time to Choose: Summary Report on the Structure of Agriculture* showed that the Executive Branch can thoughtfully examine complex public problems and identify policies to alleviate them (USDA, 1981).

Toward a New Sustainable Agriculture Policy Approach

In view of the tendencies outlined above, a rethinking of the source, nature, and scope of public policies to support a sustainable agriculture seems essential. Instead of continuing to seek ways to alter conventional agriculture by amending current federal policies, a more promising approach could be to encourage local initiatives supported by state and local policies. A sustainable agriculture would be what people and their communities want it to be, and the role of policy would be to support its implementation.

The process of developing new and imaginative policies to support a sustainable agriculture would depend on the creation and nurturing of what is called "social capital" (Youngberg, 1995, p. 6; Campbell, 1997). A Harvard political scientist, Robert Putnam, refers to social capital as the "features of social organization, such as trust, norms, and networks, that can improve the efficiency of society by facilitating coordinated actions" (Putnam, 1993, p. 167). In effect, it expands opportunities for "civic engagement", which in turn can make possible group actions in support of a sustainable agriculture.

Flora (1995), has recently examined the relationship between social capital and the sustainability of agriculture, and amplifies this relationship elsewhere in this volume. She finds that, "A pattern of problem solving guided by norms of mutual trust and reciprocity is encouraged by the sustainable agriculture movement and the various organizations that give social expression to that movement, and this is what helps to nurture and build social capital within small, agriculturally dependent rural communities" (p. 2).

The concept of social capital, and the reconnecting of people it can make possible, suggests the possibility of a fundamental change in policy strategies to guide the quest for a sustainable agriculture. Instead of relying largely on federal policy actions, it points to the need for a shift toward policy actions at lower levels of government. By enhancing community involvement and cohesion, that shift could provide the basis for a strong, new, and meaningful commitment to the sustainability of agriculture and rural communities.

Fortunately, many projects and activities underway across the country can be regarded as laboratories testing new connections, and ultimately new policy approaches favorable to the sustainability of agriculture (Flora, 1995; Campbell, 1997; and Feenstra, 1997). Three projects illustrate the diversity and promise of these exciting developments:

The **Hartford Food System** is more than a downtown cooperative farmers' market supplying city dwellers with fresh produce and local farmers with a summertime marketing outlet. It provides low-income people using food stamps access to wholesome food. It offers participants numerous educational opportunities. In effect, while connecting urban consumers to farmers it is busy producing social capital.

The **Resource Conservation and Development Program** is a growing, nationwide network of 290 locally-oriented projects in over 2,016 counties, the Caribbean, and the Pacific Basin, whose purpose is to foster mutually beneficial ties between agriculture, natural resource conservation, environmental quality, and the well-being of rural people and their communities. With staff and financial support from the USDA, RC&D is a grassroots public-private partnership of people and organizations with highly diverse, but also common, interests. It seeks a balance between rural economic development and natural resource protection. In effect, it is creating the social capital to build a sustainable future.

The **Integrated Food and Farming Systems Initiative** of the W. K. Kellogg Foundation brings together people from dozens of private non-profit organizations around the country whose programs are concerned with food, farming, community well-being, conservation, and environmental protection (W. K. Kellogg Foundation). In collaboration with other networks, IFFS is developing a common ground and building mutually reinforcing support for the sustainability of agriculture. The Henry A. Wallace Institute for Alternative Agriculture has recently joined that network to launch a nationwide process for the purpose of developing a "vision" for a sustainable agriculture. Such a vision, it is hoped, will serve to guide the identification and understanding of public policies best able to support a sustainable agriculture.

In closing, the development of policies to support the sustainability of agriculture, at all levels of government, could benefit substantially from new and imaginative support from the nation's agricultural research and extension education system. A critical question for research is, what combinations of local, state, and federal policies can effectively nurture social capital and thereby foster the kinds of civic engagement that will best support sustainability. The challenge for extension education is to take those findings to the citizenry. Addressing those needs would be more than a relevant challenge. It could provide the research and extension system with an enormous opportunity to guide the shaping of an expanded and highly relevant meaning for the 21st century.

Notes

1. Sustainable agriculture, as the term is used here, refers to an agriculture that will continue indefinitely to produce abundant and wholesome food in socially desirable ways, will not degrade natural resources and the environment, will protect human health and safety, and be economically rewarding for farmers.

2.   Occasionally, however, state policies lead the way rather than simply supplement federal policy action. For example, the Iowa Groundwater Protection Act of 1987 undoubtedly served to encourage the federal government, as well as other states, to take such action.

References

Allen, P. 1993. "Connecting the social and the ecological in sustainable agriculture", in *Food for the Future*, Patricia Allen, ed., New York:John Wiley & Sons, pp. 1-16.

Berry, Wendell. 1977. *The unsettling of America: Culture and agriculture*. Sierra Club Books, San Francisco.

Breimyer, Harold F. 1992. "Current U. S. agricultural policy in historical perspective", in *U. S. Agricultural Policy: From Changes in Washington to Changes on the Farm*. Agricultural Experiment Station, University of Missouri, Columbia, Missouri. Spec. Rept. 446, pp. 5-10.

Browne, William P., Jerry R. Skees, Louis E. Swanson, Paul B. Thompson, and Laurian J. Unnevehr. 1992. *Sacred cows and hot potatoes*. Boulder, Colorado. Westview Press.

Butz, E. 1971. "Crisis or challenge". *Nation's Agriculture*: July-Aug., p. 19.

Campbell, Dave. 1997. "Community-controlled economic development as a strategic vision for the sustainable agriculture movement". *American Journal of Alternative Agriculture*. 12:1. pp. 37-44.

Doering, Otto. 1992. "Federal policies as incentives or disincentives to ecologically sustainable agricultural systems", in Richard K. Olson, ed., *Integrating sustainable agriculture, ecology, and environmental policy*. Food Products Press, Binghamton, N. Y. pp. 21-36.

Feenstra, Gail W. 1997. "Local food systems and sustainable communities". *American Journal of Alternative Agriculture*. 12:1. pp. 28-36.

Flora, C. B. 1995. "Social capital and sustainability: Agriculture and communities in the great plains and corn belt". *Research in Rural Sociology and Development: A Research Annual*. 6:227-246.

Gallagher, Stephanie. 1997. "Organic foods: Pricier, but safer?" *Kiplinger's Personal Finance Magazine*. July 1997, 81.

Hamilton, Neil D. 1994. "Agriculture without farmers? Is industrialization restructuring American food production and threatening the future of sustainable agriculture?" Drake University Law School, Agricultural Law Center. White paper 94-1. Feb.

Hassebrook, Chuck. 1996. "The 1996 farm bill: Impacts for rural America. pp. 95 - 96, Increasing Understanding of Public Problems and Policies". Farm Foundation, Chicago, Illinois.

Henry A. Wallace Institute for Alternative Agriculture. 1993. "Clinton administration confirms plans to reduce pesticide use". *Alternative Agriculture News*. Vol. 11. No. 10. Oct. p. 1.

Jackson, Wes. 1980. "New roots for agriculture". Friends of the Earth. San Francisco, California.

Merrigan, Kathleen, 1997. "Government pathways to true food security", in *Visions of American Agriculture,* William Lockeretz, ed. Iowa State University Press, Ames, 1997. Pp. 155-72.

Putnam, R. D., 1993. *Making democracy work: Civic traditions in modern Italy.* Princeton University Press, Princeton, N. J.

Ray, Daryll E. 1996. "The FAIR act: What does it mean? Increasing understanding of public problems and policies". Farm Foundation, Chicago, Illinois. pp. 75-94.

Rodale, Robert. 1983. "Breaking new ground: The search for a sustainable agriculture". *The Futurist* 1 (1). pp. 15-20.

Schaller, Neill. 1991. "Sustainable agriculture research and education in the field. A proceedings". National Research Council, Board on Agriculture. National Academy Press, Washington, D. C. pp. 22-31.

Schumacher, E. F. 1973. *Small is beautiful.* Harper and Row, Publishers, Inc., N.Y.

Soil Conservation Society of America. 1987. *Aldo Leopold. The man and his legacy.* Ankeny, Iowa.

Smith, Stewart. 1992. "Farming—It's declining in the U.S." *Choices.* 1st quarter, p.8.

U. S. Congress, 1981. "Agriculture and food act of 1981". *Public Law* 97-98. Washington, D.C.

U.S. Congress. 1985. "The food security act of 1985". *Public Law* 99-198. Washington, D.C.

U. S. Congress. 1990. "Food, agriculture, conservation and trade act of 1990". Public Law 101-624. Washington, D.C..

U. S. Department of Agriculture (USDA). 1981. "A time to choose: Summary report on the structure of agriculture". Washington, D. C. Jan.

U. S. Department of Agriculture (USDA). 1988. "Alternative farming systems. Secretary's memorandum". 9600-1, Jan. 19.

U. S. Department of Agriculture (USDA). 1997. National Agricultural Statistics Service. Telephone communication.

U. S. House of Representatives. 1982. "Organic farming act of 1982". H.R. 5618. 97th Congress. 2d session.

U. S. Senate. 1982. "Innovative farming act of 1982". S. 2485. 97th Congress. 2d session.

W. K. Kellogg Foundation. Undated brochure. "Integrated farming systems: Making changes for a strong agricultural future". Battle Creek, Michigan.

Welsh, Rick. 1996. "The industrial reorganization of U. S. agriculture". Henry A. Wallace Institute for Alternative Agriculture. Policy Studies Report No.

6. April.

Youngberg, Garth. 1978. "Alternative agriculturalists: Ideology, politics, and prospects", in D. F. Hadwiger and William P. Browne, eds. *The new politics of food*. Lexington Books, Lexington, Mass. pp. 227-246.

Youngberg, G. 1995. " Organic farming in U. S. agriculture: A Perspective on past and future contributions". Address. Oakland, Calif. October 11.

Youngberg, Garth, Neill Schaller, and Kathleen Merrigan. 1993. "The sustainable agriculture policy agenda in the United States: Politics and prospects", in *Food for the future*, Patricia Allen, ed. John Wiley & Sons, N. Y. pp. 295 - 318.

10 Sustainability and Land Use

Winfried E.H. Blum

Introduction

In the last decade, "ustainability" has become a key word in agricultural and rural development. However, a look into international literature reveals considerable differences in the interpretation and perception of the terms "land use" and "sustainability" (Blum and Santelises, 1994; Doran and Parkin, 1994; Faeth, 1993; Gardner *et al.*, 1995; Greenland and Szabolcs, 1994; Hillel, 1991a; Hodges and Scofield, 1983; Lal, 1994; MacRae *et al.*, 1989; and Warkentin, 1995).

Most scientists define "land use" as "agricultural land use", without taking into consideration the five main other uses of land, which competitively interact with agriculture in space and time. Therefore, in the following, an attempt will be made to define sustainable land use through a comprehensive approach, distinguishing between "sustainable land use" and "sustainable agricultural land use", thus defining new approaches in the conceptualization and perception of sustainability in agricultural and rural development on a strategic, tactical and operational level, including indicators for sustainable agricultural land use conditioned in the bounds of nature and future research targets.

At a high level of abstraction, the term sustainability aims at maintaining or even improving environmental, social and economic conditions for future generations and therefore includes environmental, technical, social, and economic dimensions, as well as the dimension of time, (World Commission on Environment and Development, 1987).

Under the aspect of land use, sustainability means using land and soil in such a way that the quality and multifunctionality of both is maintained or even improved, thus leaving options for future generations. However, on an operational level, it is impossible, to define sustainability without exactly defining the land use system (including its socio-economic dimensions) and the

171

time horizon for which sustainability is aimed. Therefore, it seems necessary to begin with the question, "What is land use?". The definition of land in this context is more comprehensive than soil and includes the aspects of topography (landscape), climate, biodiversity, and others.

The Six Main Uses of Land

A definition of land use based only on agriculture is incomplete, because at least five further types of land use interact competitively with agriculture in space and time. Therefore, land use is defined as the temporarily and spatially simultaneous use of at least six main functions of soil and land. Three of these functions are more ecological, three others more linked to human activities, defined as technical, industrial and socio-economic functions (Blum 1988, 1990, 1994a).

The three ecological functions are:

(1)   Production of biomass, ensuring food, fodder, renewable energy and raw materials; these well-known functions are the basis for the existence of human and animal life.

(2)   Filtering, buffering and transformation capacity between the atmosphere, the groundwater and the plant cover, protecting the environment, including human beings, against the contamination of groundwater and the food chain. This function becomes increasingly important because of the many solid, liquid or gaseous, inorganic or organic depositions on which soils react through mechanical filtration, physico-chemical absorption, and precipitation on its inner surfaces, or microbiological and biochemical mineralization and metabolization of organic compounds, as shown in Figure 1. The latter may also contribute to global changes through the emission of gases from the soil into the atmosphere (Rolston et al., 1993) (see dotted line in fig. 1), because globally, the total pool of organic carbon in soils is three times higher than the total organic carbon in the above-ground biomass and twice as high as the total organic carbon in the atmosphere (Eswaran et al., 1993). Therefore, soils are a central link in the biotransformation of organic carbon and continually play a role in releasing CO_2 and other trace gases into the atmosphere. These

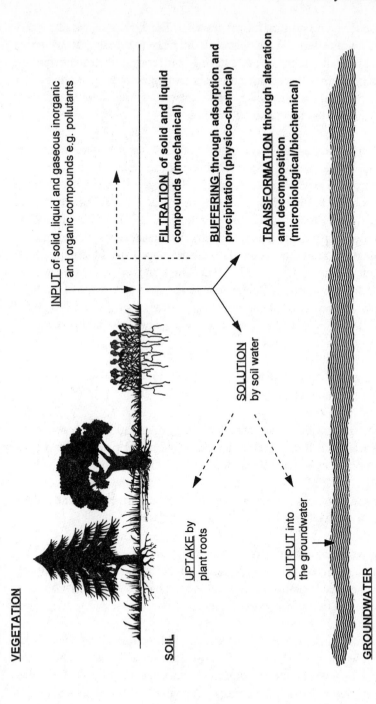

Figure 1   Soil as a filter, buffer and transformation system between atmosphere, biosphere and hydrosphere

gases are very important for processes of global change, which, in this case, involve large-scale feedback of many localized, small-scale processes. As long as the filtering, buffering and transformation capacities can be maintained, there is no danger to the groundwater or to the food chain. However, these capacities are limited, and vary according to individual soil conditions.

(3)   Biological habitat and gene reserve, with a large variety of organisms in and above the soil. Soils contain more species in number and quantity than all other biota together. Soil use is directly linked to the question of biodiversity (Constanza *et al.*, 1992; Kennedy and Papendick, 1995; Visser and Parkinson, 1992). Human life is extremely dependent on this biodiversity, considering for example, the fact that the antibiotic penicillin was developed from the penicillium fungus, ubiquitous in the soil. We do not know if we will need new genes for maintaining human life in the near or the remote future. Moreover, genes from the soil become increasingly important for many technical processes, especially biochemical, biotechnological and bioengineering ones.

In addition, soils also have three technical, industrial, and socio-economic functions and uses:

(4)   As a spatial base for technical, industrial and socio-economic structures and their development, e.g. industrial premises, housing, transport, sports, recreation, dumping of refuse and so forth.

(5)   As a source of raw materials (e.g., clay, sand, gravel, and minerals in general) as well as a source of energy and water.

(6)   As a geogenic and cultural heritage, forming an essential part of the landscape in which we live and concealing paleontological and archeological treasures of high value for the understanding of our own history and that of the earth (Hillel, 1991b).

Therefore, a definition of land use should include all these six main functions of land and soil, which we often use concomitantly in the same area.

Figure 2 shows the six functions and uses schematically. On this basis, land use can be defined as the temporarily or spatially simultaneous use of all

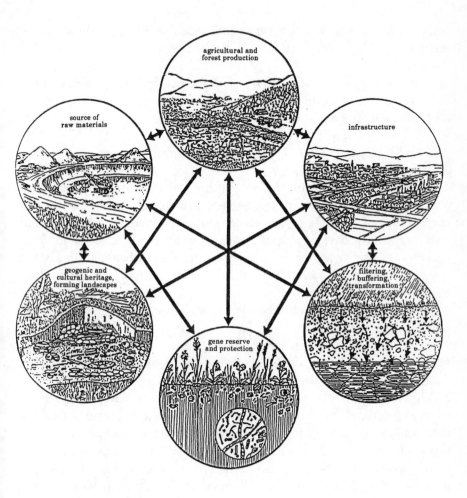

Figure 2   The six different functions of land and soil and the competition among them

these functions, although they are not always complementary in a given area. However, where specific conditions on a regional or local scale exist, this very broad and holistic definition can be reduced and adapted accordingly.

Interaction and Competition Between These Functions: A Definition of Sustainable Land Use.

To develop a comprehensive definition of sustainable land use, it seems necessary to define all the interactions and competitions which exist among these functions and their uses.

Three different categories of competition can be distinguished:

(i)   Exclusive competition exists between soil uses for infrastructure, as a source of raw materials and as a geogenic and cultural heritage on the one hand and soil uses for biomass production, filtering, buffering and transformation activities and as a gene reserve on the other hand. This becomes evident when soils are sealed through urban and industrial development, e.g. the construction of roads, of industrial premises, houses, sporting facilities or when soils are used for the dumping of refuse, all this being known as the process of urbanization and industrialization, excluding all other uses of land and soil.

The growth of urban population on a worldwide level as a measure of urbanization is shown in Table 1, demonstrating urban population increase from 1970 to 1990 on the different continents, and indicating that by 1990 South America had a higher degree of urbanization than Europe. Looking at the growth of the 35 largest cities (Blum, 1994b), we see that urbanization and industrialization have reached unprecedented levels and are continuing exponentially. Ninety percent of the increase of the global population occurs in developing countries and two-thirds of it is concentrated in urban agglomerations. Estimates of the United Nations indicate that, while in 1984, 34 metropolitan areas existed with populations higher than 5 million, in the year 2025 approximately 93 metropolitan areas of at least the same size have to be expected. A very striking example of this development is Egypt, which has all big urban agglomerations on its 3.8 percent of fertile land, in the southern Nile River valley and its delta, close to the Mediterranean Sea. It is also known that all these agglomerations are still spreading further into this fertile land, a fact that underlines the problem of sealing as an irreversible loss

Table 1. Increase of urban populations from 1970-1990

Area	1970 percent	1990 percent
Europe	67	73
South America	60	76
North America	58	71
Africa	23	34
Asia	24	29
World	37	43

Source: United Nations Environmental Data Report, 1991/1992.

of soil multifunctionality.

(ii)   A second category of competition exists through intensive interactions between infrastructural land uses and their development, and agriculture and forestry. Figure 3 shows roads and settlements in southern Germany. The scale indicates the density of this technical infrastructure, which significantly contributes to the problem of soil contamination and pollution.

These linear and point sources are loading local soils with contaminants on three different pathways: through atmospheric deposition, on waterways and through terrestrial transport. This illustrates the many possible interactions between infrastructural land use on the one hand and agriculture and forestry on the other hand. This is especially true for densely populated areas in developing countries, which grow about ten times faster than those in the northern hemisphere. The main issue is the capacity of the biota - and of human beings - to withstand these increasing loads, which - with very few exceptions - are still increasing every day (Blum, 1994 b). In this context, it also seems necessary to point out that soils are the last but one sink for many inorganic and organic depositions, the last one being the bottom of the ocean.

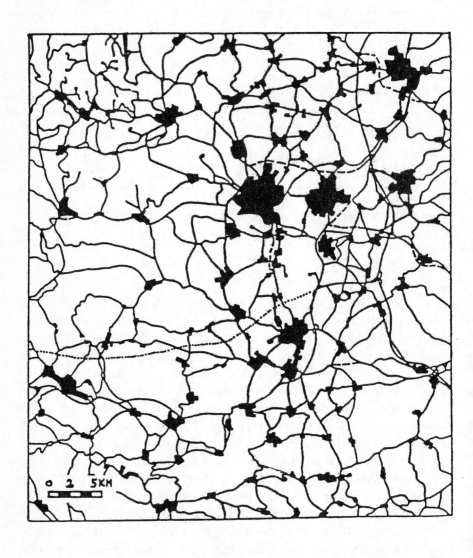

Figure 3   **Sealing of soils and landscapes by settlements and roads, Southern Germany (Blum and Schröder, 1992)**

In Figure 4, different forms of loads can be distinguished: inorganic and organic deposition from traffic and transport, as well as those from industrial and urban activities. Most of these loads, such as, severe acidification, pollution by heavy metals and other elements, pollution by xenobiotic organic compounds, deposition of non-soil materials, severe salinization, and alcalinization are more or less irreversible, because soils act as a sink (Blum, 1992). Irreversibility is defined as the non-reversibility by natural forces or technical remediation measures within 100 years, which corresponds to about four human generations. Only few processes of soil degradation, such as compaction or contamination by biodegradable organics or by small amounts of heavy metals can be regarded as reversible by technical measures or natural remediation, e.g. bioturbation and bio-accumulation processes.

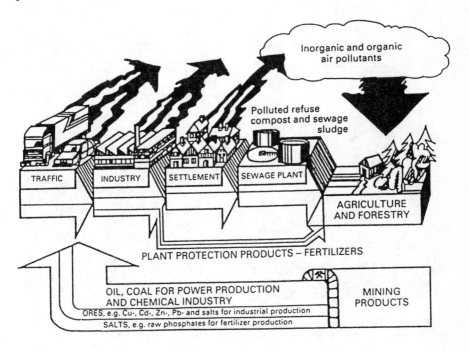

Figure 4   **Soil pollution by heavy metals through excessive use of fossil energy and raw materials (Blum, 1988)**

(iii)   A third form of competition also exists among the three ecological soil uses themselves, as shown in Figure 5. Waste and sewage sludge deposition on soils, as well as intensive use of fertilizers and plant protection products, in addition to the deposition of air pollutants (see Figure 4), may have a negative influence on groundwater or the food chain, surpassing the natural capacity of soils for mechanical filtering, chemical buffering and biochemical transformation (compare Figure 1 and see CAST, 1992; National Research Council, 1993 a, b) . This has to be taken into account when implementing or using high input agricultural systems. In this context, it should be remembered that agriculture and forestry not only produce biomass above the ground, but also influence the quality and quantity of the groundwater production underneath, because each drop of rain, falling on the land, has to pass the soil before it becomes groundwater.

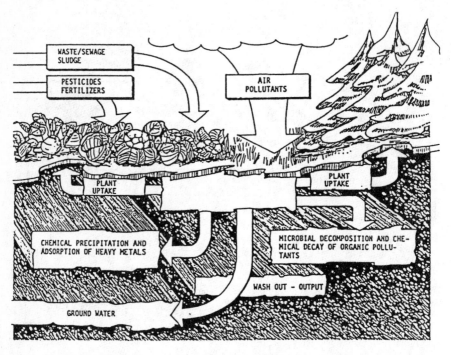

Figure 5   Competition between biomass and groundwater production, due to pollutive depositions and the use of fertilizers and plant protection products

When the groundwater is used as drinking water, the competition between the production of food on one side and the production of groundwater on the other side is a competition between the satisfaction of basic human needs. In some areas of the world, especially in Central Europe, conventional agricultural production becomes increasingly controlled by quality standards for drinking water. It is easier to transport and sell food and fodder than to do the same with the necessary amount of drinking and household water. Moreover, through erosion of agricultural soils environmental and economic damage may occur (Duda, 1985).

Based on these facts, sustainable land use can be defined as the spatial (local or regional) and temporal harmonization of all six soil functions, through minimizing irreversible uses, e.g. sealing, excavation, sedimentation, acidification, contamination or pollution, salinization and others. This definition includes the dimensions of space and time. Therefore, the harmonization of soil functions is not only a scientific question, but also a political one, which means that all people living in a given area or space have to decide which soil functions they may use at a given time. Scientists only have the possibility to develop scenarios and to explain which causes and impacts may occur when different options are exercised. One important conclusion that can be drawn from this is that the maintenance of soil multifunctionality is a precondition for the welfare of future generations.

Conclusions for the Definition of Sustainable Agricultural Land Use

The general definition of sustainable land use given above, shows clearly that agricultural land use is only one of several possible land uses and therefore depends on all other uses in a given area or region. Thus, sustainable agricultural land use is only possible when all the other land uses are sustainable as well. This means that an intensive linkage exists between sustainable agricultural use and the sustainability of all other possible uses of soil and land.

When determining the sustainability of agricultural land use we must also take into account that socio-economic factors exist, which in many cases are more important than ecological considerations. Whereas ecological factors should be defined on a local scale, regarding specific topographical, climatic, physical, chemical, biological, and other conditions of terrestrial ecosystems, especially soils, socio-economic factors are determined on a regional or even global basis. They are governed by market conditions, terms of tariffs and trade (e.g. the General Agreement on Tariffs and Trade, GATT), and are in many cases reflected by the cost of energy, raw material and labour. Often, these are the predominant factors for conventional agricultural systems. Ecological factors on the one hand and socio-economic and cultural ones on the other hand, should be clearly differentiated and not mixed up.

However, the question is, if and how indicators for sustainable agricultural land use can be defined.

Indicators of Sustainable Agricultural Land Use

Indicators of sustainable agricultural land use can be ecological ones as well as socio-economic and cultural ones (Blum, 1994a; and Hamblin, 1991).

The ecological indicators are mostly of a physical, chemical and biological nature, and should be based on the farm or local level (except for the exchange of gases, which is difficult to control on such a scale). Such indicators could be:

(1)   Soil characteristics, including products which pass through the soil into the groundwater (nutrients, pesticides, heavy metals etc.), or products which are produced above the soil, such as food, fodder, renewable energy and gases. This means that the solid, liquid and gaseous phases of soil must be controlled. Such an approach inevitably leads to the definition of soil quality or soil health (Acton and Gregorich, 1995; Constanza et al., 1992; Doran and Parkin, 1994; Doran and Jones, 1996; Doran et al., 1996; Karlen et al,. 1997; Larson and Pierce, 1994; and Papendick and Par, 1992).

(2)   Socio-economic and cultural indicators reflect two groups: one that is defined in terms of geopolitical interests at the regional or even global levels, such as terms of tariffs and trade, market conditions, costs of labour, cost of energy and raw materials, and another one that is instead defined on a farm or local level, such as cultural conditions, including education and training systems. The health conditions of the local population can also be included in this category (Blum, 1994a).

Using these two main groups of indicators, it is possible to establish a systematic approach for the definition of sustainability within a given agricultural area or region. However, according to the intensity of the use of fossil energy and raw materials, two different categories of agricultural production systems should be distinguished: low and high input systems. The indicators for both systems have to be chosen differently.

When checking ecological as well as socio-economic and cultural indicators on this basis, it becomes clear that ecological or biological indicators such as human health, species diversity or others may have different indicative values. Human health may be a very good indictor for sustainability in low input systems, because the condition of health and nutrition indicates how well basic needs such as food and water for the local population are satisfied at a farm or local level. However, under high input systems, such as those in Europe, North America or parts of Asia, South America and Australia, human health cannot be used as an indicator, because the satisfaction of basic needs, especially food, does not depend on local farming conditions but on trade and other socio-economic conditions. Species diversity, on the other hand, is a good indicator for both high and low input systems.

Therefore, the definition of indicators can only be based on their prevailing functions within a given agricultural production system. This also means that terms such as "soil health" or "soil quality" have to be specified according to the prevailing land uses, before they can be used as indicators. In general, soil characteristics should always be analyzed on the basis of their specific role in the controlling processes within a given agricultural land use system (Acton, 1993).

The question then arises, as to which soil functions dominate in a given situation. For example, soil can be analyzed in relation to very diverse functions, e.g. the production of biomass. In this case, soil functions that are important for the availability of water, air and nutrients are indicative. Soil can also be analyzed as a filtering, buffering or transforming substrate, protecting the groundwater or the food chain against contamination or pollution. In this case, totally different soil parameters should be analyzed, e.g. other soil depths, etc. Moreover, soil can be analyzed in its function as a biological habitat or gene reserve, which means that still other soil characteristics should be measured for indication purposes (Swift, 1994).

The use of physical, chemical and biological threshold values for soils, is only possible for specific local or site conditions. Threshold values for soils, applied to regional or global levels are ecologically meaningless. For example with regard to groundwater contamination, a gravely or sandy soil with low humus content cannot have the same threshold values for nitrogen turnover as a clay-loam soil, rich in organic matter, because both soil systems are functionally and therefore ecologically very different. On the other hand, threshold values on a regional or even continental scale can have intensive political impacts, in the sense of controlling and regulating.

When using indicators for the analysis or assessment of sustainability, it seems necessary to carefully check the overall system for which they should be analyzed. For example, considering the costs, time and infrastructural requirements which would be needed for the analysis of soil parameters and considering that many of them cannot be monitored so exactly as to indicate short-time changes, it may be necessary to consider material fluxes as potential indicators, instead.

Under certain circumstances, the assessment or analysis of material fluxes or loads using input/output models, can provide more useful information than using direct but costly measurements of specific parameters of an ecosystem or a soil. Such approaches have been successfully explored (Baccini and von Steiger, 1993). Several existing models in soil ecology allow us to predict impacts on soil systems through adverse material fluxes or loads, and this can help us to define sensitive indicators when needed (Bouma, 1989).

In many areas of the world, data bases for the definition of sustainable land management are already available. Therefore, new research priorities should only be defined after careful evaluation of already existing data. For the analysis and development of sustainable and agricultural land management systems, more use of existing soil information in the form of soil maps or soil data from geographical information systems is necessary (Bouma, 1989; and Kellogg, 1955).

System analyses at the local, regional or global levels have very different goals and are not always compatible, because the reliability of data differs enormously in scale and time. The output of such analyses has to be carefully checked.

Approaches for Sustainable Agricultural Land Use at the Strategic, Tactical and Operational Levels

New approaches towards sustainable agricultural land use can be achieved at either a strategic, tactical, or an operational level.

Strategic Level

Definition of constraints

When defining constraints for sustainable agricultural land use, urbanization and industrialization (including transport and the deposition of refuse material) are of great importance in many countries. In developing countries, urbanization and industrialization are progressing ten times faster than in industrial regions, and have reached such a magnitude that serious problems in agricultural areas can be observed.

Another problem is the extension of agricultural land through deforestation and other measures, and its influence on the protection of the remaining natural ecosystems. Recent data indicate that there are nearly no land reserves left for the extension of agricultural cropping or pasture land at the worldwide level, with very few exceptions, e.g. the Cerrado-areas in South America (Oldeman, 1994). Any further extension would lead to the irreversible destruction of the still remaining and more or less intact terrestrial and aquatic ecosystems, especially soils. This clearly shows that an increase in food production will only be possible by intensification on existing surfaces, which, as outlined above, diminish constantly, as revealed by recent research on human induced soil degradation, based on the worldwide GLASOD inventory (Oldeman, 1994).

Moreover, in many agricultural regions of the world, competition between the production of food, fodder and renewable energy on one hand and the production of groundwater and drinking water on the other hand exists. Therefore, primary goals have to be established, in order to maintain an equilibrium in the satisfaction of basic needs.

Definition of Procedures, Based on the Essential Governing Principles of the Biosphere

Long-term requirements for sustainable agricultural land management are conditioned on the bounds of nature and can be summarized as the essential governing principles of the biosphere, which should be considered when defining the framework for different sustainable agricultural land use systems. These important principles for sustainable land management, which are conditioned by nature, are:

- Solar orientation, reducing entropy;

- Closed cycle production and the use of energy in cascades, thus minimizing entropy production;

- Maximizing variety, which means maintenance of the greatest possible variety of species in and upon the soil (biodiversity), thus allowing a maximum of biological and technical options;

- Networking of decentralized systems, for enhancing ecological stability.

These governing principles should be taken into account when analyzing or assessing sustainable land management systems. It must be emphasized that this is a utopia, and that in most cases we are far away from those optimum conditions. Nevertheless, the targets of entropy reduction, minimization of entropy production, and increase of ecological stability can only be reached on the basis of these principles (see also Hendrix, 1987; Jackson and Piper, 1989; and National Research Council, 1989).

Tactical Level

Whereas the strategic level is aiming at a large scale approach, the tactical level deals with regional constraints. At this level, ecological, socio-economic and technical constraints have to be considered.

Ecological Constraints

Ecological constraints for sustainable food production are the limited soil surface and the constant loss of soils through soil destruction, especially erosion by water and wind, salinization and acalinization, acidification, and pollution by inorganic and organic compounds. This means that the conservation and maintenance of soil quality is one of the most important targets for sustainable agricultural land use (Sanders, 1992).

Socio-Economic and Technical Constraints:

Under this aspect, in many countries a lack of administrative and technical infrastructure can be observed, especially in countries in development, where administrative and technical support to farmers is in many cases strongly underdeveloped. The same is true for legal instruments protecting landscapes and soils or the promotion and stimulation of agricultural production through incentives.

Operational Level

Operative procedures have to focus on local or site conditions. Under such conditions, different constraints can be identified. One of them is the lack of information, e.g., because of insufficient extension services. In other areas labour is becoming scarce, e.g., through "brain drain" to urban agglomerations, which means that certain forms of alternative agriculture cannot be put into practice (Pawluk *et al.*, 1992). This and further constraints at an operative level have to be recognized. If they are not solved, such problems are generally not caused by scientific reasons, but by administrative and economic ones (Roming *et al.*, 1995).

Possible Research Targets for the Promotion of Sustainable Agricultural Land Use

A comparison of the above mentioned concept with the actual state of knowledge, reveals some targets for future research:

- Definition of criteria for sustainable agricultural production systems for local or regional ecological units, on the basis of the governing principles of biological systems.

- Development of criteria for the definition of ecologically stable and harmonic landscapes (see also Constanza *et al.*, 1997; and Pierzynski *et al.*, 1994).

- Assessment of ecologically tolerable bearing capacities of landscapes, in view of the competition from other forms of land use (see also Olson, 1981).

- Definition of crucial links between agricultural and other socio-economic and technical production systems, especially industrial ones.

Conclusions

In the 21st century, agricultural land use will occur under quite different ecological, technical and socio-economic conditions than in the centuries before. This is not only due to increasing competition for space, for example, through the still exponential growth of urbanization and industrialization, with all its socio-economic and environmental problems, especially in developing countries, but also through increasing and severe competition between biomass production on one side, and groundwater production on the other side, including problems of biodiversity and global change, e.g. through the emission of gases from agricultural areas into the atmosphere.

In many countries of the world, land surfaces for agricultural production are decreasing, due to severe soil deterioration and the loss of soil quality, which means that in the future, sustainability in agricultural land use has to be reached on increasingly reduced areas and will only meet the challenge of sufficient production by intensification. For the increase of productivity and efficiency, increasing support form renewable sources of energy will be needed, in order to avoid and reduce the existing environmental problems caused by the use of fossil energy and raw materials.

In general, a more holistic approach to sustainable land use is needed, including ecological, socio-economic and technological aspects, thus enabling science to develop more comprehensive scenarios for sustainable development.

References

Acton, D.F.1993. "A Program To Assess and Monitor Soil Quality in Canada: Soil Quality Evaluation Program Summary (Interim)". Centre for Land and Biological Resources Res. Contr. No.93-49, Research Branch, Agriculture Canada, Ottawa.

Acton, D.F., and Gregorich, L.J. 1995. "The Health of Our Soils: Toward Sustainable Agriculture in Canada". Agric. Agri-food Can., CDR Unit, Ottawa, Canada.

Baccini, P. and B. von Steiger.1993. Die Stoffbilanzierung landwirtschaftlicher Böden. Eine Methode zur Früherkennung von Bodenveränderungen. Z. Pflanzenernähr.Bodenk.156:45-54.

Blum, W.E.H.1988. "Problems of Soil Conservation". Nature and Environment series No. 33. Council of Europe, Strasbourg, France.

Blum, W.E.H. 1990. "The challenge of soil protection in Europe". *Environmental Conservation* 17:72-74.

Blum, W.E.H. and D. Schroeder, 1992. *Bodenkunde in Stichworten* (5th Ed.) Hirt-Borntraeger, Stuttgart.

Blum, W.E.H. 1992. "Treating Toxic Ground". CERES 24:42-44.

Blum, W.E.H. and A. Aguilar Santelises. 1994. "A concept of sustainability and resilience based on soil functions". p. 535-542, in D.J. Greenland and I.

Szabolcs, ed. *Soil resilience and sustainable land use*. CAB Inter. Wallingford, Oxon, UK.

Blum, W.E.H. 1994a. "Sustainable Land Management with Regard to Socioeconomic and Environmental Soil Functions - a Holistic Approach", in Wood R.C. and J. Dumanski, eds. Proceedings of the International Workshop on Sustainable Land Management for the 21st Century, Vol.2: Plenary Papers, 115-124. Agricultural Institute of Canada, Ottawa.

Blum, W.E.H. 1994b. "Sustainable Land Use for Sustainable Food Production in Africa". Proceedings of a Seminar on the Role of Science in Food Production in Africa, Accra/Ghana, p. 92-107, COSTED-IBN, Madras, India.

Bouma,J. 1989. "Using soil survey data for quantitative land evaluation". *Adv. Soil Sci.* 9:177-213.

CAST. 1992. "Water Quality: Agriculture's Role". Task Force Report No. 120. Council for Agricultural Science and Technology, Ames. IA.

Constanza, R.,R. d'Arge. R. de Groot, S. Farber, M. Grasso, B. Hannon, K. Limburg, S. Naeem, R.V. O'Neill, J. Paruelo, R.G. Raskin, P. Sutton and M. van den Belt. 1997. "The value of the world's ecosystem services and natural capital". *Nature* 387:253-259.

Constanza, R., Norton, B.G., and Haskell, B.D. 1992. *Ecosystem Health: New Goals for Environmental Management*. Island Press, Washington, DC.

Doran, J.W. and A.J. Jones, eds. 1996. *Methods for Assessing Soil Quality*. SSSA Special Publication No. 49, Madison, Wisconsin, USA.

Doran, J.W., and Parkin, T.B. 1994. "Defining and assessing soil quality", in *Defining Soil Quality for a Sustainable Environment*, J.W. Doran, D.C. Coleman, D.F. Bezdicek, and B.A. Stewart, eds. pp. 3-21. Soil Sci.Soc.Am.Spec. Publ.No.35, Madison, WI.

Doran, J.W. M. Sarrantonio, and M.A. Liebig. 1996. "Soil health and sustainability", *Adv. Agron*, 56: 1-54.

Duda, A.M. 1985. "Environmental and economic damage caused by sediment from agricultural nonpoint sources". *Water Res. Bull.* 21:225-234.

Eswaren, H. E. van den Berg and P. Reich. 1993. "Organic carbon in soils of the world". *Soil Sci.Soc. Am.J.* 57:192-194.

Feath, P. 1993. "Evaluating agricultural policy and the sustainability of production system: An economic framework". *J. Soil Water Conserv.* 48:94-99.

Gardner, J.C., Jamtgaard, K., and Kirschenmann, F. 1995. "What is sustainable agriculture?", in *Planting the Future: Developing an Agriculture that Sustains the Land and Community*, A.R. Bird. G.L. Bultena, and J.C. Gardner, eds., pp, 45-65. Iowa State Univ. Press, Ames, IA.

Greenland, D.J. and I. Szabolcs eds. 1994. *Soil Resilience and Sustainable Land Use*. CAB Inter. , Wallingford, Oxon, UK.

Hamblin, A. 1991. "Environmental indicators for sustainable agriculture". Report of a national workshop. Bureau of Rural Resources, Land and Water Resource Research and Development Corporation and Grains Research and

Development Corporation, Canberra.

Hendrix, P.F. 1987. "Strategies for research and management in reduced - input agroecosystems". *Am.J. Alternative Agric.* 2:166 - 172.

Hillel, D.J.1991a. *Out of the Earth: Soil and the Sustainability of Civilization.*The Free Press, New York.

Hillel, D. 1991b. *Out of the earth: Civilization and the life of the soil.* Univ.of California Press, Los Angeles.

Hodges, R.D. and Scofield, A.M. 1983. "Effect of agricultural practices on the health of plants and animals produced: A review", in *Environmentally Sound Agriculture*, W. Lockeretz, ed., pp. 3-33, Praeger, New York.

Jackson, W. and J. Piper. 1989. "The necessary marrige between ecology and agriculture". *Ecology* 70:1591 - 1593.

Karlen, D.L., M.J. Mansbach, J.W. Doran, R.G.Cline, R.F. Harris and G.E. Schuman. 1997. "Soil Quality: A Concept, Definition and Framework for Evaluation". *Soil Sci.Soc. Am.J.* 61, 4-10.

Kellogg, C.E. 1955. "Soil surveys in modern farming". *J. Soil Water Conserv.* 10:271-277.

Kennedy, A.C. and Papendick, R.I.1995. "Microbial characteristics of soil quality". *J. Soil Water Conserv.* 50:243-248.

Lal, R. 1994. "Sustainable land use systems and soil resilience", in *Soil Resilience and Sustainable Land Use*, D.J. Greenland and I. Szabolcs, eds., pp. 41-67. CAB Inter., Wallingford, Oxon, UK.

Larson, W.E., and Pierce, F.J. 1994. "The dynamics of soil quality as a measure of sustainable management", in *Defining Soil Quality for a Sustainable Environment*, J.W. Doran, D.C. Coleman, D.F.Bezdicek, and B.A. Stewart, eds., pp.37-51. Soil Sci.Soc.Am.Spec. Publ. 35, Madison, WI.

MacRae, R.J., Hill, S.B., Henning, J., and Mehuys, G.R. 1989. "Agricultural science and sustainable agriculture: A review of the existing scientific barriers to sustainable food production and potential solutions". *Biol. Agric. Hort.*6, 173-219.

National Research Council. 1989. *Alternative Agriculture: Committee on the Role of Alternative Farming Methods in Modern Production Agriculture*. National Academic Press, Washington, DC.

National Research Council. 1993a. *Soil and Water Quality: An Agenda for Agriculture*. National Academy Press, Washington, DC.

National Research Council. 1993b. *Ground Water Vulnerability Assessment: Predicting Relative Contamination Potential Under Conditions of Uncertainty*. National Academy Press, Washington, DC.

Oldeman, L.R. 1994. "The global extent of soil degradation", in *Soil Resilience and Sustainable Land Use*, D.J. Greenland and I. Szabolcs, eds., pp. 99-118. CAB Inter., Wallingford, Oxon, UK.

Olson, G.E. 1981. "Archaeology: Lessons on future soil use". *J. Soil Water Conserv.* 36:261-264.

Papendick, R.I. and Parr, J.F. 1992. "Soil quality—the key to a sustainable agriculture", *Am.J. Alternative Agric.* 7:2-3.

Pawluk, R.R., Sandor, J.A. , and Tabor, J.A. 1992. "The role of indigenous knowledge in agricultural development". *J. Soil Water Conserv.* 47:298-302.

Pierzynski, G.M. Sims, J.T. and Vance, G.F. 1994. *Soils and Environmental Quality.* Lewis/CRC Press, Boca Raton, FL.

Rodale, R. 1984. "Alternative agriculture". *J. Soil Water Conserv.* 39:294-296.

Rolston, D.E., Harper, L.A., Mosier, A.R., and Duxbury, A.R. 1993. "Agricultural Ecosystem Effects on Trace Gases and Global Climate Change". Am. Soc. Agronomy Spec. Publ. 55, Madison, WI.

Roming, D.E., M.J. Garlynd, R.F. Harris, and K. McSweeney. 1995. "How farmers assess soil health and quality". *J. Soil Water Conserv.* 50:229-236.

Sanders, D.W. 1992. "International activities in assessing and monitoring soil degradation". *Am. J. Alternative Agric.* 7:17-24.

Swift, M.J. 1994. "Maintaining the biological status of soil: A key to sustainable land management"?, in *Soil Resilience and Sustainable Land Use*, D.J. Greenland and I. Szabolcs, eds., pp 235-247. CAB Inter., Wallingford, Oxon, UK.

Visser, S., and Parkinson, D. 1992. "Soil biological criteria as indicators of soil quality: Soil microorganisms". *Am.J. Alternative Agric.* 7:33-37.

Warkentin, B.P. 1995. "The changing concept of soil quality". *J. Soil Water Conserv.* 50:226-228.

World Commission on Environment and Development. 1987. *Our Common Future.* Oxford Univ. Press, New York.

11 Sustainability and Information

David Zilberman and Leslie Lipper

Introduction

There are several alternative and sometimes conflicting interpretations of sustainable resource development (Batie, 1989). This diversity of interpretation can actually be beneficial, as it leads to the development of a broad spectrum of research on achieving sustainable management systems (Ruttan, 1994). Our interpretation of sustainable resource development is based upon an economic perspective - defining sustainability as the pursuit of economic development through the preservation and improvement of environmental quality and natural resources. Technological, as well as institutional innovations are necessary to achieve the twin goals of economic and environmental improvement implied by this definition.

Unsustainable resource use patterns occur primarily because of poor management, rather than a lack of technology or resources. A major cause of poor management is the inefficient provision and utilization of information. In this chapter, we address several manifestations of this problem. First, we will argue that lack of interaction between scientific disciplines which address environmental and resource problems results in research with limited practical applications, as relevant biological and physical information is not incorporated into economics and basic economic concepts are not incorporated into the decision rules of biological and physical scientists. We also argue that there is an undervaluation, and hence underutilization, of information which is not "science" based. The current research establishment does not take advantage of field-generated and indigenous sources of knowledge which could enhance research products.

Next, we will address one of the key sources of environmental damage, which is the accumulation of residues and waste products. We will argue that precision technologies which are information intensive and adjust to heterogeneity and randomness can provide outcomes which display increased productivity and decreased pollution at the same time. We proceed to describe ways in which existing institutions and policies work against the adoption of these technologies, and follow with a discussion on how incentives may be created to encourage adoption, taking into account informational constraints.

Another major source of environmental degradation is the mismanagement of common pool resources. Here we distinguish between local and global common pool resources. Information plays a major role in the design of institutions which can efficiently manage these resources. We argue that information sharing between local and regional or national managers may be a key component in attaining a socially optimal solution. In the case of global commons, monitoring and knowledge are the keys to attaining sustainable resource management.

Information and Scientific Research

Designing sustainable resource management policies is a major challenge for modern science, including both the natural and social sciences. Research in these fields provides an important knowledge base upon which practitioners and policy-makers rely. However, limitations in the practice of scientific research have negatively impacted the effectiveness of the solutions provided. In this section, we break these limitations into three categories: (a) the lack of economic literacy among policymakers and scientists; (b) the underutilization of information from biological and physical sciences in economic research; and (c) the lack of integration of field generated and indigenous knowledge into science research agendas.

Economic Literacy and Bad Policy

Developing policies and institutions for sustainability requires the use of economic information in order to understand and respond to the incentives and constraints of economic agents in their interactions with the environment. However, until now economics has not played a major role in shaping environmental and resource policies. In most countries, the prevalent environmental policy-making approach has been "command and control", where regulations rather than economic incentives are used to achieve policy goals, and often at the loss of significant social benefits. Economic analysis is often absent in the setting of environmental standards as well. Little consideration of the marginal social costs relative to social benefits is given when setting environmental and health risk standards in most cases. Frequently however, the marginal costs of eliminating risks rise steeply as risks approach zero, so societies may be significantly better off if policies allowed a small amount of risk.

A major reason for the underutilization of economic information in shaping environmental policies is the lack of economic literacy among policy makers - as well as the general public. An introduction to the basics of economic analysis should be an essential element of the educational curricula - particularly for natural scientists who often become environmental policy-makers. Economics educators need to develop appropriate educational programs for these students, as most economics classes at the college level underemphasize basic concepts which are essential for practical decision making and policy analysis. Introductory economics classes which provide useful information on applied economic analysis for scientists should aim to instill in students an understanding of basic economic tools and their role in private and public decision making.

The Scarcity of Ecological Information in Economic Research

A major source of new economic information is theoretical and applied research. Unfortunately, despite the increasingly sophisticated means of analysis which have been developed, much of the current economic research analysis lacks applicability to the practical problems being faced by society. Much of the recent literature of environmental and agricultural economics has been quite abstract, emphasizing fine points of strategic behavior while often excluding essential features of natural systems.

To be useful and relevant, economic models which address problems of agricultural, natural resource and environmental management must incorporate basic scientific rules and the stylized features of technologies applicable to these systems. In order to achieve this, a great deal more interdisciplinary work among economists and natural scientists is necessary. For example, the incorporation of the work of soil and water scientists on material balance relationships as part of the system of equations depicting the behavior of an irrigated farming system enables us to recognize and analyze the economics of input residues which have significant effects on environmental quality. Similarly, an explicit analysis of the nature of the substitutability among technological choices in agricultural input applications needs to enter economic modeling. The incorporation of physical and biological processes into economic models will also result in a much more sophisticated ability to recognize and account for the heterogeneity of agricultural production and ecological systems, and thus more realistic and useful information.

The Under-utilization of Field-generated and Indigenous Knowledge

In addition to research-generated knowledge, knowledge which is generated through field-based experiences or which has been developed by indigenous groups over time, is another major source of new information. One of the biggest challenges facing the scientific community today is the development of an information base which includes indigenous and field-generated knowledge, as well as research-derived knowledge. Scientists from all disciplines can learn from traditional technologies and institutional solutions, just as biologists and geologists access ecosystems and geosystems for new valuable materials. Feedback from field-based practitioners provides important information on the behavior of natural and social systems, which could improve the realism of models generated through research. Accessing this source of knowledge will provide useful information on a wide range of topics of interest to researchers, including the discovery of new technologies and institutional arrangements, as well as the behavior of known technologies and institutions under varying circumstances.

There is a need to devise a system where significant developments in technological or institutional innovations are reported, communicated, and documented in a manner which will make information widely available. To achieve this reality, it is crucial that field-based practitioners actively contribute to the evolution of a global information system by documenting their experience. We can conceptualize the benefits from this sort of information-sharing system by utilizing one of the most powerful concepts in modern welfare economics: network externalities. The example of telephone networks can illuminate this concept. For each additional telephone added to an existing system, marginal benefits are generated. These include the benefits both to the owner of this telephone for the information he receives and the communication activities he conducts as well as to other members of society which arise from the ability to communicate with the newly connected person. This second component of benefits represents the network externality of this new telephone. Tremendous network externalities can be generated with the expansion of modern global communication networks and the provision of basic educational and communication skills to all members of the human race.

A Microlevel Perspective on Production, Information, and the Environment

An essential avenue for economic growth with limited environmental side effects is through the development and adoption of new technologies. Existing or imminently available technologies which are information intensive and require investment in equipment and training are capable of increasing yields while decreasing environmental side effects (tradeoffs that are addressed in greater detail in Chapter 4). However, the technologies currently used in the field do not take full advantage of the entire range of available technologies. Changes in incentives and higher levels of investment into research and development will promote the widespread adoption of these technologies. We will refer to these technologies as precision technologies and in this section will present an analysis of their properties, and the associated environmental, economic and informational implications.

Input Residue Accumulation and Precision Technology Adoption

A major source of environmental degradation related to agricultural production can be understood in terms of material-balance relationships, where excessive applications of production inputs accumulate in soils and water resulting in serious environmental damage. Excessive input applications occur because the technologies traditionally used for application have two major flaws: they fail to adjust to spatial or temporal variability and they result in leakages because some of the applied input is not consumed by the crop. In many situations, the most effective way to address these problems is the adoption of precision farming, which consists of a package of technologies that allow producers to adjust production choices in response to spatial or temporal variability, or which increase input use efficiency. The term, precision agriculture, can be interpreted generically, as we do here, to include a wide array of technologies such as modern irrigation technologies (sprinkler and drip irrigation), integrated pest management techniques, and low-level and precision pesticide applications. Precision agriculture may also be interpreted in a narrow sense as that which is commercially referred to as "precision agriculture" technologies, including geographic positioning system (GPS) devices, yield monitors, and technologies that rely on remote sensing. Precision farming techniques are usually information intensive relative to traditional technologies. In the following section we discuss the relationship between agricultural pollution and precision technology adoption and the role information plays in this process.

As the cost of data collection and analysis declines and the ability of science to address complexities increases, scientists are increasingly capable of recognizing variability within systems that were previously treated as homogenous. Our increased understanding of complex systems has lead to the development of new technologies and policies. For example, until recently, many of the studies conducted on the economics of farming sought optimal solutions at the field level, e.g., which crops to grow, how much input per acre to apply, etc. Improved monitoring technologies have allowed for the identification of heterogeneity within plots and fields, as well as the recognition of the suboptimality of uniform input application when spatial heterogeneity exists. Spatial variability includes the differences in fertility and waterholding capacity which occur at the sub-field level and which arise due to variations in the rate of chemical decomposition, topography and soil texture. Precision agriculture technologies adjust input use levels in response to these varying conditions. Similarly, precision technologies allow producers greater responsiveness to random events which occur over time, in comparison with traditional farming practices, which often involve rigid input application schedules unresponsive to changes in weather conditions and other variables that vary over time.

The ability to adjust to heterogeneity and randomness results in a decrease in input residue accumulation under most production conditions. This effect is realized because frequently producers are applying inputs based upon average conditions across a field, so that some areas receive too much input application, while others receive too little. Adjusting application to reflect heterogeneity in production conditions reduces over-application in the areas of low input requirement, thus decreasing residual accumulations.

In some cases precision farming techniques may actually upgrade the physical characteristics of a field, resulting in greater input use efficiency in the production process. For example, drip irrigation may improve the waterholding capacity at different locations within a field, as well as the use efficiency of other inputs applied through irrigation water such as fertilizer and agricultural chemicals. In some cases, the transition from drip to gravity irrigation methods, has been found to increase input use efficiency from .6 to .95 (Boggess *et.al.*, 1993). Thus, the fraction of applied water that ends up as runoff or deep percolating water that may cause drainage and other pollution problems is considerably lower under the precision technology, in comparison with traditional technologies.

Recent research conducted by Khanna and Zilberman (1997) modeling the economic and environmental impacts of precision technology adoption has indicated that:

- The adoption of precision technologies is likely to result in an overall increase in output. It's very unlikely that the use of more advanced technologies will result in a reduction of output.

- Under a wide range of circumstances, precision technology adoption will result in an overall savings in input applications. There may be circumstances when the output effect is very substantial, where an overall increase in input use may occur with the adoption of precision technologies. However, the usual case will be a net decrease in input use.

- Under a wide range of circumstances, the adoption of precision technologies will result in less pollution. There are situations where a significant increase in input use will result in increased pollution. Generally however, pollution is likely to decrease.

The profit-maximizing producer will select more advanced precision technologies if the gains in terms of extra revenues and lower variable input cost are less than the fixed and variable costs associated with the new technology. The monitoring and adjustment capacity of precision technologies require intensive data collection and interpretation which represents a major share of the costs associated with many precision technologies. Thus, profit-maximizing farmers will choose the precision technology components for which the marginal benefits of additional information are equal to the marginal costs of acquiring the information.

Decreasing costs of information acquisition will lead to higher rates of precision technology adoption. In addition, because of their output-increasing effect and the likely input-saving effect, increases in output and input prices can also be expected to result in increased adoption rates as well. Greater incentives for precision technology adoption would also result if residue accumulation were taxed. With a penalty or tax leveled on pollution, the pollution-saving effects of precision technologies will serve as an extra incentive for the adoption of such technologies.

Information Requirements of Precision Technologies

The Global Positioning System (GPS) is an important class of precision technology which addresses spatial heterogeneity. It allows mechanical devices such as tractors and sprayers to identify their locations at a given moment in time. Combined with data generated by geographic information systems on the specific characteristics of each location, input applications can be adjusted accordingly. Since there may be several dimensions of heterogeneity within the field that may require different responses, precision technology packages may include several layers of geographic information, all of which require a great deal of data collection, storage, retrieval and interpretation capacity.

There are several difficulties associated with the use of GPS and GIS technologies. First, the accuracy of remote sensing information may be far from perfect, requiring significant interpretation before action can be taken. Remote sensing cannot completely substitute for the human monitoring of field conditions. For example, inaccuracies and lack of precision of remote sensing make it very difficult to identify the early stages of insect infestations. As efforts to reduce pesticide use continue, there will be an increased use of human scouts as a key element in integrated pest management strategies. These strategies emphasize responsive rather than preventive applications of pest controls.

Secondly, unless information about heterogeneous production conditions is accompanied by the capacity to respond at the same level of detail, the benefits of the information are negligible. For example, successive rounds of remote-sensing photography result in increasingly detailed information, but each round is quite costly. It is therefore important to develop protocols determining the number of times during the season remote-sensing monitoring activities should be executed, based upon the capacity to respond to the information in the field.

The continuous monitoring of weather patterns is a common way in which variability over time - or randomness - in agricultural production is addressed. A case in point is the California Irrigation Management Information System (CIMIS), which provides information on weather variation and that is widely used by farmers to adjust irrigation levels. This sort of information is especially effective in situations where the response can be immediate and the changes in input levels are not costly. Precision technologies play a role here as farmers who operate drip or sprinkler irrigation systems are more capable of responding to CIMIS information than those using gravity methods. The precision systems are documented to have a significant yield-increasing and cost-saving effect (Osgood *et. al.*, 1997) Their main drawback is the high fixed cost of capital, making them primarily appropriate for high value crops such as fruits and vegetables.

Even when farmers have information on the variability of production conditions over space and time, and have effective means to respond to this information, uncertainty about production relationships or market conditions may impair the effectiveness of precision farming. Thus, designing optimal response strategies which account for heterogeneity requires a significant amount of information. There is a high degree of uncertainty regarding the responsiveness of crops to inputs, especially under varying conditions. The design of optimal input application schemes that take into account new information is a tricky problem given the dynamic nature of production systems and the limited information that we have about them.

The ability to take advantage of information on heterogeneity which precision technology affords results in an increase in the value of information on crop productivity and optimal crop management. To obtain more accurate yield response parameters, more data on input use and yield response under various conditions is needed. Thus, one key feature of precision agriculture systems in the future will be the accumulation of information that can be fed into computerized systems, and which can adjust application rates as new knowledge is accumulated. Optimal precision farming systems will have an element of feedback, monitoring changes in field conditions and using this information to better estimate response parameters.

There are obviously increasing returns to scale from knowledge, and the integration of information obtained from a large numbers of locations is essential to derive better estimates of response parameters. Thus, the need to compute exact formulas to effectively utilize precision farming will lead to an increased demand for professionals that combine knowledge in management and biological sciences. Since the design of parameters for precision farming is data intensive, farmers located within a region may exploit the scale effect associated with establishing networks of information. These networks may share information on the performance of the agricultural production system which can be used for estimating parameters needed for management of precision farming.

The design of management systems that combine economic and environmental objectives and provide the principles for software design for precision farming is a new research challenge in farm management. Unfortunately, farm management has been underemphasized in agricultural economics departments, and with the reduction in government involvement in agriculture and the importance of agricultural policies, it may be timely to increase the emphasis on farm management and to develop systems that will be able to increase the economic efficiency in the farm sector while addressing environmental problems. Additional research challenges are addressed in the following chapter.

Role of Information in Overcoming Market Failures

Thus far, the analysis has demonstrated how information-intensive technologies improve productivity and reduce environmental side effects at the micro level. However, information considerations play a major role in designing policies to address residues and waste at the aggregate level of industries and sectors as well. The standard textbook solution for policymakers seeking to promote environmentally sound agricultural production is a tax based upon the environmental cost of production. Specifically, the tax is set at the intersection of the social marginal benefit and cost curves, where the marginal benefit is due to increased production and the marginal cost is due to environmental side effects. Despite the potential benefits of such first-best solutions, the introduction of optimal taxation to issues of environmental quality is extremely difficult due to several informational problems described below.

Lack of Information on the Cost of Pollution Damage

One of the major challenges of policy analysts is to provide policymakers with sound cost estimates of various types of environmental pollutants. Two types of information are needed to estimate such costs:

Information about the quantitative relationship between waste material disposal and environmental and human health damage: For example, we know little about the relationship between nutrient disposal areas near a farm and fish kills in nearby lakes or water-borne diseases. Environmental and health damages are caused by the transportation of waste material, the exposure of victims, and vulnerability. Estimates of key parameters of these processes are fraught with uncertainty. Lichtenberg and Zilberman (1988) argue that much of the disagreements regarding health risk regulation is the result of inconsistent estimation of the parameters of the environmental damage generation functions and provide a methodology for the consistent treatment of the uncertainties associated with these functions. Obviously, they also demonstrate that better knowledge of health generation will make the regulatory process more accurate and less controversial.

Information on the value of environmental and health damages: There is a large literature on attempts to develop methodologies to quantify the cost of losses in terms of human health and environmental quality (Randal, 1990). Both human health and environmental quality are non-market goods, and there is only a limited amount of information obtainable about their values through techniques such as hedonic pricing and travel cost methods. However, methodologies that are used to infer the existence value of environmental goods such as contingent valuation, are subject to considerable disagreement and controversy.

The lack of good information on the costs of pollution has led to the adoption of the Baumol and Oates approach of setting aggregate target levels for environmental quality and health and designing policy instruments to attain these target levels. Political debates on how these target levels should be set continuously arise, and better information on either damage generation or valuation of environmental damage will improve policymaking significantly.

Lack of Information About Pollution Generation

Baumol and Oates (1974) show that taxes are the most efficient tool to restrict residues below a target level. However, even in these cases, two types of information problems make it very difficult to implement pollution taxes.

Nonpoint source problems: The monitoring of residues and wastes or the overexploitation of a resource is very difficult. In many cases, there is no easy way to trace individual sources of aggregate waste materials or environmental damage. Agricultural pollution problems are frequently viewed as nonpoint source problems which are much more difficult to address than point sources because of the inability to assign liability to individual users. The distinction between source and nonsource problems depends on monitoring technology and information, and new research over time can lead to the development of technologies which can provide information on residue or waste accumulations at low cost and facilitate the regulation of agricultural residues.

There are several approaches to address nonpoint solution problems in agriculture, especially if the industry is regulated so aggregate pollution would not exceed the ambient target level. In these cases, the nonpoint pollution problem can be viewed as a local public "bad" problem. It can be addressed efficiently by collective punishment, an ambient tax paid by all polluters once the regional target level is exceeded (Segerson, 1991), or by randomly penalizing some of the polluters when the regional target level is exceeded. These and other solutions are presented by Xepadeades (1992) but they have implementation problems because of heterogeneity among producers and for political and economic reasons. In particular, both collective and random punishment may be opposed by producers because they are too harsh.

Asymmetric information. One major obstacle to the introduction of pollution taxation is that individuals have incentives to conceal information from policymakers and tax collectives about their production and pollution activities. There is a significant literature on the design of truth-revealing incentives (Green and Laffont, 1979; Holmstrom, 1979). These incentives aim to induce the producer to reveal her true behavior, as any attempt to conceal it will result in a worse punishment. Smith (1995) developed a truth-revealing tax to address agricultural pollution problems. However, the implementation of such truth-revealing mechanisms in cases of agricultural pollution problems is very challenging since such policies tend to be complex, nonlinear, and very sensitive to specifications of production and pollution technologies. Policymakers are interested in simple solutions to complex problems. Therefore, they prefer policies that are not first best but are easy to implement with information that is readily available.

Taxes and Information Requirements

In the following paragraphs a brief discussion on tax policies which create incentives to address pollution and waste problems is presented. These may include:

Output tax. Such a tax may be easy to implement because information about output is readily available. If all producers use the same type of technology, then producers with more output are likely to also be responsible for more pollution. However, if there are differences in production technology, producers that apply precision technologies may be more productive that those applying less environmentally-friendly technologies. In this case, an output tax will be counterproductive and may actually lead to a decrease in the adoption of precision technology.

Sales tax on input. This tax is applicable when the environmental or resource problem with which a policymaker is concerned is linked to the use of a specific input, such as irrigation water, or pesticides. Depending upon the producer's risk characteristics, and those of the input (i.e., risk reducing or risk increasing), this tax may reduce input use and even encourage the adoption of precision technologies. This tax is also relatively easy to implement and may be collected from agricultural input dealers. Indeed, many countries have imposed taxes on pesticides or fertilizers. But as Khanna and Zilberman (1997) argue, individuals who adopt precision technologies cause less damage and are more productive with the use of agricultural inputs than individuals who use traditional technologies and therefore input taxes may lead to inefficiency.

Technology-dependent input tax. The efficiency of input taxes may be increased by varying the tax according to the choice of technology. For example, a farmer using a precision technology for pesticide application will pay a lower pesticide tax than a farmer that uses an aerial spray. However, the implementation of technology-dependent taxes requires considerably more information than sales tax, and therefore are more expensive to implement.

Technology tax. In some cases, it is difficult to obtain information on input sales, but information on land use and technology use are more readily available. In these cases a per acre tax or subsidy which distinguishes farmers according to their technology may lead to the adoption of precision farming. Such a tax may be inefficient as it will not affect input use within a technology, and may lead in some cases to over-adoption.

Transferable permits. Distributional and political considerations may lead to the replacement of any of the above taxation schemes by transferable permits. For example, policy-makers may set a target level of chemical use which is distributed among farmers according to the historical use levels and then farmers may trade the permits. Alternatively, transferable permits for output will have the same efficiency effect as with input effects, but with different equity effects. One may also develop transferable permits for input use that are technology dependent, where more polluting technologies require more permits per unit of applied input.

Other Forms of Environmental Regulation and Information

Policies of uniform taxation may create problems because of heterogeneity and the multi-dimensionality of environmental impacts. Environmental damage prevention in a riparian zone may be much more valuable than in less-sensitive environments. Therefore policy design must take into account the distribution of environmental benefits across locations, and adjust accordingly. The same resource contamination may be multi-dimensional by affecting both humans and wildlife populations. Policies that may address one or both of these aspects include:

Restricted use policies. Policy-makers may find that the cheapest approach to addressing problems with multi-dimensional features is to impose restrictions on input use. In particular, zoning is a response to spatial heterogeneity. In some cases, policy-makers may disallow certain productive activities. For example raising black goats is forbidden in some areas of the Middle East because of the damage they inflict on vegetation. In others cases, there may be restrictions on input intensity, such as the number of head of cattle allowed per land unit. These policies are not first best policies. However, if transactions costs are taken into account, they may be quite efficient.

Another form of use restriction arises when governments allow only certified individuals to prescribe and apply certain materials. Certified consultants should be informed about both environmental and production considerations, so that their prescriptions can balance the two. They also should record their activities, and be held liable for mis-prescriptions. The emerging industry of chemical consultants will ideally fill this niche.

Purchasing fund. It may be socially optimal to preserve ecosystems that are especially valuable and sensitive through the use of government sponsored purchasing programs. One example of this type of program is the Conservation Reserve Program (CRP) in the United States, which has been transformed from a soil conservation to an environmental preservation program. The success of this program depends on the use of sound economic criteria for purchases, the availability of good information on environmental amenities, and the capacity to balance between different dimensions of environmental quality in purchasing decisions (Babcock *et. al.*, 1996).

Incentives for the adoption of monitoring equipment. The introduction of equipment to monitor both emissions and environmental quality may transform pollution sources from nonpoint to point problems. Millock *et. al.* (1997) develop a scheme where individuals who do not adopt monitoring equipment are assessed a high per acre tax, in contrast to those who do adopt and are taxed according to their emissions. This scheme will induce the adoption of monitoring equipment among the lighter polluters, and over time the tax may be increased to gradually encourage wide-scale adoption. A variation of this scheme will be the use of tax proceeds for the subsidization of monitoring technology adoption.

Safety standards. When the control of the generation and movement of pollution is difficult and costly, society may apply a diversified strategy to reduce environmental damage by supplementing or replacing source control with exposure reduction. This may be accomplished through protective clothing or containment measures. The development of such measures requires information on pollution transport and exposure and their control.

Education. It may be that the most effective manner for averting pollution behavior is the education of individuals about environmental damage and the damage generation process and to internalize environmental values.

Information and the Management of Common Pool Resources

Another major source of environmental degradation arising from agricultural production occurs with the mismanagement of common pool resources[1]. Common pool resources are characterized by difficulty of exclusion, and rivalry in consumption (Ostrom and Gardner, 1993). Difficulty of exclusion may arise due to the physical indivisibility of the resource, as with groundwater aquifers or fisheries, or due to the presence of economies of scale, as with grazing lands. Common pool resources are vulnerable to over-exploitation, as the gains from over-use are realized by the individual, while the costs are shared among all present and future users. Thus, production decisions are based upon the private, rather than the social costs and benefits of resource exploitation.

Solutions to the problems associated with common pool resource management have generally focused on the design of property rights systems which will create the correct incentives for sustainable management. Widely varying prescriptions have arisen from the findings of theoretical and applied research; however the importance of information in determining the appropriate method emerges as a dominant theme.

In analyzing the role of information in the sustainable management of common pool resources, it is useful to distinguish between local and global commons. In general, local commons are governed at the community or village level, and access to the commons is restricted in some fashion, so there is not free entry to the use of the resource (Dasgupta, 1993). In contrast, global commons are more frequently characterized by open access to the resource. Users of the commons are not known to one another, and there is no barrier preventing access to any potential user of the resource. The primary difference between the two types of commons lies in the feasibility and expense of monitoring resource use patterns (Dasgupta, 1993) and the ability of agents to act strategically to affect a collective result (Baland and Platteau, 1996).

In many cases, local commons have exhibited the capacity to regulate use among its membership, resulting in sustainable systems of resource management. Theoretical and empirical studies have indicated the importance of information in the success of these schemes (Baland and Platteau, 1996; Seabright 1993, Bardhan 1993, Meinzen-Dick *et. al.*, 1996). Among local commons, especially those with a limited group membership, monitoring of resource use is generally possible and within financially feasible ranges, allowing the group to set resource management standards. Since trespasses upon collective norms can be detected, sanctions may be devised and imposed at relatively low costs. In addition, members are known to one another and have the ability and incentives to build long-standing relationships and refrain from over-exploitation in order to maintain-going mutually beneficially relationships (Seabright, 1993). Under these conditions, communities have shown the capacity to devise and enforce sustainable systems of collective management (Ostrom and Gardner, 1993; Meinzen-Dick *et.al.*, 1996). It is important to note, however, that even though the group may have the capacity to manage the resource sustainably, they may not have sufficient information on ecological processes which is necessary for successful long-term management.

Game theoretic and empirical studies have also indicated that as group size becomes larger, the incentives and capacity to cooperate in the management of common pool resources become diluted, in part because of greater difficulty in monitoring use patterns (Bardhan, 1993; Baland and Platteau, 1996). Additionally, local systems of commons management may break down as a result of exogenous pressures such as population growth and migration, commercialization of the economy, and government policies.

Information—or, more specifically, the lack of it—has been particularly important in the institution of government policies which have contributed towards the failure of local common property schemes.

In recent years, many governments have moved to centralize the management of local commons under state regulated systems, based upon the belief that local management either was absent, or if in place, incapable of sustainable resource management. However, most experience with state management of local common pool resources has shown poor results (Meinzen-Dick et. al., 1996; Baland and Platteau, 1996). Information asymmetries are a major cause of the poor performance. Detailed information on the spatial heterogeneity and randomness over time which occurs in local ecosystems is necessary in order to make sound management decisions and this information is difficult and expensive for state agencies to collect and process. Monitoring of resource use patterns is also difficult to accomplish, resulting in a weakened capacity of state agencies to impose sanctions upon trespassers. As a result of these problems with information, together with other factors such as the presence of corruption and budgetary constraints, common pool resources managed by state agencies have often deteriorated into situations of de facto open access, exhibiting high rates of resource degradation.

Privatization is another policy which has been put forward in an attempt to improve the management of common pool resources (Demsetz, 1967). Information plays a key role in determining the potential efficiency of privatization schemes. The efficiency of resource privatization depends on the ability to define and enforce property rights, as well as the level of transactions costs which may arise in bargaining. Information on the location, quality and quantity of resources is necessary in order to define a property right and to institute a properly functioning market. In cases where the costs of defining and trading common pool resources is high, or where there are high transactions costs and increasing returns to scale, privatization of the resource will not necessarily result in greater efficiency, and may even cause greater resource degradation through the creation of new externalities.

It is important to note that privatization may have negative distributional consequences as well, which in turn will affect the efficiency of resource use. In many cases, the privatization of resources has also resulted in the expropriation of resources from the poorest members of society (Dasgupta, 1993; Jodha, 1987; Blaikie and Brookfield, 1987). The disenfranchisement of poor members of society from their traditional resource base in the process of privatization has forced these users to access increasingly marginal and fragile resources, resulting in high rates of resource degradation, as well as increased impoverishment (Dasgupta, 1993). The privatization of some common resources may put additional pressure on remaining commons, triggering a loss of management capacity and a deterioration into a situation of open access on the remaining commons (Blaikie and Brookfield, 1987). Resistance among the traditional users to the expropriation of their resources will also result in an increase in transactions costs, thus decreasing the efficiency of privatization schemes (Baland and Platteau, 1996). Clearly, a critical piece of information that is necessary for policy-makers in assessing the efficiency and equity implications of a privatization program, is the status of current users of common pool resources, the value of the resource to them, and the potential impacts of a change in property rights schemes upon them. This information may indicate that the privatization of common pool resources does not result in an increase in social welfare.

The above analysis indicates that the appropriate property rights and management scheme for the sustainable use of local common pool resources depends on the characteristics of the ecosystem, as well as socio-economic and political conditions. In some cases, local user groups may be in a better position than state bureaucracies to manage local commons due in part to their greater information on local environmental conditions and the use patterns of the membership. However, in the presence of rapidly changing ecosystems, and with the increase in the quantity and complexity of knowledge on ecosystem behavior generated through research, local communities may not have the capacity to obtain and process sufficient information to design long-term sustainable resource management schemes. Information sharing among state and local user groups may result in decreased costs to both parties, and enhanced efficiency. In cases where no local user group is functioning, then state agencies may play an important role in fostering their development, as with the creation of local water districts in California for the management of irrigation water. In still other cases, privatization may provide the best potential for common pool resource management, with the state providing a framework that allows markets to operate with suitably low transactions costs. The potential for cooperation between state, local communities and private parties in the management of common pool resources is an area of research which is just beginning to be explored, but one which shows considerable promise (Evans 1996; Lam 1996; Baland and Platteau 1996).

With the global commons, the key impediments to achieving a sustainable system are the lack of information about the causes and consequences of global externalities and the lack of monitoring and enforcement capacity. Considerable uncertainty exists about the ecological processes underlying the generation of many global externalities. For example, modeling of the extent of global warming and the impact of various pollutants on climate change is still in the initial stages, with considerable debate surrounding the correct approach and data to adopt (Pearce and Turner, 1990). The lack of information on the sources and extent of potential damage has greatly hindered efforts to address the problem, as governments are reluctant to incur costs for investments whose benefits are highly uncertain.

However, even when greater information about the sources and impacts of global externalities is available, problems in monitoring may preclude successful intervention.   Technological innovations and advancements in information technology constitute an important solution to this problem. Precision technologies are essential in the monitoring of resource use patterns and changes in the global environment. Without this information, enforceable international agreements on global commons management will not be possible. In order to make such systems credible to all parties, monitoring must be shared.   The development of independent monitoring and information networks, as provided by many non-governmental organizations, is another factor which can contribute to successful cooperation in the management of the global commons.

A major problem which has been encountered in the management of the global commons has been the claim on the part of many developing countries that the industrialized countries are unwilling to pay for the costs of conservation efforts from which they will benefit. One solution which has been put forth is the use of transferable payments, including the "debt for nature" swaps, from rich countries to developing countries in order to finance resource conservation efforts. Information plays a key role here as well. In order to be capable of designing efficient and enforceable transfer schemes, it is necessary to have information on the sources of the problem and the value of conservation to the various parties involved.

Dynamic Systems and Uncertainty

One of the most basic characteristics of living systems is their tendency to evolve and change over time. This is true for human society, as well as for local and global ecosystems. These dynamic systems are also subject to random shocks and there is a significant amount of uncertainty surrounding their parameters. The ability to track these changes and respond to them is a key component of a sustainable resource management system. Information gathering and learning is a critical feature of a management system for dynamic stochastic systems. In particular, the following three aspects are important:

The importance of early detection. The identification and detection of phenomena which have catastrophic potential is an important component of an effective management strategy. Early detection may enable low cost solutions, as well as more time to develop technological and other solutions to address the problem. Therefore designing an institutional set up which facilitates monitoring and leads to a quick response capacity is a crucial element of sustainable development.

Adaptive management. It may be politically attractive and seem less expensive to design policy solutions that are predetermined and based upon average future outcomes. However these solutions may be much inferior to strategies that are capable of adjusting to a state of nature and a wide array of contingencies. This is the main idea underlying the concept of adaptive management which many ecologists view as essential to achieve sustainability (Odum 1992; Christensen 1996). The advantage of flexible policies is especially apparent in systems with a high degree of randomness (Rausser and Hochman, 1980), when choices are irreversible (Fisher *et.al.*, 1992), or when reversibility is extremely costly (Zhao and Zilberman, 1997). Arrow and Fisher (1974) introduced the notion of option values which is the expected value of the economic gain from delaying irreversible decisions which allow policy-makers to adjust to new information. In some cases, irreversibility considerations may lead to not only delay but also to smaller-scale activities.

Active learning. Rausser and Hochman (1980) argue that policy actions should be assessed in terms of their impact on the performance of the system as well as the value of the extra information they provide. Thus, the optimal management of dynamic systems may entail a continuous research effort and sometimes the modification of policies that increase variability to provide better information on the responsiveness of parameters of the system.

Conclusions

A major theme which arises from our analysis is that the notion of "weak sustainability" (defined as the maintenance of environmental quality while pursuing economic growth) is not sufficiently ambitious, as there exists a vast potential to achieve economic growth while actually improving the environment. Contrary to the belief of many that economic growth and environmental quality are inversely related, we have argued that with better generation and utilization of information improved resource allocation in terms of both environmental quality and economic productivity may be achieved.

However, improving environmental quality and economic well-being requires changes, both in terms of research and policy management. Improved research products for sustainable policy making will require the integration of economic and biological considerations in research. We should build knowledge networks to take advantage of field-generated knowledge and incorporate them into the knowledge base from which new technological and institutions solutions are derived.

Adoption of precision technologies that use information to more accurately apply inputs, can lead to both increased productivity and decreased pollution. These technologies are in their infancy, and still need considerable refinement. Their efficient utilization requires innovations in management practices, as well as the development of institutional support to provide the necessary information.

Inappropriate incentives are the main reason for pollution and environmental degradation, but textbook environmental economic solutions may not work because of a lack of information. Workable solutions must be simple and responsive to information availability, as well as the features of production technology and pollution generation. Our analysis indicates that optimal policies will combine financial incentives with some direct control and education.

Information clearly plays a critical role in designing and implementing sustainable strategies for the management of the commons. Essentially, three types of information are necessary: information on resource use patterns, information on current management and institutions, and information on the value of resources. The acquisition of these types of information requires monitoring efforts and extra research, but may provide the foundations for policy reforms for both local and global commons.

Natural systems are evolving and subject to random events. Therefore, we should develop management strategies that are adaptive and incorporate active learning. Adjusting decisions as information is revealed will prevent premature irreversible choices, resulting in more efficient and environmentally sound outcomes.

Resource degradation is not an inevitable side effect of economic growth, but rather it is a by-product of bad policies and the poor use of information. With the improvement of information generation and utilization, the ability to achieve a form of "strong sustainability" where both economic growth and an improvement in environmental quality may be obtainable.

Note

1.   Following Ostrom and Gardner (1993) we distinguish between the resource itself and the property rights regime governing it. Here, we use common pool resources as any resource which exhibits the characteristics of indivisibility and subtractability of use, which may be under one of several types of property regimes, including private, common property (communal ownership) or open access.

References

Arrow, K. and A. Fisher. 1974. "Environmental Preservation, Uncertainty and Irreversibility". *Quarterly Journal of Economics.* 88:312-319.

Babcock, B.A., P. G. Lakshminarayan, J. Wu and D. Zilberman. 1996. "The Economics of a Public Fund for Environmental Amenities: A Study of CRP Contracts". *American Journal of Agricultural Economics.* 78:961-971.

Baland, Jean-Marie and Jean-Phillipe Platteau. 1996. *Halting Degradation of Natural Resources, Is There A Role for Rural Communities?* Rome, Italy.: The Food and Agriculture Organization of the United Nations.

Bardhan, P. 1993. "Analytics of the Institutions of Informal Cooperation in Rural Development". *World Development.* 21:633-9.

Batie, S. S. 1989. "Sustainable development: challenges to the profession of agricultural economics". *American Journal of Agricultural Economics* 71:1083-1101.

Baumol, W. J. and Oates, W. E. 1974. *The Theory of Environmental Policy*, New Jersey: Prentice Hall.

Blaikie, P. and H. Brookfield. 1987. *Land Degradation and Society.* London; New York: Methuen.

Boggess, W., R. Lacewell and D. Zilberman. 1993. "Economics of Water Use in Agriculture", in *Agricultural and Environmental Resource Economics*, G. Carlson, D. Zilberman and J. Miranowski, eds. New York, Oxford: Oxford University Press.

Christensen, N. et. al. 1996. "The Report of the Ecological Society of America

Committee on the Scientific Basis for Ecosystem Management". *Ecological Applications.* 6: 665-691.

Dasgupta, Partha, (1993) *An Inquiry Into Well-Being and Destitution*, Cambridge: Oxford University Press

Demsetz, H. 1967. "Toward a Theory of Property Rights". *American Economic Review*, 57:347-59.

Evans, P. 1996. "Government Action, Social Capital and Development: Reviewing the Evidence on Synergy". *World Development* 24: 1119-1132.

Fisher, A., T. Krutilla, and C. Cicchetti. 1992. "The Economics of Environmental Preservation: A Theoretical and Empirical Analysis". *The Economics of the Environment.* International Library of Critical Writing, Vol. 20. 1992.

Green, J. and J.J. Laffont. 1979. *Incentives in Public Decision Making.* New York: North-Holland Publishing Co.

Holmstrom, B. 1979. "Groves' Scheme on Restricted Domains". *Econometrica.* 47:1137-1144.

Jodha, N.S. 1986. "Common Property Resources and the Rural Poor". *Economic and Political Weekly* 21.

Khanna, M. and D. Zilberman. 1997. "Incentives, Precision Technology and Environmental Quality". *Ecological Economics.* Forthcoming.

Laffont, J. J. 1988. *Fundamentals of Public Economics*, Cambridge Massachusetts: MIT Press

Lam, W.F. 1996. "Institutional Design of Public Agencies and Coproduction: A study of Irrigation Associations in Taiwan". *World Development.* 24:1039-1054

Lichtenberg, Eric and D. Zilberman. 1988. "Efficient Regulation of Environmental Health Risks". *Quarterly Journal of Economics.* 103:167-178.

Meizen-Dick, Ruth, et. al. 1996. "Local Organization for Natural Resource Management: Lessons From Theoretical and Empirical Literature" Unpublished Document: Food Policy Research Institute, Washington DC.

Millock, K., D. Zilberman, and D. Sunding. 1997. "Incentives for Monitoring Nonpoint Source Pollution. Mimeo". Department of Agricultural and Resource Economics, U. C. Berkeley.

Odum, E. 1992. "Great Ideas in Ecology for the 1990s". *Bioscience* 42: 542-545.

Osgood, Daniel, D. Cohen, D. Parker and D. Zilberman. 1997. "Forecasting the Production Benefits and Incidence of a Public Program: An Integrated Survey and Estimation Procedure Applied to Study the California Irrigation Management Information System" *Advances in Econometrics.* 12:303-317.

Ostrom, Elinor and Roy Gardner. 1993. "Coping with Asymmetries in the Commons: Self-governing Irrigation Systems Can Work". *Journal of Economic Perspectives*, 7:93-112.

Pearce, David W. and R.K. Turner. 1990. *Economics of Natural Resources and the Environment.* Baltimore Maryland: Johns Hopkins University Press.

Randal, A. 1990. "Thinking About the Value of Biodiversity". Unpublished

Manuscript. Department of Agricultural Economics and Rural Societies, Ohio State University.

Rausser, G.C. and E. Hochman. 1980. *Dynamic Agricultural Systems: Economic Prediction of Control.* New York: North Holland Publishing Co.

Ruttan, Vernon. 1994. "Constraints on the Design of Sustainable Systems of Agricultural Production". *Ecological Economics* 10: 209-219.

Seabright, Paul. 1993. "Managing Local commons: Theoretical Issues in Incentive Design". *Journal of Economic Perspectives,* 7:113-134.

Segerson, K. 1991. "Air Pollution and Agriculture: A Review and Evaluation of Policy Interactions", in *Commodity and Resource Policies in Agricultural Systems.* R. Just and N. Bockstaiel, eds. Berlin: Springer-Verlag.

Smith, R. 1995. "The Conservation Reserve Program as a Least-Cost Land Retirement Mechanism". *American Journal of Agricultural Economics.* 77:93-105.

Xepapadeas, A.P. 1992. "Environmental Policy Design and Dynamic Nonpoint-Source Pollution". *Journal of Environmental Economics and Management.* 23:22-39.

Zhao, J. and D. Zilberman. 1997. "Irreversibility and Restoration in Natural Resource Development". Unpublished Manuscript. Department of Agricultural and Resource Economics, University of California at Berkeley.

12 Sustainability: Challenges of Cross-Disciplinary Research

Mary C. Ahearn and Gerald W. Whittaker

Introduction

Nowhere is the call for cross-disciplinary collaboration more explicit than it is for issues dealing with agricultural sustainability. Mainstream definitions of agricultural sustainability recognize the links among agricultural production activities, the environment, communities, and society at large. The purpose of this chapter is to discuss the motivation of this call for collaboration and to relate the level of sustainability analysis to the extent of cross-disciplinary collaboration and critical research issues. Barriers to cross-disciplinary efforts will be briefly reviewed and, finally, the chapter will discuss the development of integrated physical and economic models as an example of cross-disciplinary efforts for addressing agricultural sustainability issues.

A common theme in current discussions of science policy is the importance of, and often the increased need for, cross-disciplinary work. Recent expressions of this view for agriculture can be found in the latest National Research Council report on the USDA-Land Grant System (NRC, 1996). It is also reflected in the Request for Proposals (RFP) for competitive grants (e.g., the Fund for Rural America, the National Research Initiative, and the Sustainable Agriculture Research and Education programs) (USDA Web Site, 1997). Evidence suggests that individual researchers share the view that there is a need for more cross-disciplinary research. For example, among agricultural economists, a 1996 survey regarding professional priorities indicated that the profession overwhelmingly (92 percent) believed there is a need for more cross-disciplinary collaboration (Ahearn, 1996). In addition, a 1993 survey of agricultural economists who had participated in multidisciplinary research projects found that the respondents believed that multidisciplinary work had a greater value to society than their uni-disciplinary work (Young, 1995). Finally, a further indication of the recognition of a need for greater cross-disciplinary work is the genesis of at least two new disciplines which seek to integrate disciplinary frameworks, namely agroecology and ecological economics (Gliessman, 1990; Constanza, Daly, and Bartholomew, 1991).

Agenda Setting

In conventional terms, U.S. agriculture is among the most productive sectors of the U.S. economy (Ahearn et al., 1997). But, it is also recognized that agriculture has a variety of negative impacts on the environment. Many of the physical processes of these impacts are not well understood by physical scientists, let alone quantified. Some of the most serious impacts include sheet and rill erosion, plus other soil quality factors, such as soil compaction, and declining levels of organic matter; and surface and groundwater quality effects, such as sediments in waterways, and agriculture as the major contributor to nonpoint sources of pollution (NRC, 1993). In addition, the organization of U.S. agriculture has changed significantly over time (as outlined in Chapter 1), and has been accompanied by social and farm community changes (some of which are addressed in Chapters 5 to 7) that some would label as problematic.

A major reason for the increasing interest in cross-disciplinary work is because the general public, who are the beneficiaries and major financial sponsors of publicly-supported research, have demanded that science focus on "real world" problem-solving research. Solutions to real world problems generally benefit from contributions from a variety of disciplines. Furthermore, there is a recognition that science and technology advances commonly include secondary, and unwanted, impacts. These secondary impacts are often in the "domain" of disciplines other than the original one, quite frequently in the domain of the social science disciplines.

Delivering real-world problem solving research does not imply that there is no role for basic or disciplinary research in addressing issues of agricultural sustainability. It is widely recognized that applied research and education activities cannot proceed without a sound basic, disciplinary program. Basic, disciplinary, research is very much an intermediate input into the real-world solutions demanded by the beneficiaries of research. Rather than a disassociation from disciplinary work, what is called for is, first, an identification of research and education priorities that recognize the comprehensiveness of the sustainability agenda. After years of relative stability, the process for how science priorities get specified is currently very dynamic. In particular, recommendations have been made to directly solicit the views of customers of the USDA-Land Grant System about the agenda of the system (for example, NRC, 1996). No clear consensus has yet emerged on how the views of the public should best be distilled and integrated into the planning process, although several models have been implemented (e.g., C-FARE, 1997).[1]

A second stage in planning a program for agricultural sustainability research is to evaluate when uni-disciplinary or cross-disciplinary research is required to address the particular research question at hand. In other words, research in the agricultural sustainability area must be designed in recognition of not only where a contribution can potentially be made in the disciplinary literature, but also where the research will potentially contribute to solving "real world" problems of sustainability. In the USDA-Land Grant system, the responsibility to provide socially valuable research is shared by individual scientists and research administrators.

The Level of Analysis and Cross-Disciplinary Research

A fundamental contribution of the sustainable agriculture agenda is to explicitly recognize the linkages of agricultural production to the environment and society. These linkages are explored at multiple levels: the field level, the farm level, the ecosystem (e.g., watershed) level, and at major geopolitical levels, such as the state or nation (Lowrance, Hendrix, and Odum, 1986; PCSD, 1996). Each level of analysis has an associated set of research and education issues which determines the extent to which a particular disciplinary framework dominates, the extent to which cross-disciplinary approaches are utilized, and the extent to which the cross-disciplinary approaches are integrated (Castle, 1970; Lockeretz, 1991; Stark, 1994).

The field level of sustainability analysis addresses agronomic sustainability, that is, the ability of a field to maintain production over time with minimal environmental degradation. This level of analysis is generally the domain of physical scientists and focuses on quantifying the relationships between yields and levels of selected environmental indicators, such as soil erosion. The next level of analysis, the farm sustainability level, considers the market position of the farming business in concert with the environmental impacts of the production process, generally embracing the concept of the farming system. The physical sciences contribute information about the environmental impacts of a farming system, while the economic analysis contributes information about the likelihood and/or rate of adoption of the associated technologies and impacts on economic health of the farm. A research design which uses the frameworks of a variety of physical sciences and economics is a requirement at this level.[2]

The next two levels of analysis--the ecosystem and the major geopolitical boundary level--offer the greatest insights for policy analysis. Social sciences offer important links from field and farm level analysis to policy because of the information they may provide on human behavior and attitudes. Perhaps the most significant contribution of economics, in particular, in a cross-disciplinary effort is the overall assessment and integrative framework. Monetary valuation offers the ability to quantify and aggregate over impacts, plus provides the link to the incentives of private agents in the market place. And while the central focus is on the market, economics provides concepts and tools that address nonmarket activity and market failures. The tools of economics are critical for designing policy mechanisms that are consistent with private incentives. On the other hand, in real world situations social issues, such as income inequality, may be more important to society at large or to policy makers than economists' emphasis on maximizing private economic surplus.

The ecosystem level provides for the aggregation of the environmental relationships identified in the field and farm levels to a level which is meaningful to society. Society is concerned with the actual impact of an alternative production system on farm and environmental sustainability. Only through the consideration, i.e., modeling, of the complexity of environmental factors in an ecosystem framework do the environmental results of interest have credibility. Unfortunately, the current lack of knowledge regarding the complexity of the environmental relationships severely limits the ability of this level of analysis to provide results. However, this level of sustainability analysis is also receiving a great deal of attention and is poised to yield more productive results in the near future. Attempts to integrate frameworks across disciplines at the ecosystem level will be elaborated on below.

Because policies are developed and enforced at geopolitical boundaries, a focus at this level is an ultimate goal for sustainability research and education activities. Traditional results of economic performance and organizational structure are commonly reported at geopolitical levels (such as, state or national farm income statistics or the size and distribution of farms). Similarly, key social indicators (such as, migration patterns, income inequality, and crime rates) are reported at geopolitical levels. However, geopolitical boundaries generally bear little relationship to meaningful ecosystem boundaries. An additional challenge, therefore, for analysts focusing on policy implications of sustainability issues is to integrate the ecosystem-level results with the economic and social analyses in the traditional geopolitical boundaries of relevance for policy design (an issue that is also addressed in Chapter 9).

Resource accounting is an example of an economic framework that allows for the integration of economics and environmental impacts associated with agriculture at a policy-relevant level of analysis. Resource accounting is an effort to adjust the traditional National Income and Product Accounts to reflect relevant nonmarket activities and to account for the depreciation of natural capital, as well as the traditional flows of manufactured capital. Therefore, the resource accounting framework is recognized as an important tool for monitoring sustainability (PCSD, 1996). The resource accounting concept is not a new concept. Conceptual work on the accounting framework remains very much a work in progress (some recent developments in this area are explored in Chapter 8). The United Nations, the Bureau of Economic Analysis, and most currently, the National Academy of Science, have all convened groups of analysts in an attempt to recommend accounting practices. The greatest obstacle to empirical applications of resource accounting systems in sustainability analysis has been the lack of information on (1) the science-base of the environmental relationships and (2) the value that society places on the related nonmarket goods and services. Resource accounting can be viewed as a value-added activity. Unless the, largely, disciplinary work has been completed, resource accounting applications are severely limited. However, numerous examples exist to provide evidence that significant progress is being made that will allow for future empirical applications using the resource accounting framework (BEA, 1994; Bartelmus, et al., 1991; Hrubovcak, LeBlanc, and Eakin, 1995).

The question of the relationships among farm structure, community viability, and quality of life is a high profile issue for sustainability. Critical questions include: how much does society value the higher personal and community quality of life, and social stability that a small farm structure is purported to provide, relative to a large farm structure (an issue that is explored in Chapter 2)? What will a small-farm structure cost in terms of environmental impacts and food sufficiency? In addition, is agricultural land use, relative to an alternative land use, a preferred land use, in terms of providing long-term environmental and social benefits (issues that are addressed elsewhere in this volume, especially in Chapter 10). These "big-picture" issues are best dealt with at the macro level.

Challenges to Collaboration

Challenges to collaboration can be labeled as institutional or substantive in nature, although it is recognized that obstacles within and across these two categories are not unrelated.

Institutional. There is a great deal of consensus in the thinking of several authors on the organizational and institutional barriers to effective cross-discipline collaboration (for example, Stark, 1994; Young, 1995; Zilberman, 1994). These include: inadequate communication, particularly in articulating different methodologies without a common technical language; funding conflicts among departments; sharing of credit for the products of a project; and disciplinary chauvinism. Other institutional barriers to cross-disciplinary collaboration commonly identified include the reward system of research institutions and competition among scientists. In the case of cross-disciplinary work, it is likely very important to have an institutional structure that allows for bottom-up, as well as top-down direction.

Substantive. The greatest challenges faced by researchers interested in participating in cross-disciplinary research are subject-matter oriented, including: (1) the technical integration of conceptual models, (2) the differences in the level of certainty associated with scientific knowledge bases, thereby impeding empirical applications based on integrated frameworks, and (3) the lack of consistent or compatible primary data. Each of these challenges is addressed next.

Disciplinary frameworks will vary in the ease to which they can be integrated. This is because of conflicts, or incompatibilities, among underlying patterns of thought. For example, disciplines will vary based on what is to be assumed and what is to be established empirically. Zilberman (1994) observed that economists, in comparison to other scientists, are inclined to be less engaged in the details of a particular problem. He writes:

> I think the most important issue we *(economists)* have to address is our tendency to abstract from reality and to rely on second-hand data and to remove ourselves from primary data collection and from learning and communicating with people associated with the problem (p. 41).

To the extent that he is correct, economists may experience the greatest shift in their culture, relative to other disciplines, in response to the new science policy focus on addressing real world problems.

Assuming a unifying framework is identified, cross-disciplinary work may be hampered by uneven scientific knowledge bases at all levels of sustainability analysis. At the field level, little information exists about how technologies that are purported to be "green", that is to reduce environmental degradation relative to conventional practices, actually do affect the environment. An example is the set of practices that fall under the Integrated Pest Management (IPM) label, which may or may not lead to reduced chemical use (Norton and Mullen, 1994). Again, the literature is mixed for individual practices, but for the most commonly agreed upon component of IPM, scouting, strong evidence exists about its relationship to chemical use. Most empirical evidence indicates that increased use of scouting is associated with increased chemical use.

At the farm-level, estimating the private costs and returns of alternative systems is key to understanding farmers' adoption of practices, as well as the key to the proper role for government action. The obvious first step in understanding the economics of alternative practices is to define them. This is primarily a challenge for physical scientists, although a task that is best tackled in a cross-disciplinary team to ensure usefulness in future integrated analysis. Another critical challenge in determining the economics of alternative practices is to correctly measure the labor and management component of the production inputs. Often times, alternative practices are more management and information intensive than conventional practices. Whether an alternative practice is adopted over a conventional practice may very well be based on the cost of the additional labor and management input requirements, especially in light of the increasing share of farmers with off-farm employment responsibilities.

At the macro-level, the science base which informs relationships regarding the complexities of ecosystem health is not as conclusive. Although a scientific base of information may be growing at the field level regarding how agricultural production practices and inputs affect the environmental quality of that particular field, much less information is available that indicates how the same production practices and input use affect ecosystem health and human health (issues that are also addressed in Chapter 10). Even the relationships that are widely considered as fundamental in ecology have been called into question. For example, an "established" concept in ecology is the role of biodiversity to buffer and provide resilience to ecosystems (Saterson, 1995). This concept has recently been called into question, thereby turning a fundamental component of the ecological paradigm into an interesting and controversial empirically-based debate (Grime, 1997).

The third substantive obstacle to cross-disciplinary collaboration is the availability of adequate data. This is true at the field, regional, or national level, although the deficiency is greatest at the national level. Since a goal of agricultural sustainability is to consider the extensive impacts—market and nonmarket—of agricultural production, the data requirements for the ideal data set are enormous. There are modest successes toward constructing comprehensive data bases that capture farm economic, production, and environmental variables at the regional level (USDA, 1991-93; Setia, 1997). Resources have not been forthcoming to develop even such basic data sets at the national level. Even sparser, are data sets that allow for the relation of the economic values of the nonmarket environmental impacts to the associated alternative production systems. GIS tools, coupled with statistical techniques to estimate data surfaces from partial data sets may offer the greatest hope for the development of comprehensive national or, ecosystem-based, constructed data bases.

Sustainability Analysis through Cross-Disciplinary Efforts: An Example

The linking of physical process models with economic optimization models provides an example of where cross-disciplinary efforts have proven to be quite productive in analyzing sustainability issues, and represents an attempt to overcome some of the obstacles described above. Each model used by itself, either economic or physical, is incomplete for analysis of agricultural policy and the environment. An economic model used in isolation will offer insight into human behavior in the face of policy changes affecting input use, production, profitability, and agricultural emissions to the environment; but no assessment of the physical consequences of the behavior will be forthcoming. The physical model can be used to assess the effect of different agricultural management practices and input-output combinations on the environment, but the practices are accepted as given, with no ability to analyze the behavior underlying the practices. The motivation for linking economic models to physical process models is to specify models which can simulate the effect of policy on human producers, and the resulting effects of the human behavior on the environment. Because we expect this progress to continue to expand the ability of agricultural physical and social scientists to collaboratively contribute to the sustainability agenda, we briefly summarize the development of the integration of economic and physical models.

The fundamental paradigm followed in linking economic models to physical process models is quite simple: one matches the physical parameters of one model to those in the other. For example, the profit maximizing amount of nitrogen fertilizer as estimated by the economic model will serve as the amount of nitrogen applied in the physical process model. As a result of model characteristics, there is quite a variety in implementation of integration of economic and physical models. Some major categories of economic models include disaggregate (micro-unit decisions) and aggregate (regional or national), parametric econometric, parametric linear programming, and nonparametric linear programming (Data Envelopment Analysis). Srinivasan and Arnold (1994, p. 453) categorize physical process models as "non-spatially distributed (EPIC, CREAMS), or spatially distributed (ANSWERS, AGNPS, SWRRB); single-event (AGNPS, ANSWERS), or continuous-time scale (EPIC, CREAMS, SWRRB, ROTO); field-scale (WEPP, EPIC, CREAMS), or watershed/basin-wide (ANSWERS, AGNPS, SWRRB)".[3]

The Erosion Productivity Impact Calculator (EPIC), has been the most popular choice for a physical model in integration with an economic model.[4] EPIC is a comprehensive model of crop production at the field (Williams et al., 1990), and applications illustrate different approaches to integration. EPIC has been integrated with micro-unit models (Johnson et al., 1991) and representative farms with aggregation to regions (Mapp et al., 1994) by solving the economic model and using the output therefrom as an input in EPIC. An alternative method is to use EPIC to generate a distribution of physical parameters based on different scenarios, then include these "data" with economic observations in a data set, and, subsequently, to use the data set in the estimation of a parametric model which includes both economic and physical characteristics (Wu and Segerson, 1995; House, Helfand and Larson, 1997). This last approach has been referred to as micro-parameter distribution models (Hochman and Zilberman, 1978; Just and Antle, 1990; Opaluch and Segerson, 1991). Applications using these approaches to integration of economic models with EPIC include nitrogen taxes and regulation of application (Helfand and House, 1995; Johnson, Adams, and Perry, 1991; Larson, Helfand, and House, 1996), ambient water quality taxes (House, Helfand, and Larson, 1997) and commodity programs (Wu, Mapp, and Bernardo, 1996).

Ecosystem-based models are very important to the environmental agenda of sustainability. As the scale of the ecosystem modeled increases so, too, does the heterogeneity of the resource base. Newer physical process models, such as landscape models (e.g., Geoghegan and Bockstael, 1996) and the Soil and Water Assessment Tool (SWAT), provide ever more complete simulation of heterogenous ecosystems, such as a watershed. SWAT combines many of the desirable capabilities of the other models. Following the Srinivasan and Arnold (1994) categorization of physical process models, SWAT is watershed-based; it is spatially distributed, e.g., allowing for the transport of chemicals from fields; and it models time continuously, rather than modeling only a single event, such as a rainstorm. Moreover, SWAT allows for a wide variety of management practices and is appropriate for use in modelling ungauged basins. With the ability to model ungauged basins, SWAT is suitable for analysis of large watersheds on the order of hundreds of square kilometers or more or for analysis of multiple large watersheds. The unit of analysis is a watershed, where the size of the watersheds making up the basin is specified by the user and determined by topography. The model provides quantitative estimates of the standard environmental indicators which would result from economic-based, optimizing human behavior. Of course, the sustainability researcher or policy maker is still left with the major task of weighing (e.g., conducting an economic valuation of) the environmental impacts relative to the quantified market impacts.

The ideal circumstance to link SWAT to an economic model would be physical and financial information on all micro-units within each watershed. Since these data do not exist, links to models such as SWAT require spatial statistics techniques. The application of spatial statistics to link physical and economic models requires the assumption that the values at each location (either from observation or an economic model) are representative of the population in the area from which they were drawn. Then, a 3-dimensional surface can be fit to the data. There are several techniques available, including kriging, loess, local regression, and the averaged shifted histogram (Scott and Whittaker, 1996). Once a surface has been estimated for each variable, a summary statistic of the surface within each watershed is used as an input into the model. The link is completed by either the direct entry of the result of the economic model, or results of the SWAT simulation can be combined with results from the surface estimation for use in a micro-parameter distribution model.

A geographic information systems (GIS) interface is an especially nice feature for cross-disciplinary efforts because it allows nonspecialists to use the model with comparatively little effort, and exponentially reduces the time to create an application. Although the newer methods of linking require extensive statistical estimation and manipulation of data in a GIS system, inexpensive computing power and cheaper, easier to use, GIS software make the sort of analysis outlined here quite reasonable. In fact, it is possible to link an economic model to SWAT using the averaged shifted histogram version of nonparametric regression using public domain software on an entry level personal computer.

Concluding Comments

Sustainability poses no threat to a discipline-based research and education system. Disciplinary input is an essential input into sustainability research. Interest in extending the rich scientific knowledge base of our research and education institutions to real world problems of sustainability will only continue, resulting in an increased emphasis and institutional recognition of high-quality cross-disciplinary efforts. Institutional inertia has likely been an obstacle to collaboration in the past. However, quality management concepts have taken hold in public institutions and will likely facilitate the process by which cross-disciplinary efforts are implemented in the future.

The U.S. President's Council on Sustainable Development has recommended that participants in decision making processes regarding important social, economic, and environmental issues be broadened to include representation of all affected groups (PCSD, 1996, p. 7). The Council labeled this finding as their most important one in an extensive review of the issues. The knowledge base generated through sustainable agriculture research should be an important component of the information considered in such a participatory management process. Moreover, problem-solving research, like sustainable agriculture research, can potentially benefit from the feedback provided from a broad-based decision making process by providing realistic and agreed upon goals for sustainability. A similar approach to sustainability has been implemented in countries such as the Netherlands (Gilbert, 1996), where progress towards sustainability is measured with respect to how close the country is to attaining their currently defined goals.

Notes

1. This is not to imply that the concept of greater public participation in the agenda is universally embraced. For example, recently Beattie and Innes (1997) argued against "greater 'stakeholder' influence over the research and education agenda and process" due to the greater politicization that may ensue.

2. See Roberts and Swinton (1996) for a review of the literature with respect to the alternative economic methods used in comparing the sustainability of crop production systems.
3. The models cited here are only a part of the available physical process models, and are only meant to give an indication of the variety available. The characteristics and proposed use of each model pair determines the method of integration.
4. The 6 regional studies funded under the Sustainable Agriculture Economic Impact Study, for example, relied on EPIC as the common physical process model (Setia, 1997).

References

Ahearn, M.C. 1996. "The Views from the Inside". Paper presented at the C-FARE conference on Priorities for Agricultural Economics, Annapolis, MD: Nov. 16, 1996.

Ahearn, M.C., J. Yee, E. Ball, and R. Nehring. 1997. "Agricultural Productivity in the U.S.", Agric. Infor. Bull., Econ. Res. Serv., USDA, forthcoming.

Antle, John M. And Richard E. Just. 1992. "Conceptual and Empirical Foundations for Agricultural-Environmental Policy Analysis", *Journal of Environmental Quality*, Vol. 21, No. 3, pp. 307-316.

Bartelmus, P., C. Stahmer, and J. van Tongeren. 1991. "Integrated Environmental and Economic Accounting: Framework for a SNA Satellite System". *Review of Income and Wealth*, Series 37, No. 2, pp. 111-148.

Beattie, B. R. and R. Innes. 1997. "Federal Funding of Agricultural Research, Education, and Extension in the Land Grant Universities". *Choices*, Second Quarter, pp. 8-12.

Bureau of Economic Analysis (BEA). 1994. "Integrated Economic and Environmental Satellite Accounts". *Survey of Current Business*, April, pp. 33-49.

Castle, Emery N. 1970. "Priorities in Agricultural Economics for the 1970's", *American Journal of Agricultural Economics*, Vol. 52, Dec., pp. 831-840.

Costanza, Robert, Herman Daly, and Joy Bartholomew. 1991. "Goals, Agenda and Policy Recommendations for Ecological Economics". Chapter 1 in Robert Costanza, ed.: *Ecological Economics: The Science and Management of Sustainability*. New York: Columbia University Press.

Council on Food, Agriculture and Resource Economics. 1997. *Economics Research and Education Priorities for an Efficient and Sustainable Food System*. Wash., D.C.: C-FARE Board of Directors.

Geoghegan, J. and N. Bockstael. 1996. "Human Behavior and Ecosystem Valuation: An Application to the Patuxent Watershed of the Chesapeake Bay". Chapter 7 in *Ecosystem Function and Human Activities: Reconciling Economics and*

Ecology. Simpson, R.D. and N.L. Christensen, Jr., eds. New York:Chapman & Hall, pp. 147-174.

Gilbert, A. 1996. "Environmental Accounting, Materials Balances and Sustainability Indicators--Cadmium Accumulation in Soil", Chapter 7, in van den Bergh, Jeroen C.J.M., ed. *Ecological Economics and Sustainable Development: Theory, Methods, and Applications*. Cheltenham, UK: Edward Elgar.

Gliessman, S.R. 1990. *Agroecology: Researching the Ecological Basis of Sustainable Agriculture*. New York, NY: Springer-Verlag.

Grime, J.P. 1997. "Biodiversity and Ecosystem Function: The Debate Deepens". *Science*, Vol. 277, 29 August, pp. 1260-1261.

Helfand, Gloria E. and Brett W. House. 1995. "Regulating Nonpoint Source Pollution Under Heterogeneous Conditions". *American Journal of Agricultural Economics*, 77:1024-1032.

Hochman, E. and D. Zilberman. 1978. "Examination of Environmental Policies Using Production and Pollution Microparameter Distribution". *Econometrica*, 46:739-60.

House, Brett W., Gloria E. Helfand, and Douglas M. Larson. 1997. "What is the Right Ambient Water Quality Tax". Paper presented at the 1997 American Agricultural Economics Association Annual Meeting, Toronto, Canada

Hrubovcak, J., M. LeBlanc, B.K. Eakin. 1995. "Accounting for the Environment in Agriculture". Tech. Bull. No. 1847, Econ. Res. Serv., USDA, Oct.

Johnson, Scott L., Richard M. Adams, and Gregory M. Perry. 1991. "The On-Farm Costs of Reducing Groundwater Pollution". *American Journal of Agricultural Economics*, 73(Nov.):1063-1073.

Just, R. and J. Antle. 1990. "Interactions Between Agricultural and Environmental Policies: A Conceptual Framework". *American Economic Review*, 80:197-202.

Larson, Douglas M., Gloria E. Helfand, and Brett W. House. 1996. "Second-Best Tax Policies to Reduce Nonpoint Source Pollution". *American Journal of Agricultural Economics*, 78(Nov.):1108-1117.

Lockeretz, William. 1991. "Multidisciplinary Research and Sustainable Agriculture". *Biological Agriculture and Horticulture*, Vol. 8, pp. 101-122.

Lowrance, R., P.F. Hendrix, and E.P. Odum. 1986. "A Hierarchical Approach to Sustainable Agriculture". *Amer. J. of Alternative Agric.*, Vol. 1, No. 4, pp. 169-173.

Mapp, H.P., D.J. Bernardo, G.J. Sabbagh, S. Geleta, and K.B. Watkins. 1994. "Economic and Environmental Impacts of Limiting Nitrogen Use to Protect Water Quality: A Stochastic Regional Analysis". *American Journal of Agricultural Economics*, 76:889-903.

National Research Council (NRC). 1996. *Colleges of Agriculture at the Land Grant Universities: Public Service and Public Policy*. Board on Agriculture, Committee on the Future of the Colleges of Agriculture in the Land Grant University System. Wash., D.C.: National Academy Press.

National Research Council (NRC). *1993. Soil and Water Quality: An Agenda for Agriculture*. Board on Agriculture, Committee on Long-Range Soil and Water Conservation. Wash., D.C.: National Academy Press.

Norton, G.W., and J. Mullen. 1994. "Economic Evaluation of Integrated Pest Management Programs: A Literature Review". Pub. No. 448-120, Virginia Cooperative Extension. Virginia State University.

Opaluch, J.J. and K. Segerson. 1991. "Aggregate Analysis of Site-Specific Pollution Problems: the Case of Groundwater Contamination from Agricultural Pesticides". *Northeastern Journal of Agricultural and Resource Economics*, 20:83-97.

President's Council on Sustainable Development (PCSD). 1996. *Sustainable America: A New Consensus for Prosperity, Opportunity, and A Healthy Environment for the Future*. Wash., D.C.: U.S. Govt. Printing Office, Feb.

Roberts, W.S. and S.M. Swinton. 1996. "Economic Methods for Comparing Alternative Crop Production Systems: A Review of the Literature". *Amer. J. of Alternative Agric.*, Vol. 11, No. 1, pp. 10-17.

Saterson, Kathryn. 1995. "Ecological Principles as Informed by Economics". In Sandra S. Batie (ed.): *Developing Indicators for Environmental Sustainability: The Nuts and Bolts.* Proceedings of the Resource Policy Consortium Symposium, Wash., D.C., June 12-13.

Scott, David W. and Gerald Whittaker. 1996. "Multivariate Applications of the ASH in Regression", *Communications in Statistics*, 25:2521-2530.

Setia, P. 1997. "Sustainable Agriculture Economic Impact Study". Draft report on the SARE Project. Econ. Res. Serv., USDA, Aug.

Srinivasan, R. and J.G. Arnold. 1994. "Integration of a Basin-Scale Water Quality Model With GIS". *Water Resources Bulletin*, 30:453-462.

Stark, C. R. 1994. "Adopting Multidisciplinary Approaches to Sustainable Agriculture Research: Potentials and Pitfalls". *Amer. J. of Alternative Agric.*, Vol. 10, No. 4, pp. 180-151.

U.S. Department of Agriculture (USDA). 1997. World Wide Web Site. [http://www.usda.gov/].

Williams, J.R., P.T. Dyke, W.W. Fuchs, V.W. Benson, O.W. Rice, and E.D. Taylor. 1990. *EPIC - Erosion/Productivity Impact Calculator: User Manual*. United States Department of Agriculture, Agricultural Research Service, Technical Bulletin Number 1768.

Wu, JunJie, Harry P. Mapp, and Danile J. Bernardo. 1996. "Integrating Economic and Physical Models for Analyzing Water Quality Impacts of Agricultural Policies in the High Plains". *Review of Agricultural Economics*, 18:353-372.

Wu, JunJie and Kathleen Segerson. 1995. "The Impact of Policies and Land Characteristics on Potential Groundwater Pollution in Wisconsin". *American Journal of Agricultural Economics*, 77:1033-1047.

Young, Douglas L. 1995. "Agricultural Economics and Multidisciplinary Research". *Rev. of Agr. Econ.* 17: 119-129.

Zilberman, David. 1994. "Economics and Interdisciplinary Collaborative Efforts". *J. of Agr. and Applied Econ.* 26 (1): 35-42.

List of Contributors

Mary C. Ahearn, Chief, Economic Indicators and Resource Accounting Branch, Resource Economics Division, Economic Research Service, U.S. Department of Agriculture.

William Amponsah, Associate Professor of Agricultural Economics and Rural Sociology, North Carolina A & T State University.

John M. Antle, Professor of Agricultural Economics and Economics, and Director, Trade Research Center, Montana State University; and University Fellow, Resource for the Future, Washington, D.C.

Sandra S. Batie, Elton R. Smith Professor in Food and Agriculture Policy, and Head, Department of Agricultural Economics, Michigan State University.

Winfried E. H. Blum, Professor and Head, Department of Soil Science, Universität für Bodenkultur, Vienna, Austria, and Secretary General, International Society of Soil Science.

Donald G. Bullock, Associate Professor, Department of Crop Production, University of Illinois, Urbana-Champaign.

Susan M. Capalbo, Associate Professor of Agricultural Economics and Economics, Montana State University.

Ralph D. Christy, Professor, Department of Agricultural, Resource, and Managerial Economics, Cornell University.

Daniel C. Clay, Professor of International Agriculture, Institute of International Agriculture, Michigan State University.

Gerard E. D'Souza, Associate Professor of Agricultural and Resource Economics, Division of Resource Management, West Virginia University.

Richard L. Farnsworth, Associate Professor of Environmental and Natural Resource Economics, Department of Agricultural and Consumer Economics, University of Illinois, Urbana-Champaign.

Cornelia Butler Flora, Professor of Sociology and Director, North Central Regional Center for Rural Development, Iowa State University.

Tesfa G. Gebremedhin, Professor of Agricultural and Resource Economics, Division of Resource Management, West Virginia University.

John Ikerd, Extension Professor of Agricultural Economics, Department of Agricultural Economics, University of Missouri.

Lynndee Kemmet, Research Associate, The Jerome Levy Economics Institute, Annandale-on-Hudson, New York.

Margaret Kroma, Graduate Research Assistant, Department of Sociology and North Central Regional Center for Rural Development, Iowa State University.

Erik Lichtenberg, Associate Professor of Agricultural and Resource Economics, University of Maryland.

Leslie Lipper, Graduate Research Assistant, Department of Agricultural and Resource Economics, University of California at Berkeley.

Thomas Reardon, Associate Professor of Agricultural Economics, Michigan State University.

Sonya Salamon, Professor of Family Studies, Department of Human and Community Development, University of Illinois, Urbana-Champaign.

Neill Schaller, Associate Director, Henry A. Wallace Institute for Alternative Agriculture, Greenbelt, Maryland.

Luther Tweeten, Anderson Professor of Agricultural Marketing, Policy, and Trade, Department of Agricultural Economics and Rural Sociology, The Ohio State University.

Gerald W. Whittaker, Agricultural Economist, Resource Economics Division, Economic Research Service, U.S. Department of Agriculture.

David Zilberman, Professor and Chair, Department of Agricultural and Resource Economics, University of California at Berkeley.

Index